PREPARING FOR A CAREER IN EDUCATION

Challenges, Changes, and Issues

PREPARING FOR
A CAREER
IN EDUCATION

Challenges, Changes, and Issues

ROBERT W. RICHEY
Dean of Continuing Education
Director of Summer Sessions, and
Professor of Education, Indiana University

McGRAW-HILL BOOK COMPANY

New York   St. Louis   San Francisco   Düsseldorf
Johannesburg   Kuala Lumpur   London   Mexico
Montreal   New Delhi   Panama   Rio de Janeiro
Singapore   Sydney   Toronto

Library of Congress Cataloging in Publication Data
Richey, Robert William, date
  Preparing for a career in education: challenges,
changes, and issues.

  "Consists of nine chapters selected from the 19
chapters in the fifth edition of [the author's]
Planning for teaching: an introduction to education."
  Bibliography: p.
  1. Teaching as a profession. I. Title.
LB1775.R523   371.1'0023   73-11261
ISBN 0-07-052346-0

Preparing for a Career in Education
Challenges, Changes, and Issues

1 2 3 4 5 6 7 8 9–MAMM–7 6 5 4 3

This book was set in Caledonia and Helvetica by Black Dot,
Inc. The editors were Robert C. Morgan and Helen Greenberg;
the designer was Joseph Gillians; and the production
supervisor was Sally Ellyson.
The printer and binder was The Maple Press Company.

CONTENTS

Preface **vii**
1 The Challenge of Teaching **1**
2 Planning a Career in the Teaching Profession **38**
3 Opportunities in Education **70**
4 The Changing Role of the Teacher **96**
5 Educational Technology, Change, and Transition **132**
6 The Teaching Profession: Its Status, Organizations, Publications, and Code of Ethics **151**
7 Legal Liabilities and Responsibilities of Teachers **180**
8 Recurring Controversial Issues and Problems in Education **215**
9 Current Controversial Issues and Problems in Education **237**
References **263**
Index **271**

PREFACE

Anyone interested in teaching usually wishes to become the most competent teacher possible. This task becomes increasingly difficult as the role of schools and of teachers become more demanding and complex. Furthermore, the abundance of teachers in some areas today adds incentive for prospective teachers to excel in their preparation for entering the profession. An introductory course in education, therefore, should be designed to help students plan with care and insight their preparation for teaching, as well as their professional growth after entering the profession.

The members of the National Council for Accreditation of Teacher Education recognized the importance of having students plan their careers in education in their statement of *Standards for Accreditation of Teacher Education,* which was adopted in January 1970. Standard 3 states: "The institution owes it to the student to determine as objectively and systematically as possible specific strengths and weaknesses as they affect his continuing in a teacher education program." Students need assistance "in assessing their strengths and weaknesses in planning their programs of study. Prospective teachers need to be informed about professional organizations and agencies as well as current school problems. They also need to know about the wide variety of options available to assist them in teaching."

Preparing for a Career in Education: Challenges, Changes, and Issues is designed to assist colleges and universities in fulfilling their obligations to students as prescribed by Standard 3. It is intended for use in an introductory course in education. The first chapter deals with the tremendous amount of change taking place in our society and the challenges that educators will face in the future. Chapter 2 should assist a student in understanding more fully the concept of career planning, as well as the fundamental and sequential steps involved in this process. Attention also is given to competencies considered to be essential for success in teaching. The wide range of current as well as emerging opportunities that a career in education provides are explored in Chapter 3 with the hope that the interests and abilities of each prospective teacher may best be utilized and his success and happiness in the profession may be proportionately increased. Chapters 4 and 5 are concerned with such vital questions as: What are the normal duties and responsibilities of teachers and how might they change in the future? What are some of the newer instructional patterns and procedures? How will educational technology affect the work of teachers? How can a teacher cope with change? Chapters 6 and 7 are concerned with the status of teaching, the role of professional organizations in the improvement of the profession, the obligations and responsibilities of teachers, and some of the legal liabilities and responsibilities with which teachers are faced. In Chapters 8 and 9 some of the persistent and current problems and issues in education are examined. The student is encouraged to plan ways to help solve these problems and contribute effectively to the fuller realization of the school's function in a democratic society.

Throughout the book the needs of both prospective elementary and secondary school teachers are taken into consideration. Special efforts have been made to include research findings related to teachers and teaching, and to indicate probable changes in the role of schools and of teachers. Attention has been given to such topics as curricular innovations, ecology, differentiated staffing, middle schools, flexible scheduling, nongradedness, educational technology, accountability, national assessment, performance contracting, vouchering, racism, and the education of blacks and other minority groups. The need for humanizing the educational process has been emphasized. Topics have been approached from the point of view of encouraging students to explore them further and to expand their understanding of the teaching profession.

In the end-of-chapter material, the "Questions for Consideration" are designed to stimulate thoughtful concern and discussion on basic ideas, concepts, problems, issues, and plans for teaching. The primary purpose for including the "Problem Situations" is to provide an opportunity for students, through group participation, discussion, and debate, to gain skill in identifying relevant factors stated (as well as those not stated) in a problem situation, sensing the variety of possible solutions to a problem, weighing the issues involved, and deciding upon the most appropriate course of action. An instructor may wish to use other problem situations, appropriate for each chapter, with which he or his students are familiar. The "Activities to Pursue," which emphasize *doing*, are designed to encourage students to work independently or in groups along lines of special interest in their explorations of teaching as a profession. The self-appraisal forms and lists should prove helpful in appraising one's fitness and general competence for teaching and thus aid one to plan more effectively his preparation for entering the profession.

The content of *Preparing for a Career in Education* consists of nine chapters selected from the nineteen chapters in the fifth edition of *Planning for Teaching: An Introduction to Education.* The main purpose of this adaptation is to reach in a limited manner the career planning needs of students enrolled in a one-semester hour (rather than a two- or three-semester hour) introductory course in education, or of students in an introductory course in which a number of paperback books are used as text material. As such, the content of *Preparing for a Career in Education* reflects some of the questions and concerns that tens of thousands of students have expressed as they entered their first course in teacher education. It also reflects some of the understandings, insights, and convictions gained by the author as a result or more than twenty-five years of intensive exposure to the problems and concerns of students planning to become educators.

Of those who helped revise various chapters of the fifth edition of *Planning for Teaching*, the following should be recognized for the corresponding chapters in *Preparing for a Career in Education*: Drs. Edward G. Buffie and John W. Vaughn of Indiana University—Chapters 4 and 5; Dr. Maurice A. McGlasson of Indiana University—Chapter 6; Dr. Lowell C. Rose, Executive Secretary of Phi Delta Kappa—Chapters 7, 8, and 9. Dr. James E. Hertling of Indiana University served as a sounding board and a critic of the manuscript, and prepared the problem situations at the end of each chapter. Dr. Norman R. Dixon of the University of Pittsburgh carefully checked the manuscript for relevance on the education of minority groups and made many excellent suggestions. The author is grateful to these people for their past contributions and their enthusiasm for the publication of this paperback edition. Appreciation also is extended to the many publishers, and especially to the National Education Association and the American Association of Colleges for Teacher Education, for their willingness to grant permission to use various materials again.

As has been true in the preparation of the five editions of *Planning for Teaching*, I am forever grateful to my wife Eloise, who typed much of the manuscript, checked on many details, proofread, criticized copy, made many helpful suggestions, and shared in the sacrifices, problems, and pleasures of producing another book which may help others in the formulation of plans for moving effectively and happily into the teaching profession.

Robert W. Richey

1 | THE CHALLENGE OF TEACHING

Congratulations upon your interest in becoming a member of the teaching profession. In addition to being the largest of the professions, teaching may be considered to be basic to all the other professions. In other words, other professions are made possible through the work of teachers in elementary and secondary schools, colleges, and universities.

Becoming a successful teacher presents a greater challenge today than at any previous time in history. Students expect more from schools and their teachers than they did in earlier days. Pressures applied by them, as well as by parents and by the profession itself, to find improved ways of teaching have led to the development of new programs and instructional strategies such as inquiry approaches, simulation games, contract approaches, computer-assisted instruction, and programmed learning materials. Teachers are being challenged to utilize new approaches in an effort to improve learning results. Furthermore, schools and teachers today are dealing with a clientele which is considerably more knowledgeable than previous students due to such factors as mass media, population mobility, population shifts from rural to metropolitan areas, and the economic ability to travel widely.

But a genuine challenge serves to attract people equipped to accept and meet the challenge. As a result, better-qualified persons today are being attracted to teaching. They also have the benefit of improved teacher preparation programs. For those who are personally and professionally qualified, teaching offers a genuine challenge and an opportunity to make a major contribution to the improvement of society.

In addition to the increased challenge, your interest in the possibilities of becoming a teacher also is commendable in view of the frequent criticisms that are being voiced about schools and teachers. It is not uncommon to hear that schools are irrelevant and have failed in their mission of educating the youth of America. You may have read about the abundance of requests for increased school taxes which have been defeated by voters. You may have heard about some school districts which, frustrated in their efforts to provide an effective educational program, have contracted with private business firms to operate all or part of their instructional programs. You may have sensed some anger upon the part of the general public toward teachers who engage in collective bargaining over salaries and working conditions. You may have been told that it will be very difficult, if not impossible, to get a position as a teacher. In the face of what might appear to be discouraging conditions, your interest in pursuing a career in the teaching profession therefore is commendable.

In some respects this negative climate may seem to be a function of the times. In contrast to the optimistic growth pattern of the past, Stinnett makes the following assessment of the current scene [124:5–6][1]:

Something has gone sadly awry. On every hand the quality of life is diminished by blight, pollution, noise, and over-crowding. Our streams are fouled, our soils eroded, our forests cut down, our traffic snarled. As one quipster put it, "not only is there no God, but try getting a plumber on weekends."

Man may walk on the moon in safety and security, but not on the streets and in the parks of our big cities. There is hunger in the midst of plenty; poverty abrades the nation's conscience. Riots, violence, pickets, marches, and dissent mar our days and nights. We seem suddenly to have come upon visions of our limitations; earlier visions of better tomorrows seem now obscured or jaded. The infinity of our powers and possibilities seems, at least momentarily, to be giving way to frustration. We despair that there are no more mountains to climb, no more rivers to cross, no more virgin forests to devastate. Above all, we have lost our identity in the anonymity of the mob. The individual is only a number in the soulless conscience of an error-prone computer.

The much-ballyhooed American goal of uninterrupted, eternal growth—in GNP, in ever bigger cars, in income, in large cities, in population—is proving to be a delusion. The price of bigness is too big to pay. Our cities are becoming unlivable and ungovernable. Population growth, already outrunning our natural resources, is still climbing dangerously. We can no longer believe in the gospel of growth. Faith in the miracles of technology has sustained our giddiness. But technology cannot defy the limitations of nature. For every technological advance there have been corresponding adverse effects—fouled air, polluted waters, impossible transportation problems.

Within this negative context it might be easy for any teacher aspirant to become discouraged. But so frequently the abundance of criticism tends to blur the massive educational accomplishments of the past and the vision of the future. It is true that there are many weaknesses and problems existing in our educational system and in the profession which warrant critical analyses. And constructive criticism should always be encouraged, since it serves many useful purposes. "But criticism that is based on erroneous assumptions, that uses slogans rather than facts, or that takes the form of wild accusations does not further the public interest" [92:13]. It may be helpful, therefore, to note briefly some

[1]References indicated by number are listed in an alphabetical reference section beginning on page 263.

The advent of the space age highlights the importance of quality education in a demanding and rapidly changing world. *(Photograph from National Aeronautics and Space Admininstration.)*

contributions of the American school system, as well as some future challenges facing teachers, as a means of gaining perspective for planning a career in education.

SOME POSITIVE CONTRIBUTIONS OF AMERICAN EDUCATION

Teachers, and the school systems in which they work, do not pretend to make exclusive claims for the tremendous gains that have been made in our society. But few people would ever deny that they have played a significant role in making possible the rapid and monumental growth of our nation.

From the founding of the first common school in America, largely of the public subscription type, a hardy breed of poorly educated, poorly equipped teachers kept the feeble flame of learning alive, under the most adverse circumstances, until the founding of our state school systems. . . .

With the advent of special schools for the preparation of teachers, there went out from these substandard institutions an ever enlarging stream of dedicated people, to plant and nurture the seeds of the American dream. By present standards, their preparation was meager, their learning sketchy. But they made up in zeal and devotion to the goals of this country for their deficiencies in scholarship . . . under great handicaps, they were able to impart a significant measure of learning, enough to enable the people to become self-governing people, thus developing and nurturing one of the world's few constitutional democracies [126:2].

Unification of the Nation

It is difficult to comprehend the prodigious task with which the public schools have been confronted in their attempts to fulfill one of the greatest dreams a society has ever dreamt—universal educational opportunities. Inscribed on the base of the Statue of Liberty is the following:

> Give me your tired, your poor,
> Your huddled masses yearning to breathe free,
> The wretched refuse of your teeming shore,
> Send these, the homeless, tempest-tossed, to me:
> I lift my lamp beside the golden door.

In response to this open-door approach, more than 30 million immigrants have come to our shores—vastly different in backgrounds and culture. Through the process of bringing these people into our schools, teachers over the years have been able to impart a measure of literacy to them and assist them in becoming a part of the developing American culture—its ideals, behavorial patterns, customs, hopes, and aspirations.

Just as the purposes of the American school are unprecedented, so are its achievements. To it the American people owe the unity which has enabled them to master a continent and to forge from immigrant diversity a single people. It has helped to prevent the formation of rigid class barriers. It has fostered the diversification of talents, the ingenuity, and productivity which has brought this society to the highest level of economic prosperity ever known. On it are based many of the great American scientific and technological advances. And, perhaps most important of all, the spiritual stamina and fervor for freedom which have preserved individual liberty and guarded equality of opportunity through war and hardships have been derived from American education. This majestic record has set the standard against which the rest of the world judges the value of universal education [16:6–7].

Although much remains to be done in American society in recognizing and unifying people whose races, religions, creeds, national origins, as well as ethnic, cultural, and economic backgrounds, are so diversified, undoubtedly public schools will continue to be perhaps the most effective integrating and unifying force within our total society.

Opportunities for Education

Throughout the years educators have fought vigorously for the establishment, preservation, and improvement of the free public school system. This fight has been based upon a fundamental tenet of a democratic society—respect for the dignity and worth of the individual. In a democratic society each individual should have the opportunity to achieve the promise that is within him—to be worthy of a great society and capable of strengthening it. Education is the medium through which this belief can best be realized. In other words, a democratic society is committed to the proposition that educational opportunities must be provided for all youth in our society [Figure 1–1].[2]

The greatness of a nation may be manifested in many ways—in its purposes, its courage, its moral responsibility, its cultural and scientific eminence, the tenor of its daily life. But ultimately the source of its greatness is in the individuals who constitute the living substance of the nation.

A concern for the realization of individual potentialities is deeply rooted in our moral heritage, our political philosophy, and the texture of our daily customs. It is at the root of our efforts to eliminate poverty and slums at home and to combat disease and disaster throughout the world. The enthusiasm with which Americans plunge into projects for human betterment has been considered by some critics to be foolishly optimistic. But

[2]Figure credits may be found at the end of each chapter.

FIGURE 1–1   Per cent of youth 15 to 19 years of age enrolled in school in various countries. The United States excels by far other countries in the percentage of secondary school youth engaged in formal education.

Per cent

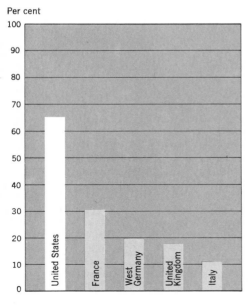

though we may have gone to extremes in a naive belief that we could cure all of mankind's ills, we need not be ashamed of the impulse. It springs from our deepest values. We do not believe that men were meant to live in degradation and we are foes of the poverty and ignorance which produces that result. We deplore the destruction of human potentialities through disease, and we are prepared to fight such destruction wherever we meet it. We believe that man—by virtue of his humanity—should live in the light of reason, exercise moral responsibility, and be free to develop to the full the talents that are in him.

Our devotion to a free society can only be understood in terms of these values. It is the only form of society that puts at the very top of its agenda the opportunity of the individual to develop his potentialities. It is the declared enemy of every condition that stunts the intellect, moral and spiritual growth of the individual. No society has ever fully succeeded in living up to the stern ideals that a free people set themselves. But only a free society can even address itself to that demanding task [100:1].

In commenting upon some accomplishments in American education, a prominent state superintendent of public instruction has presented the following comparisons [92:13]:

Public education in America is essentially free and is, in many respects, almost universal. Our concept of what these basic features are has been expanding for the past hundred years, and we strive to make the reality match the concept. In 1870, high school graduates composed only two per cent of the population of 17-year-olds. This percentage has increased by leaps and bounds; by 1968 it was almost 77 per cent. The numbers of graduates make interesting reading too: In the year 1869–1870, it was 16,000; in 1967–1968 it was 2,672,000. In this period U.S. population increased approximately fivefold, whereas the number of high school graduates increased 167 times.

It is instructive to note how we compare with other nations in retaining students through the final year of high school. The United States retains 70 per cent of its age cohorts. Japan holds second place, retaining 57 per cent. England and Germany retain 12 and 11 per cent respectively.

These data hold considerably more meaning than the mere percentages suggest. Scholars have developed a retentivity index to show the relative chances that students from families with different occupational backgrounds will reach the last grade of the secondary school. This index shows that the U.S. is less selective or discriminatory than other nations. For example, more than two-and-a-half times as many pupils from working class families reach the final year of secondary school in the United States as in England. As a more extreme example, the same ratio for the U.S. and Germany is more than seven to one.

Thus the United States provides education for a greater percentage of its young people than do most industrial nations. And it does so with the least social bias.

When we look at data for higher education, we find again that the U.S. provides substantially more opportunities for its citizens to enroll in institutions of higher education and to earn degrees than do other advanced nations. The UNESCO Statistical Yearbook for 1967 shows that the U.S. has 2,840 students enrolled in higher education per 100,000 population. In a list of seven industrial nations, the Soviet Union is second, with 1,674. The other five are Canada, 1,651; Japan, 1,140; France, 1,042; Germany, 632; and England, 480.

Reports on the number of graduates per 100,000 population for the year 1960 again show the U.S. with a commanding lead; the figure is 268. In the same year Japan was second with 165. The other five industrial nations were reported as follows: Soviet Union, 163; United Kingdom, 133; Canada, 128; Germany, 78; and France, 55.

These data for the secondary schools and for higher education emphasize that the

Per cent

FIGURE 1–2   Percentage of 17-year-olds who graduate from public and nonpublic schools in the United States. What factors have fostered this phenomenal increase?

U.S. makes educational opportunities substantially more available to its citizens than do other major nations. The figures confirm that public education is almost universal at the elementary and secondary levels. But this result has been achieved only after many decades.

Other evidence of educational opportunities is to be found in the fact that American schools have become almost universally coeducational at all levels. "The U.S. has been in the forefront in recognizing the educational rights of the female and in providing opportunities for women to develop their full potential. Unfortunately, it is true that we have not been as successful in utilizing the talents of women as in developing them" [92:14].

Polley calls attention to another contribution of the American educational system [92:14–15]:

American education has not been stratified in the European sense, and largely because of that fact it has produced another outstanding achievement: social mobility. Social mobility contributes not only to a healthy and growing economy but to the maintenance of a free political system. Sons of immigrant fruit peddlers become owners of restaurants or doctors; sons of poor farmers become university presidents or bankers; and the sons of police officers and plumbers are elected mayors or members of Congress. Without a system of comprehensive and high quality education, social mobility would be a far less significant factor in our economic and political life.

While the goal of equal educational opportunities for all has not been reached, much progress, especially in recent years, has been made. As will be indicated in other sections of this book, many complex factors are involved in achieving this goal. Indeed, it must be a concern of the total society.

Economic Returns of Education

The economic returns of education are reflected in the unparalleled economic growth of this nation. Although the people of the United States constitute only about 6 per cent of the world's population and occupy less than 7 per cent of the world's land area, they create over one-half of the world's wealth, produce over 40 per cent and consume nearly one-third of the total energy produced in the world, and own one-half of the world's telephones, radios, and television sets [20:iv]. "We provide more material things, such as food, clothing, and houses, more health services, more cultural and recreational outlets for more people than any other nation, past or present" [145:1].

The striking relationship between education and economic growth in various nations throughout the world is revealed through a comparison of educational development, natural resources, and per capita income. As may be noted in Table 1–1, Denmark and Colombia present an interesting contrast. Colombia has abundant natural resources. Until recently, it had neglected education. Its per capita income in 1965 was the equivalent of $284. A century ago Denmark had a very low per capita income, and its soil was not rich. It had few minerals, and the growing season was short. But the people decided to place much emphasis upon developing good schools for their children. The per capita income in 1965, in contrast with Colombia's, was $2,066. Likewise, Brazil, very rich in natural resources but low in education, produced only $270 per capita. On the other hand, Switzerland, with limited resources but a well-

FIGURE 1–3 Relationship between lifetime income of men and the level of education.

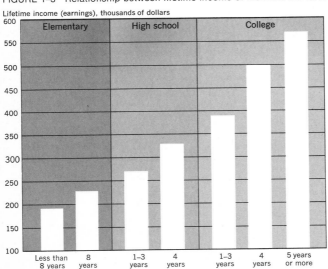

Years of school completed

TABLE 1–1   **RELATIONSHIP OF NATURAL**
RESOURCES, EDUCATION,
AND INCOME IN SELECTED
COUNTRIES

Nation	Natural Resources	Educational Development	Per capita Income, 1965
Brazil	High	Low	$ 270
Colombia	High	Low	284
Denmark	Low	High	2,066
Mexico	High	Low	455
New Zealand	High	High	1,986
Switzerland	Low	High	2,343
United States	High	High	3,501

Source: What Everyone Should Know about Financing Our Schools,
National Education Association, Washington, 1968, p. 8.

developed educational program, ranked first in Europe in per capita income in 1965. Similar examples can be illustrated by many other countries. They show clearly that regardless of natural resources, the development of educational potential increases per capita income.

The manifold ways in which good schools strengthen society are summarized in the booklet *Education Is Good Business* [20:46–47]:

1. Well-documented evidence indicates that schools have made a magnificent contribution to our economic growth. More education means a more highly skilled work force; gains in worker efficiency achieved through education have accounted for 20 to 23 per cent of our growth in national product. Education is the base upon which the quality of research and development activities of American industry rests; the "advance of knowledge" achieved through research accounts for an additional 20 per cent of our prosperity.
2. Investments in education, accordingly, mean bigger markets for American businessmen. Rising markets give us strength in our economy.
3. Just as we want our economy to be generally strong, we want the many special benefits that education-based research helps to provide: freedom from disease, better communications, faster travel, clean water, and clear air in our growing cities.
4. We want a national government and an economic structure that can cope with chronic unemployment, a problem which appears to be characteristic of periods of rapid technological change. We believe that education, properly directed, is the chief means whereby people can find new kinds of jobs when the old kinds disappear. Labor, industry, and government must be sensitive to this fact.
5. For our whole system of government to function properly, we need strength and fiscal stability in our local governments. Good education is an important safeguard against economic stagnation and decay of local areas.
6. Of great importance are the benefits that education yields to the student as an individual. For the student, the zealous pursuit of education leads to higher income; the opportunity to choose among a variety of interesting and challenging kinds of work; a greater chance to participate in on-the-job training (in order to keep one's skills fresh and up-to-date); and, finally, job security.

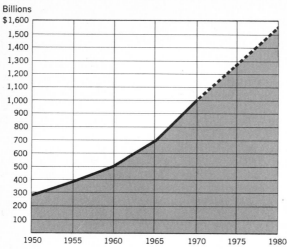

Billions

FIGURE 1-4 Past and projected gross national product. In comparison with other countries, the United States has a high standard of living, and is capable of raising this standard. Approximately 4 per cent of the GNP is expended for public elementary and secondary education. In what way has public education contributed to the enormous growth of the GNP?

7. By no means, however, are all the individual benefits of education in material form. Education promotes stability of family life, the improvement of educational opportunities for one's children through the early learning experiences that educated parents offer their boys and girls, and a vastly greater capacity to enjoy leisure. Furthermore, the attainment of full cultural maturity may be a central purpose of education.
8. Education is one of the chief ways by which we come to value human life in all its complexity. Through education, our children are led to develop a feeling of compassionate regard for their fellowmen—to be willing, on the one hand, to walk the extra mile to alleviate our neighbor's distress; and to be able, on the other, to share gracefully our friend's happiness in times of joy.

Frequent criticisms are made of our educational system. Much of this criticism is sincere and justified. Some of it is mixed with half-truths, misinformation, and ill-founded generalizations. There are those who would have us believe that European educational systems are far superior to our public school system. But it should be remembered that [51:4]:

The educational system which is criticized today is the same one from which came the people who built the first atomic bomb, who flew the first airplane, who launched the first atomic submarine, who led the world in thermonuclear experiments, who developed mass industrial production of automobiles, bathtubs, and telephones. And, by the way, gave the world sulfa drugs, terramycin, and Salk vaccine.

Yet, in the face of this phenomenal growth, problems remain. Many are still hungry, poorly housed and clothed, in need of medical attention and more education. To these and other problems, teachers must address themselves as they guide the educational growth of future generations.

Promotion of the Democratic Way of Life

The founding fathers clearly recognized that education is fundamental to the preservation of freedom and self-government. For example, George Washington, in his "Farewell Address" in 1796, strongly encouraged the spread of knowledge: "Promote then, as an object of primary importance, institutions for the general diffusion of knowledge. In proportion as the structure of a government gives force to public opinion, it is essential that public opinion is enlightened." Thomas Jefferson warned that "if a nation expects to be ignorant and free in a state of civilization it expects what never was and never will be." He felt that "if the condition of man is to be progressively ameliorated . . . education is the chief instrument for effecting it." Indeed, almost every president of the United States has made strong statements regarding the importance of education. In recent years especially, they have worked vigorously to provide various types of federal support in order that the public schools, colleges, and universities might be better able to fulfill their mission.

In order to perpetuate and to strengthen our democratic way of life, youth must gain a clear understanding of the values and traditions that have emerged from mankind's search for desirable ways of living. They must have an operational understanding of the democratic ideals and values that guide free people in acting responsibly, so that, ultimately, the welfare of society is seen as the combined welfare of all individuals. Factual knowledge alone does not ensure wise decision making since

FIGURE 1–5 Trends in the level of educational attainment of persons 25 years old and over in the United States. Between 1940 and 1969, the proportion of high school and college graduates more than doubled, raising the median number of school years completed by persons 25 years of age and over from 8.6 to 12.1. What effect will this trend have upon schools and the role of the teacher?

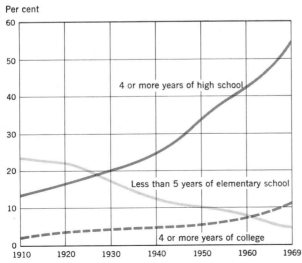

Per cent

decisions are made largely in terms of the ideals and goals an individual cherishes. How can our schools do an even better job in meeting this basic need in a free world?

John W. Gardner, in his book titled *Excellence* [38:159–160], sounds a warning which has significance for all teachers as they work with boys and girls:

The importance of competence as a condition of freedom has been widely ignored (as some newly independent nations are finding to their sorrow). An amiable fondness for the graces of a free society is not enough. Keeping a free society free—and vital and strong—is no job for the half-educated and the slovenly. Free men must be competent men. In a society of free men, competence is an elementary duty. Men and women doing competently whatever job is theirs to do tone up the whole society. And a man who does a slovenly job—whether he is a janitor or a judge, a surgeon or a technician—lowers the tone of the society. So do the chiselers of high and low degree, the sleight-of-hand artists who always know how to gain an advantage without honest work. They are the regrettable burdens of a free society.

Individual competence, however, is not enough to ensure a strong, vibrant, creative, and productive society. Teachers should help boys and girls value the dignity of work and the establishment of high standards of performance in all phases of life. Youth must learn to accept the responsibility for setting their own high standards of performance, for serving as their own hard disciplinarians, and for demanding quality performance upon the part of their fellowmen. They must feel that satisfaction at the level of mediocrity will result in the decay of the ideals that have made this country great. They must feel a sense of pride in and dedication to their work and to the basic ideals of our society.

In the history of our country we have never faced a period in which the demand for education has been greater. It seems obvious that, barring world catastrophe, the demands for educated intelligence will increase.

In order to add strength to our nation and survive the strong threats to our way of life, increasing numbers of our most able young people must become teachers. Our future welfare rests so heavily upon the quality and quantity of education received by the young that only the best should teach. We, as a nation, can afford no less since our most important resources are the capacities, the energy, and the character of our people.

Alvin C. Eurich very effectively summarized the challenge with which we are faced [26].

America still means promise; it is still a land of opportunity. At this juncture of our history perhaps our greatest opportunity is in the education of our children. If we fail in this, we fail all succeeding generations. But there can be no bright future—as there never has been in any field—if we maintain the status quo. We cannot stand still. Every nation in the history of mankind has been defeated totally and miserably when it strove merely to protect what it had. New nations, including our own, have risen to the top through hardship and struggle, through ingenuity and the courage to create new patterns.

Innovation has been basic to our economic well-being and growth. It is also basic to education, for creative imagination in education will determine our future and the future of our children.

AMERICAN LIFE IN TRANSITION

In view of these major contributions, one may ask "Why do some people feel that major changes should be made in the American school system?" A great portion of the answer to this question lies in the fact that we are in a major period of transition which appears to have begun in the 1940s and has continued to accelerate. This transition essentially is "a move from an industrial to a post-industrial society, from a pluralistic to a more centrally (or technocratically) directed nation in which traditional concepts, institutions, and practices are being challenged, negotiated, traded, or held on to" [17:5].

In making its forecast for the 1970s and 1980s, the National Industrial Conference Board indicated that this transition which we are encountering is compounded by the following complex considerations [17:5]:

(1) the rate of change which is shrinking research and planning time; (2) outdated criteria used to examine new problems and opportunities; (3) micro and piecemeal ways of dealing with problems at macro scale; (4) public insistence on "instant" solutions and leader impatience with problems that demand attention over longer periods of time; (5) inexperience in bringing about large-scale collaboration on the part of leaders in and between the private and public sectors; (6) the pushing and pulling on the part of those who, through fear or selfish interests, resist change, and those who want to lead and accelerate it; (7) competing demands for scarce talents and resources, and the increasingly frequent absence of needed skills; (8) uncertainty on the part of decision makers and institutions as to the nature of their new roles and responsibilities in a changing society; (9) the temporary inability of our systems of checks and balances, of regulations and controls, to function effectively during the transition; and (10) the question of how to regularize the irregular.

The American school system, an agency of society, is being affected by the profound changes which have been taking place during this period of transition and which will continue to occur in the future. Educators are becoming more aware of these changes as phenomenal events draw attention to the new conditions under which we live. The increasing use of automation and computerization, the expanding use of atomic energy, the phenomenal growth of population, the explosion of knowledge, the launching of communication satellites, the landing of men on the moon, and a host of other sensational developments have been experienced within the space of a third of a century. These have focused attention upon the rapid, pervasive, and fundamental changes in our cultural scene.

Educators can appreciate and aid in planning the proper role of the schools in today's affairs only when they understand the consequences of these basic changes in living conditions. This understanding will help avoid the tendency of educators to impose upon youth the same values, beliefs, and modes of behavior that have characterized the past—thereby transmitting increasing incompetence for dealing with the future. In the swift flow of change there are those among us who would have us feel that whatever exists is irrelevant—that only tomorrow is relevant [126:1].

How does our contemporary culture differ specifically from that of the past? An examination of some of these differences may provide clues to the new competencies that will be required of youth in order to make creative approaches to, and to deal more adequately with, the changing character of the future. The statements that follow should be considered as only the beginning of many with which all thoughtful prospective teachers should be concerned.

1. *Community life has been affected increasingly by industrial and technological processes.* Inventions and new ways of making the basic commodities of life have moved from hand manufacture to a machine process which is largely automatic and highly technical in nature. Through mass production, enormous factories now turn out great quantities of products. The simple agrarian life and modes of production of our forefathers (and in many other parts of the world today) are in sharp contrast with this industrial and technological proficiency. We note the creation of "new relationships between people, education, and work, with technical skills and knowledge, mental alertness, and creative capacities taking priority over capacities to endure hard physical labor" [54:2]. To what extent has the school's curriculum been modified in order to reflect these changes?

2. *Extreme ease of production has led to a high standard of living for many.* In spite of the range of differences existing within our society, we now enjoy the highest standard of living in the world. The results of

FIGURE 1–6 Number of farms in the United States. Between 1952 and 1970 the number of farms declined from 5.2 million to 2.9 million—resulting in a corresponding decrease in rural population.

Millions of farms

FIGURE 1–7   Changes in productivity of workers, 1850–1975. In 1975 each worker will produce almost twelve times as much as the worker of 1850.

our scientific and industrial knowledge have provided us with more of the material things than ever before. As compared to the past, we live in better houses, take more and longer vacation trips, engage in more outdoor activities, dine out more often, attend more sports activities, read more books, periodicals, and newspapers, listen to more records, engage in more hobbies, and attend more concerts, art galleries, and museums. In brief, the pattern of our lives has changed very significantly as a result of this increase of abundance.

3. *Modern living has become increasingly urban.* In 1950, 59 per cent of our population lived in urban areas. This percentage had increased to over 70 in 1970. The major portion of the remaining 30 per cent live in nonfarm rural locations and commute to urban areas for employment. During this period of time, decided increases have occurred in such occupational groups as professional and technical workers, proprietors and managers, clerical and sales workers, skilled and semiskilled workers, and service workers. For the most part, these occupations are located in urban areas. What changes in the character of living and the education needs of youth have resulted from this increase in urbanization?

4. *Vast differences exist in the educational opportunities afforded children.* Large numbers of boys and girls, especially those living in the slum sections of cities, may be considered to be educationally disadvantaged. Often finding little relevance in the school experiences, many of them either drop out or graduate from school without any hope of continuing their education, regardless of their abilities. They may experience major difficulty in finding employment and a role to play in an increasingly complex, technological society. To what extent are teachers attempting to understand the backgrounds and values held by disadvantaged children and their families? To what extent are teachers respecting the racial and ethnic differences which these boys and girls hold and, at the same time, helping them to become effective citizens?

5. *Increased standardization of policies, procedures, and products has resulted in increased pressures toward conformity.* The frontiersman

and the farmer lived close to the land. Their welfare depended heavily upon the use of individual initiative, hard work, and ingenuity in solving problems and in improving their status in life. Mechanization, unionization, standardization, and pressures toward conformance tend to inhibit individuality and creativity at a time when these qualities are especially needed. To what extent is the school assisting the young in making creative approaches to the solution of the increasingly complex problems in our society?

6. *Productivity, new markets, new economic and distributive occupations, communication, and urbanization have been influenced by new patterns of ownership.* Yesterday's society was characterized mainly by individual ownership and direct proprietary control over the means of production. Today the ownership of industry is diffused. The stockholder or bondholder rarely understands or manages to any appreciable degree the enterprises in which his money is invested. Labor groups have become highly organized and are corporate in character. The forces which direct our economic and productive affairs are corporate groups that are increasingly directed by professional managerial experts. Today the individual functions more and more in terms of the group with which he comes in contact. Youth has difficulty in being able to identify, to find purpose, to develop feelings of responsibility, to become effective citizens.

7. *Our population has become highly mobile.* Modern transportation facilities and a generally high standard of living in an economy which is extremely productive make it possible for people to move about with great ease. This means that people no longer may be educated to fit the requirement of only one restricted community. They are much more in touch with each other and consequently know more about how others live. Personal aspirations are altered as the possibilities of a better life are experienced firsthand.

Millions of workers change jobs every year. Today, approximately 20 per cent of all the families in the United States move yearly to gain better jobs, health, or climate, or for other reasons. Much of the mobility of people is "from the open country and small towns and villages to large centers of population and from the centers of cities to the suburbs, with the inevitable consequences of culture clashes that shake institutions, disturb long-established customs, set values in new perspective, color political action, disrupt systems of school support, and leave indelible marks on the behavior patterns and characters of children" [54:3].

8. *We are now living in a highly interdependent world community.* A dislocation in one major industry today may affect the industrial actions, health, and economic well-being of large numbers of people in distant areas. War today is a concern of all the people; depression is global in proportions. We now face the need for the skills and knowledge necessary to enable us to live together in this complex, interdependent

society—accepting without prejudice people of other races, creeds, and religions.

9. *The older controls in our social life no longer operate as they did in our earlier agrarian period.* The family, for instance, was at one time an institution around which centered the production and marketing of goods, personal services, recreation of all members, and a large part of the group's education and worship. Today practically all these activities are performed through some other community institution or organization. The parent used to supervise the chores of the young, but today if work is available, children are generally without the supervision of a parent or teacher. What is the responsibility of the school in providing for these learnings?

10. *Today's community life for many has become highly impersonal compared with small-town agrarian life in the past.* In the contemporary metropolitan area the individual is often unknown to his neighbor; personal identity frequently is lost in the confusion of urban life. Here one is less accountable for his actions, less subject to the pressures of a society in which every individual is well known by his neighbors. The problems of finding an adequate sense of belonging and adequacy seem to become more difficult under such conditions. Why are there 20 million mentally ill persons in our society, 6 million alcoholics, 44,000 suicides a year, increasing incidence of juvenile delinquency and drug addiction? To what extent are schools responsible for promoting desirable physical and mental health in this world?

11. *Technological advancements have made possible greater amounts of leisure time.* Since 1859, the amount of leisure time for the average worker in our society has increased from 12 to 52 hours per week. Today Americans spend more income for leisure-time pursuits than for all public elementary and secondary schools. In spite of the constructive benefits that have been derived from the increased amount of leisure time available to the average individual, some questions having educational significance may be raised. How can we account for the low state of physical fitness of children, youth, and adults throughout America? Why, according to the late J. Edgar Hoover, has serious crime reached the highest point in history, and, why is it increasing four times as fast as the population? How constructively do those over 65 years of age spend their time? Why have so many homes, the basic unit in our society, disintegrated because of the high divorce rate?

12. *American society has become one in which an understanding of totalitarianism and an ability to meet its challenge are imperative.* With the current trend toward dictatorship, an enlightened citizen should study the significance of the suppression of the individual's thoughts and actions, not only in the international scene but also in our domestic affairs, and be prepared to oppose tyrannies over free men's self-government. This ability to lay bare the basis of totalitarianism is of

crucial importance today; in our technological society the bigotry of the demagogue may immediately reach a whole people rather than be merely disseminated by word of mouth from one speaker to a handful of others. The forces which make for tyranny over the minds of men may use the devices of modern science for their own purposes. To find ways of disclosing the purposes and evaluating the efforts of totalitarianism of all kinds is an imperative need in modern society.

13. *The citizen today needs to make finer and more subtle discriminations in what he says and hears than did his ancestors.* Through radio, movies, television, and the press, modern citizens receive opinions and attitudes which tend to be uncritical expressions of emotion and exhortation rather than critically examined statements of conviction. "Different ethnic, racial, and cultural groups of people are vigorously struggling for recognition, full rights, fair employment practices, nondiscrimination in housing, and higher levels of living. Pressure tactics, emotional displays, and florid propaganda displace reason and the exercise of sober judgment in approaches to the solution of common problems" [54:3].

We are asked to distinguish between groups, interests, and pressures whose purposes are not always explicit and whose avowals may be different from the intentions which underlie them. To avoid a feeling of hopelessness, anxiety, and frustration, it is necessary to have the techniques and skills by which a thoughtful evaluation may penetrate to the real significance of what goes on in contemporary society. What is the difference between liberal and subversive activities, indoctrination and education, freedom and license, control and dictatorship?

These characteristics of modern living are of course not exhaustive of the changes that have occurred in our culture, but they are representative. They reveal some of the modern conditions with which prospective teachers are faced. They set the stage on which teachers are to act. They define the requirements of the context in which teachers must develop professional proficiencies. If schools are to keep pace with the conditions of modern life, they should consider how well they will be able to meet the demands of the contemporary social scene. To what extent have educators been aware of the pervasive changes of modern living, and to what extent have they defined the content and methods of formal education in terms of these conditions?

THE CHALLENGE OF THE FUTURE

The changing nature of our culture, as indicated in the preceding section, represents only a prelude to the rate and the scale of change that may take place in the future. We will be encountering the future so rapidly that the ordered and familiar patterns of living may seem to be inadequate to provide direction for us [117:67]. Toffler maintains that this rate of change may become so great that we may experience a state of future shock—"the dizzying disorganization brought on by the premature arrival of the future" [143:13]. In his opinion, "it may well be the most important disease of tomorrow"—a breakdown in communication, a misreading of reality, an inability to cope [143:13]. This possibility raises some fundamental problems for mankind: How much change can he accept and assimilate? How can he retain some familiar clues that, in the past, have guided him into the future? How can he gain and maintain any sense of competence for determining the direction in which this change will take place?

Increasing attention is being given to forecasting the future—sometimes called *futuristics.* As the National Industrial Conference Board points out, many current acute problems—air and water pollution, transportation, inner-city deterioration—might have been lessened if better forecasting had been done twenty or thirty years ago [17:1]. Unless we do more long-range forecasting and planning in all areas—business, industry, government, education, etc.—we will be "backing into the future" [17:1].

The purpose of forecasting is to enable people to make better choices. In brief, it is the process of (1) anticipating what occurrences are possible and assessing their probabilities; (2) identifying the occurrences that can be controlled and the extent of such control; and (3) evaluating alternative future possibilities, considering varying degrees of control that are within our power [17:2]. It is a deliberate process of planning the future rather than planning for the future.

Educators are faced with the challenge of being in the forefront of forecasting the future and planning educational programs that will enable their products—the students—to live constructively in a world that will become increasingly different from the world of today. Unfortunately much of the curriculum in schools today is geared to the past, with little attention being given to the futuristic type of thinking and skill development that future generations must have if, perhaps, they are to survive. Furthermore, with the "premature arrival of tomorrow," it seems certain that education in the future will not be a straight-line extrapolation of the past (Lecture of Alvin Toffler, Indiana University, April 26, 1971).

A number of educators are devoting much thought to education in the future. For example, Donald N. Michael, in his challenging book *The Next Generation* [70], indicates some changes that most likely will take place within the next few years and which will affect greatly the role of the school in society and the work of teachers. Much of the discussion that follows is adapted from three lectures he gave to prospective teachers in an introductory education course.[3]

A generation is a convenient span of time in terms of which teachers

---

[3]Permission granted by Donald N. Michael.

can project on probable changes since (1) the pace of change in politics, technology, society, and the world is so great that it is difficult to make useful predictions much beyond this period of time; (2) this is the period in which you as a teacher will assume major responsibilities as a citizen and as a mediator, moderator, and transmitter of the culture to the pupils you will teach; and (3) the next generation of young people will share, to a greater or lesser degree, the various value systems that exist in today's society. If we go much beyond this time period, it is highly probable that the people who will be growing up and becoming adults will be emphasizing values that are importantly different from those we share.

The speculations that follow apply basically to the United States. What may happen in regard to the rest of the world is vague, extremely complex, and uncertain. It should be held in mind, however, that what happens to us in the future may be affected enormously by what happens in the rest of the world. Michael feels that "whether we live or die over these years may depend more upon what happens in the emerging nations, for example, than on what we do at home."

What, then, may happen during the next few years that has significance for a teacher? Many of these probable happenings are well known and represent only the continuation of current visible trends. *But frequently it is as important to be encouraged to think further upon matters with which we may be familiar as it is to be exposed to new ideas and information.*

1. *Our population will increase considerably, and its composition will change significantly.* The population of the United States reached the historic point of 200 million November 20, 1967. By 1985 it is expected to

FIGURE 1–8   Past and projected population of the world. Note that the population approximately doubled between 1760 and 1880 (120 years) and again between 1880 and 1960 (80 years). What new educational problems will arise if the population doubles between 1960 and the year 2000 (40 years)?

Millions

Year   1900   1930   1970   2000

FIGURE 1–9 Growth in the number of people over 65 years of age in the United States. What educational needs does this increasing population age group present, and how should schools and teachers attempt to meet these needs?

be between 235 and 250 million, with the strong probability of increasing to over 300 million by the turn of the century. In 1975 almost 50 per cent of the population will be less than 25 years of age, and this percentage is expected to increase. In 1970 there were approximately 20 million people 65 years of age and older. It is predicted that this 65 and older age group will grow to 25 million in 1985 and from 28 to 33 million by the year 2000. This condition increases the polarization of our population. We face the increasing problem of meeting the pre-work force needs of the young and the needs of those who are retired. Definite trends toward lowering the age of retirement will increase the percentage of the population who are in the post-work force. From an educational standpoint these two large populations represent decidedly contrasting needs and conflicting value systems. Both between and within these groups there are the well-educated and the ill-educated, the haves and the have-nots, the laggards and the leaders, the concerned and the indifferent. These vast contrasts pose enormous educational problems with which educators will need to grapple. What changes will need to be made in our educational structure to meet the challenge which this situation will present?

   2. *A much greater percentage of our population will be living in*

urban areas. By 1980, approximately 80 per cent of the population in the United States will be living in urban areas, with about 70 per cent living on approximately 5 per cent of the land area. Most of them will be living in four major urban areas, called megalopoli, which will consist of smaller cities that have become fused together. One such area will stretch from Maine to Virginia; another, from Minneapolis and Chicago to Buffalo; a third, from San Francisco to San Diego; and a fourth, from Miami, Florida to Houston, Texas. As a result, there will be unprecedentedly large urban complexes—a situation historically unfamilar, especially to the older generations.

As towns and cities fuse together across state lines, the conventional forms of city and state government will be inadequate to meet the problems and potentials of the regional cities. During this time period, interesting and hopefully successful experiments in new forms of government, school districting, and the like will emerge. At the same time, some urban areas will be growing while others will be decaying—each presenting different needs and value patterns. Density populations in metropolitan areas may reach 700 per square mile as compared to 400 in 1970. If present trends continue, further problems most likely will be generated with respect to crime, pollution, transportation, polarization of black-white communities, housing, simple privacy, social interaction, natural beauty, outdoor recreation, individual freedom, and equal economic and educational opportunities.

How will these changes affect the perspectives and values of youth as well as parents and other adults? In what ways may the organization and financing of school systems be changed? What changes may need to be made in teacher certification procedures, in programs of instruction, and in the preservice and in-service preparation of teachers?

3. *It will become increasingly difficult for the individual to establish and maintain identity, dignity, and purpose in life.* With the trend toward urbanization and the formation of very large cities, parents and children may be less inclined to identify themselves with other people, as well as institutions and communities. Interpersonal relationships may become highly transient. Physical uprooting of families most likely will increase because of the need for parents to change jobs more often. Values may change and life-styles may become more complex. Increased feelings of isolation may exist in the midst of great numbers of people, rapid communication, and transportation. It may become increasingly difficult for the individual to relate to others, to feel a cause or purpose in life, to sense a feeling of adequacy and worth. All these probable conditions may result in the teacher having to play an increasingly significant role in helping youth to establish identity as well as values in terms of which they will direct their lives. How will teachers be able to provide more humanizing experiences for their students without sacrificing opportunities for the students to gain the fundamental knowledge and skills needed

for effective living? How will teachers aid in the development of the twenty-first-century man described by Goodlad [42:4]:

We would have him be a man with a strong sense of himself and his own humanness, with awareness of his thoughts and feelings, with the capacity to feel and express love and joy and to recognize tragedy and feel grief. We would have him be a man who, with a strong and realistic sense of his own worth, is able to relate openly with others, to cooperate effectively with them toward common ends, and to view mankind as one while respecting diversity and difference. We would want him to be a being who, even while very young, somehow senses that he has it within himself to become more than he now is, that he has the capacity for lifelong spiritual and intellectual growth. We would want him to cherish that vision of the man he is capable of becoming and to cherish the development of the same potentiality in others.

4. *The influence of parents upon the educational growth of their children may decrease.* A number of factors will affect the relationship between parents and children. For example, there may be more physical separation of parents and children. More mothers may find it necessary to work, either to satisfy career aspirations or to supplement the family budget. Greater emphasis undoubtedly will be given to preschool experiences which may lessen the contacts of parents with children under six years of age. Ease of transportation may cause children and youth to spend more time away from home in camping, using recreational facilities, traveling, and studying abroad.

There is the possibility, however, that advanced technology may tend to return the family to the center of the stage as a basic learning unit. As Goodlad points out [42:4]:

Each home could become a school, in effect, via an electronic console connected to a central computer system in a learning hub, a videotape and microfilm library regulated by a computer, and a national educational television network. Whether at home or elsewhere, each student, of whatever age, will have at the touch of a button access to a comprehen-

FIGURE 1–10 Past and projected number of women in the work force. The trend toward more women being in the work force will continue. How should the public schools seek to meet their vocational needs? What are the implications for the education of children of working women?

Millions of women in the labor force

sive "learning package," including printed lessons, experiments to be performed, recorded information, videotaped lectures, and films.

5. *There may be a definite increase in the number of women in the labor force.* Between 1969 and 1980 the number of women in the labor force is expected to increase from a total of 30 million to a total of 37 million—employed either full-time or on a part-time basis [50:5]. It is estimated that 22 million of these 37 million women in 1980 will be married. A relatively high percentage of them will be between the ages of 20 and 44 years, having children under 18 years of age at home. In what ways may the educational needs and objectives of girls change? How may the work of a teacher be affected by this tendency for an increasing number of mothers to work at least part-time in the labor force? What are the implications for the establishment of day-care centers?

6. *The percentage of culturally deprived children may increase, especially in the central part of large metropolitan cities.* By 1980, 50 per cent of the children living in the central part of our large metropolitan cities may be considered to be culturally deprived. Unless rather drastic measures are taken to curtail the development of this condition, a very significant percentage of young people will never be able to develop fully their potential for effective democratic living. Benjamin Bloom, in his book *Stability and Change in Human Characteristics,* finds that the intellectual and emotional deprivation of many children begins early. From his studies [6:104–105], he finds that half of a person's "intellectuality," as well as general intelligence, is formed by the age of four. By the age of six, when a child enters school, he has developed as much as two-thirds of the intelligence he will have at maturity. Even with regard to purely academic achievement, at least one-third of the development at age 18 has taken place prior to a child's entrance into the first grade at school. If children are deprived of early intellectual stimulation, they may never reach the heights of which they might be capable.

Bloom maintains that the environment has a maximum impact on the development of a specific trait during the period of time in which that trait experiences the most rapid growth. For example, a starvation diet would not affect the height of an eighteen-year-old, but could severely retard the growth of a one-year-old baby—a loss that might never be recovered. Other studies indicate that poor diet in very young children also can permanently damage intellectual growth.

What measures are being taken and what new steps should be taken in order to overcome the problems of cultural deprivation of people in our society? How can educators help in solving this problem?

7. *In terms of the way we shall be living (life-styles), there will be opportunities for greater diversity in the midst of conformity.* A study of life in various communities will reveal that the level of anonymity for the individual tends to increase as the population of a city increases. As the population of urban areas increases, therefore, people will have greater

freedom to experiment with the styles of living they desire. They will be developing and experimenting with different sets of values which will affect how they live, what they aspire to, how they want their children educated, what kinds of education they want for themselves, and where they want to live.

Within this context of anonymity, the individual may become increasingly self-centered and demanding. He may tend to use people with careless indifference of the consequences to them; take from the material world whatever he wishes, but seldom if ever give anything in return; insist upon being permitted nearly everything and being held accountable for nothing; become increasingly disrespectful of law and order—frequently resorting to violence, lawlessness, and crime; and become insensitive to the need for any environmental controls.

Concurrent with this probable change in life-styles, there may be a tendency for values to become negotiable items. As the National Industrial Conference Board points out [17:51]:

Goals, values, and ethics in U.S. society are being questioned, modified, and traded. This state of flux grows out of and accompanies transitions from a "yesterday" controlled by adults to a "today" dominated by young people; from a production to a service economy; from a concern for quantity and status to a quest for quality and equality. Schizoid situations proliferate. "The establishment" sees traditional values as eroding; the young believe that many of these values have lost their relevance, and that "the establishment" obstructs change. The sweep of power from individuals and single units to groups and conglomerates, from a pluralistic power base to a powerful apex, throws up in its wake serious questions concerning cherished American ideals. The question is: Which values will be traded and which held?

Teachers will have the opportunity to work with students who represent a greater variety of life-styles. They will be confronted with the more difficult task of helping youth as well as adults clarify their values in terms of which their behavior will be governed and to build more meaningful concepts of freedom and responsibility in a democratic society.

8. *More and more demands will be made for high-level social competence.* In the past our lives have been related basically to our local environments. In the future our lives will be affected more by our continental and world environments. So many things will be happening in so many places that the environment in which teachers and students live will become quite complex. The number of significant social interactions will become almost overwhelming.

Only recently have we begun to take seriously first-class citizenship for blacks, as well as the recognition of the need to do something about poverty in our society. There are many other social requirements which we must set for ourselves. We are only beginning to recognize that we must be more humane and prepare sensible and meaningful lives for older people. There are questions regarding air and water pollution,

26

traffic control, population control, conservation of resources, etc. All these interact with one another, and all these have assets and liabilities with regard to carrying out each of them. A teacher will not be able to concentrate totally on the discipline he is teaching or on the community in which he is located. To be a good teacher, he will have to transcend subject-matter disciplines as well as local attachments. These conditions will put a much greater burden upon teachers than in the past, when life was less complex, less closely coupled, and less loaded with events of enormous implication.

9. *Leisure will become an increasingly important part of the lives of many.* Automation, shorter work weeks, earlier retirement, and longer life-spans will provide even greater amounts of free time for the individual to spend as he wishes. Increasing affluence will extend the scope of ways in which he may choose to spend this free time. Free time, therefore, will become a very important part of life. It will take on a legitimacy and a significance that our Protestant ethic-oriented society has not had in the past. Even though work will still be considered a moral obligation of the individual, leisure will be considered a more virtuous part of life. For some people, increased free time will present a wonderful opportunity in which they may grow—a time for personal fulfillment. For others it may be a period of boredom, frustration, and anxiety—or a time for dangerous and sometimes criminal activities as a way of getting a "kick" out of life. If children are to avoid the undesirable results of increased leisure time, they need to learn before they grow up how to find

FIGURE 1–11 Projected changes in the spending of family income. Between 1968 and 1980, it is estimated that the amount of money spent on nondurables (clothing, food, paper goods, etc.) will increase 50 per cent; expenditures for services (laundry, restaurants, recreation, health, repairs, etc.) will increase 75 per cent; but expenditures for durables (cars, appliances, furniture, etc.) will increase 100 per cent. At the turn of the century, about half of the average wage earner's weekly pay was spent on food. In 1980 less than one-fifth of his wages will be needed for food. What are the social, economic, and educational implications of these changes?

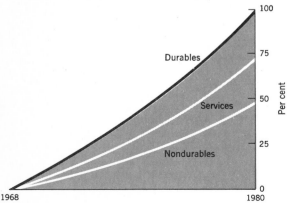

personal enrichment in their free time. Toynbee, the great historian, warns that never in the history of man has any nation been able to accumulate a vast amount of leisure time for its people and survive.

How to help both young and old learn to use leisure time for personal enrichment and fulfillment presents exciting and important opportunities for the teacher. How will the work of a teacher be affected? How might the role of the school in the community change? What changes may be made in the school's curriculum? Will cocurricular activities in the school take on added significance? What changes might take place in the use of the school's library, auditorium, playground, or fine arts and music departments? Will the use of the school's facilities tend to follow the 24 hours per day pattern of operation that more industries and businesses may adopt as a result of automation? What new requests for the services of teachers may be made by industries, businesses, recreation centers, and government agencies?

10. *We will become increasingly aware of the need for environmental controls.* Although environmental scientists have been concerned for some time about the serious, perhaps irreversible, deterioration of the ecological conditions that support life on this earth, mankind received its first shocking realization of the problems on Christmas Eve 1968 when the astronauts sent back pictures of the earth. For the first time, in the words of Von Braun, "We saw the beautiful little blue silver sphere on which we live shining forth against the blackness of infinity. The peoples of the earth saw for the first time how finite our habitat really is; they sensed its essential frailty" [129:5].

The threat to human survival comes from several interrelated problems: (1) the explosive increase in human population; (2) an awesome increase in man's ability to alter the environment (largely through the release of vast quantities of gaseous, liquid, and solid effluent), and (3) rapid depletion of resources that are in finite supply. If man is to survive, it is imperative that all three of the problems be dealt with simultaneously [149:10].

Although the population of the United States is only a fraction of the world's population, we proportionately are by far the most serious "pollutants" since we are the largest per capita consumers of goods and materials. What should be the role of educators in assisting mankind to establish bases for survival?

11. *The educational attainment of our population will continue to rise.* Between 1965 and 1985 the percentage of men 25 years of age and over who have completed four years or more of college is expected to increase from 11.4 to 19.4 per cent, and the increase for women is expected to be from 6.4 to 9.7 percent [97:1]. During this period of time the total number of high school graduates is expected to rise from about 47 million to 87 or 88 million among persons 25 years old and over. At the same time it is anticipated that there will be a sharp reduction in the percentage of persons 25 years old and over who have had less than five

When viewed from the surface of the moon, the earth appears as a giant space ship carrying its own life support system. Learning how to preserve this finite system has become a major educational responsibility. *(Photograph from National Aeronautics and Space Administration.)*

years of formal schooling. The expected increase in the median years of school completed by those 25 years old and over may also serve as an indicator of improvement in educational attainment. Between 1960 and 1985 the median is expected to increase from 10.5 to 12.4 years of formal schooling [97:2]. What effect may this expected increase in educational attainment have on the pupils as well as on the parents and other adults with whom teachers will work? How will our economy and social structure be affected?

12. *Both basic and applied knowledge will expand at a very rapid rate.* "If we start with the birth of Christ as the base point, it is estimated that man's knowledge doubled for the first time around 1750. The second doubling of man's knowledge occurred by 1900. . . . With the acceleration of an industrial and business economy, man's knowledge doubled a third time by 1950 and a fourth time by 1960" [68:11]. We may expect this trend in the expansion of knowledge to continue, especially when we consider that, for example, 90 per cent of all the scientists who have lived since the dawn of history are living and working today [17:21]. Bentley Glass, a distinguished scientist and past national president of Phi Beta Kappa, states [39:44]:

The obsolescence of education in rapidly developing fields of knowledge has become about equal in rate to the obsolescence of an automobile. In five to seven years it is due for a complete replacement. It follows that our times, to a degree generally quite unrecognized, demand a major reconstitution of the educational process, which must become one of life-long renewal. Perhaps a month out of every year, or three months every third year, might be an acceptable new pattern. Indeed, instead of cramming the educational years of life into adolescence and early maturity, a more efficient plan might be to interrupt education with work periods after elementary school, high school, and college. In any case, programs of continuing education for all professional people must become mandatory, and the educational effort and expenditures must be expanded by at least a third to permit adequate retraining and reeducation.

How will the school system be affected by the continuing education needs of all ages of people? What kinds of skills and attitudes should teachers attempt to develop in students so that they may be effective citizens, competent to deal with the problems they will face in life? What implications does this rapid increase in knowledge have for the in-service education of teachers—how can they be relevant in content, process, and procedures?

13. *Significant technological changes will take place as a result of more automation and the use of computers.* The term "cybernation" refers to the use of computers in automation. Through the use of a procedure known as numerical control, computers will replace many skilled workers who, in the past, have designed and fabricated complex components for such things as shipbuilding and automobile manufacturing. Much of what is called design work, in such areas as architecture and engineering, is a fairly routine task of working through a series of alternatives. This type of design can now be done by computers. As a result, a person may try out different models of how an airplane might be designed, how a certain kind of economic system might operate, how a particular national strategy might be construed, or how some type of educational program might function. In other words, a computer may be used to try out various ideas and refine them before they are actually put into operation.

It is easy to see that job opportunities, as well as the lives of many people, will be affected greatly by cybernation.

Many unskilled workers will lose out to machines, and some extension of the antipoverty program may be needed to provide them with the services they cannot afford. However, some unskilled jobs will remain and some new ones will be created. Automation will turn some jobs that now require skill into jobs that merely require watching a meter or a dial; other jobs which now require a high level of skill will be split into simpler ones that will be done in part by semiskilled workers and in part by machines.

Many skilled workers will be forced to retrain. Already, skilled machinists' jobs have begun to be abolished as computer-controlled machine tools take over their tasks. Gradually, many bank clerks, office workers, auditors, draftsmen, and middle-level managers and engineers will find their work being done by computers [71:8–9].

The work of highly creative persons will not be threatened by cybernation. Rather, they will have more latitude for being creative. For example, creative people in such areas as economics, political science,

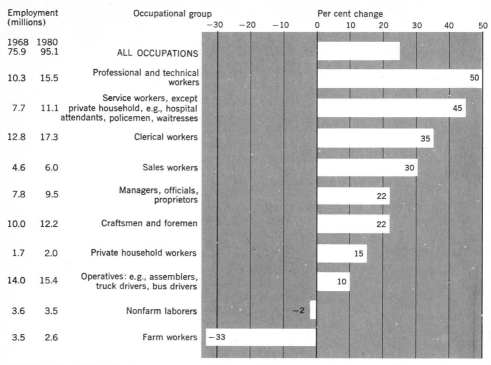

Employment (millions)		Occupational group	Per cent change
1968	1980		
75.9	95.1	ALL OCCUPATIONS	
10.3	15.5	Professional and technical workers	50
7.7	11.1	Service workers, except private household, e.g., hospital attendants, policemen, waitresses	45
12.8	17.3	Clerical workers	35
4.6	6.0	Sales workers	30
7.8	9.5	Managers, officials, proprietors	22
10.0	12.2	Craftsmen and foremen	22
1.7	2.0	Private household workers	15
14.0	15.4	Operatives: e.g., assemblers, truck drivers, bus drivers	10
3.6	3.5	Nonfarm laborers	−2
3.5	2.6	Farm workers	−33

FIGURE 1–12 Estimated changes between 1968 and 1980 in occupational groups. What are the educational implications of these changes?

and the behavioral sciences will be able to conceptualize about man and his environment in a much higher and different manner from that which is available without the assistance of the computer. Likewise, the demand for people in most of the professions will increase greatly, and the hours of work per week will tend to be longer than at present.

The person who does a routine kind of physical or mental work, on the other hand, will be potentially subject to displacement. This means that, in the years ahead, we shall find many people being continually displaced from their jobs, having to learn new jobs, and having to live in a number of different locations and to learn new ways of life. It means that children will grow up recognizing the fact that many of them will have two or three careers which will involve seven or eight different jobs during their work years. It means that they may spend a significant amount of their lives in school being retrained and reeducated. Obviously, the vocational education programs in our schools will need to undergo considerable reorientation. It also means that the demands upon teachers and vocational counselors will increase greatly. How should teachers attempt to counsel and educate youth for a work world that is becoming so complex—when many of the jobs that will exist in the year 2000 are not

now known? How can we absorb effectively another 15 million into the
labor force during the 1970s and early 1980s in spite of the decreasing
number of man-hours required for the production of goods?

14. *There will be a decided increase in management technology.*
Management technology refers to a set of procedures, techniques, and
approaches to organizing, on a national scale and over long periods of
time, the manpower brawn and brains to accomplish major tasks. In other
words, brain power may be organized administratively and procedurally
in much the same way as men have been organized to use their muscles in
the past. Management technology makes it possible to plan ahead and to
undertake activities that may literally change the nation in terms of how
various resources and agencies are used.

Management technology started after World War II as a new approach to the development of our weapons system, and has been applied
more recently to the space program, to city building and rebuilding, to
oceanography, to the construction of school buildings, and in a number
of other areas. Undoubtedly this trend will continue. This means that
more and more people will be meshed in larger and larger administration

FIGURE 1–13   Estimated percentage changes between 1968 and 1980 in various industries. State and
local government and service industries will experience the most rapid gains. What effect will these
changes have upon the occupational needs of youth?

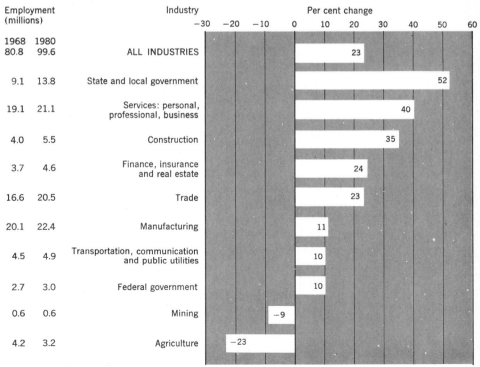

Employment (millions)		Industry	Per cent change
1968	1980		
80.8	99.6	ALL INDUSTRIES	23
9.1	13.8	State and local government	52
19.1	21.1	Services: personal, professional, business	40
4.0	5.5	Construction	35
3.7	4.6	Finance, insurance and real estate	24
16.6	20.5	Trade	23
20.1	22.4	Manufacturing	11
4.5	4.9	Transportation, communication and public utilities	10
2.7	3.0	Federal government	10
0.6	0.6	Mining	−9
4.2	3.2	Agriculture	−23

complexes. How will an individual in this type of complex maintain a sense of loyalty, dignity, and worth? What new skills, understandings, and attitudes will be needed?

15. *We probably will experience a greater degree of social engineering.* The term "social engineering," refers to the systematic application of social science to the organization, control, direction, and motivation of man and his institutions. The computer enables the social scientist to do two things he has never been able to do before. First, he can build enormously complex models about man and his institutions. In the past, his work was done using only simple models because he was unable to keep the many variables in mind and manipulate them. But the computer has the capacity to manipulate very large numbers of variables. This means that very complex and subtle models of how men behave in groups and organizations can be conceived of and simulated on computers. Second, by virtue of the computer, he can collect data about society as it is now, check the computer models against them, and determine whether the models represent reality. In the past the social scientist was not able to do this type of verification, since it took a long time to collect the data and to process them. Because of the rapid processing of data, there exists the potential for developing far more sophisticated social sciences.

We inevitably will have available, for good or for bad, many more opportunities to control or be controlled than we have had in the past. More funds will be available for research to evaluate and understand what is happening as growth takes place in federal programs dealing with such areas as education, poverty, unemployment, pollution, population, counterinsurgency, and guerrilla warfare. It will be necessary to conduct this research in order that we will not flounder in our own complexity. This raises a basic problem of determining who is going to do the job of deciding what is to be controlled as well as that of controlling it. What are going to be the ethical bases for deciding what is to be controlled? Who is to be controlled and under what circumstances? This kind of power carries with it a potential for corruption, even for destroying our whole democratic system. Since education is bound to be affected to some extent, this profound ethical question will confront teachers in the future.

16. *There may be an increasing professionalization of the government and all activities having to do with the planning and administration of society.* Almost everyone will admit that, as our population increases, the task of governing ourselves will become more complex. We note the increasing role being played by the government in solving the complex and technical problems faced by our society. The solution of many of these problems calls for the services of people who are highly competent in governmental affairs. Perhaps the greatest challenge for our society over the years ahead is going to be meeting the increasing professionalization of the government and of all other activities having to do with the

planning and administration of our society. This condition raises the very important question of the role played by the citizen who is not part of the professional governmental processes by which our society will be conducted. Is there a danger of following the same plan that has been formally approved in Russia for the establishment of a national computer network for the collection and processing of information essential for the control, the planning, and the management of the country's economy—in fact, all aspects of that nation's life? How will teachers be able to face the critical challenge of helping pupils and adults identify themselves with and play significant citizenship roles in the direction of the nation and in other democratic processes?

17. *Major and dramatic advancement most likely will be made in biological engineering.* It is generally agreed that the developments in biological science and their application over the next two decades will be at least as spectacular as the development of atom smashers and the like in the field of physics. One development will be that of the increased ability to alter brain processes, modify personality, and control behavior through the use of chemical agents, drugs, and electronic devices. Krech [62:48] feels that in the not too distant future teachers will be "talking about enzyme-assisted instruction, protein memory consolidators, antibiotic memory repellers, and the chemistry of the brain." There is much evidence that memories can be enhanced or wiped out. Biologists probably will be able to change characteristics that might be inherited. They may be able to predetermine the sex of a baby. They will be able to help the aged to revitalize their memories, skills, and abilities. They undoubtedly will find ways to manipulate the emotional and cognitive characteristics of human beings.

This raises several questions: Who has the right to make these changes? What are the implications of these advancements for dealing with behavior problems, psychological disorders, juvenile delinquency, potential school dropouts, crime, and the like? Will there be possibilities of motivating more young people to develop their capacities for democratic living to the fullest extent possible? What new educational needs and economic and social complexities may arise if it becomes possible to revitalize the memories and abilities of older people?

Some Major Professional Challenges Facing Teachers

In addition to those already mentioned, what are some other major professional challenges which the future holds for teachers?

1. How should a teacher balance his role between being the agent for conserving the styles of the past and acting as the cutting edge for disrupting traditions and inventing new ones? It has always been a

question whether the task of education is to prepare people to fit the society or to prepare them to change the society. In the past, teachers have been able to be rather casual about the problem because the nature of society did not change very fast. But the future is going to change society fast and radically, and a teacher is going to be confronted perpetually with the problem of determining his role as a conserver of the past and as an innovator so far as the future is concerned.

2. What will be an appropriate role model for a teacher? In the future the status of the teacher in society will increase because the welfare of society will be more and more dependent on education of all sorts and at all ages.

Education will be available almost on a cradle-to-grave basis. More children of all economic groups will attend nursery school and kindergarten. Post-high school educa- tion will be more widely available and, with increased recognition that a well-educated population is a national necessity, government subsidies for higher education will be more general.

Many different kinds of institutions will provide opportunities for lifelong education. Community colleges, vocational schools, centers for instruction in recreation activities, and institutions attached to industry, business, and government will cater to all individu- als, regardless of age: Indeed, we will see more and more intermingling of age groups as education becomes a general condition of living rather than just early preparation for it [71:11–12].

As a result of these highly probable conditions, a teacher will play an exceedingly important role in the lives of his pupils as well as in those of many adults. To his pupils a teacher will be an expression of adulthood and the opportunities which being an adult presents. Expressing the adult world through what one teaches and relating it to society become a very interesting, difficult, and challenging task for the teacher.

3. How should a teacher attempt to promote the growth and devel- opment of wisdom in his pupils? We shall need people who are more than skilled engineers, scientists, and technicians. We shall need people who are humanists, who have the intuition that is necessary to under- stand the human predicament, and who have the insight to do the things that the large society with its high aspirations sets for itself. It is going to take wise men and women, indeed, to act in such ways that save the individual from being lost sight of in the mass. In the past we have been able to bumble through and manage to get along with only a few wise people. No man could do very much good or evil to mankind. But this will not be the case in the future. To do good in the future will require more than technological skill. It will require wisdom. "Without wisdom, technical brilliance alone could lead to social or physical disaster and the destruction of the democratic way of life. Somehow, our schools and homes must educate for and practice wisdom, compassion, courage,

tolerance of uncertainty, and appreciation of the unique and different" [71:14].

SUMMARY

In the first part of this chapter an attempt was made to indicate briefly some contributions that education has made in the growth and development of our nation. More than ever before in the history of mankind, our future progress will depend upon how well schools fulfill their role. Stated differently, the need for quality education has never been greater, and, in the years to come, the need will increase still more. This, therefore, constitutes one of the important reasons for becoming a teacher.

The second part of the chapter was concerned with a number of changes that have taken place in our culture during the past quarter of a century. These changes have called for major modifications to be made in school organization, procedures, and practices.

In the third part of the chapter, an attempt was made to indicate some of the technological and social changes that may take place in the future and the need for teachers to help those of the next generation acquire the knowledge, skills, and attitudes that will enable them to deal successfully with the increasing complexity of life. Teachers face the challenge of discovering new ways of helping youth as well as adults gain the competencies they will need to cope adequately and effectively with the complexity of problems they will face and to preserve and refine the basic freedoms that characterize our way of life. Never in the history of mankind has the need for education been greater. Never have teachers faced so great a challenge.

QUESTIONS TO CONSIDER

1. What features of the American school system have especially contributed to the phenomenal growth and success of America?
2. Have you ever experienced any school practices and procedures that showed a lack of respect for the dignity and worth of the individual? How will you attempt to avoid the use of such practices and procedures?
3. Does the concept of equal educational opportunity mean that all pupils should receive the same kind and amount of education?
4. John W. Gardner has stated: "At this moment in history, free institutions are on trial." What evidences would support (or not support) such a statement?
5. In the second part of this chapter you noted some major changes that have taken place in our society. What educational implications do you see in each of these changes?
6. In an age of advancing technology, upon what bases can you defend a program of general education as a part of your college education?

7. How will technological changes that may take place during the next few years affect the function of the school and the role of the classroom teacher?
8. If greater emphasis is placed upon helping youth "learn how to learn," how will the nature of the teacher's work change?
9. How will you attempt to educate youth for the effective use of leisure time?
10. In what ways should public schools attempt to meet the educational needs of adults?

PROBLEM SITUATION FOR INQUIRY

The school system in Bayview is faced with a crisis. The school district treasury has been depleted, and the regular distribution of tax funds from the state will not be available for three months. The district has gone to the voters of Bayview four times during the last two years asking for additional taxes to operate the schools. Each time the voters have rejected the proposal. A fifth vote is to be taken within the next four weeks. If the issue is not approved by two-thirds of the voters, it will be necessary to close the schools in Bayview for a period of two months until the distribution of taxes is received from the state.

Bayview is a retirement community in which a large number of the residents do not have children attending the Bayview schools. An analysis of the previous four defeats indicates that the request for new taxes has been defeated by the segment of the community which does not have children enrolled in the schools.

If you were the superintendent of the Bayview school district, what would you do in an effort to convince *all* the voters that education is a worthwhile community investment?

ACTIVITIES TO PURSUE

1. List what you consider to be the major challenges that teaching holds for you. Discuss these challenges with some of your college teachers, or with other students who plan to teach, to see whether they agree with your challenges.
2. Read *Future Shock,* by Alvin Toffler, and *The Next Generation,* by Donald N. Michael. Discuss the contents of each with your colleagues. Make a list of implications for education which emerge from their projections.
3. Make a list of new opportunities that will open to teachers during the next few years as a result of technological and social changes that most likely will occur. Check your list with some of your colleagues and professors.
4. Confer with some leading executives in business and industry regarding their views on the importance of education to our economy. Ask them to indicate what educational responsibilities their businesses and industries may need to assume in the future.
5. Confer with employment agencies in your community regarding the changes in employment patterns they have noticed during the past few years. What changes do they anticipate so far as the future is concerned?
6. Visit one or more preschool projects especially designed for culturally deprived children. Observe the kinds of activities being provided for children, and discuss with the teachers what they hope to accomplish.
7. Talk with one or more social workers and with those working in various welfare agencies regarding the importance of education. What solutions do they see for welfare problems? In their opinions, how will the lives of children whose parents are on welfare be affected?
8. Discuss with your colleagues the educational role, if any, that our federal government should take in alleviating the problems of people who are culturally deprived, who are unemployed, who have unequal educational opportunities.
9. Ask some Appalachian whites, blacks, Puerto Ricans, Chicanos, or American Indians

how education can improve their lives and their people. Discuss your findings with your colleagues.

10. Discuss with your colleagues the changes that most likely will take place in the United States within the next 10 to 20 years. What modifications in the elementary and secondary school curriculum do these changes suggest?

FIGURE CREDITS

FIGURE 1–1 (*Source: 200 Million Americans,* U.S. Department of Commerce, Bureau of the Census, Washington, November, 1967, p. 57.)

FIGURE 1–2 (*Source:* Data from "Ranking of the States 1971," *Research Report 1971–R6,* National Education Association, Research Division, Washington, 1971, p. 28.)

FIGURE 1–3 (*Source:* Adapted from "Does Increased Education Produce Increased Income?" *NEA Research Bulletin,* vol. 46, no. 4, National Education Association, Research Division, Washington, December, 1968, p. 103.)

FIGURE 1–4 (*Source:* Data from *Statistical Abstract of the United States,* U.S. Department of Commerce, Bureau of the Census, Washington, 1970, p. 312, and *The Realities of School Finance,* American Association of School Administrators, Washington, 1970, p. 10.)

FIGURE 1–5 (*Source:* Kenneth A. Simon, and W. Vance Grant, *Digest of Educational Statistics,* U.S. Office of Education, National Center for Educational Statistics, Washington, 1970, p. 10.)

FIGURE 1–6 (*Source:* "Farms in U.S.," *The Wall Street Journal,* Dow Jones and Company, Inc., New York, Mar. 30, 1971, p. 1.)

FIGURE 1–7 (*Source:* Arnold B. Barach, *USA and Its Economic Future,* Twentieth Century Fund, Inc., New York, 1964, p. 3.)

FIGURE 1–8 (*Source:* Harrison, Brown, and E. K. Fedorov, "Too Many People in the World?" *Saturday Review,* Feb. 17, 1962, p. 18.)

FIGURE 1–9 (*Source:* Data from "Our No. 1 Priority," *NRTA Journal,* vol. 20, no. 96, National Retired Teachers Association, Ojai, California, July–August, 1970, p. 4.)

FIGURE 1–10 (*Source:* J. D. Hodgson, "Manpower Patterns of the 70's," *Manpower,* vol. 3, no. 2., U.S. Department of Labor, Washington, February, 1971, p. 5.)

FIGURE 1–11 (*Source:* Reprinted by permission from *Changing Times,* the Kiplinger Magazine, (January 1970 issue). Copyright 1970 by The Kiplinger Washington Editors, Inc., 1729 H Street, N.W., Washington, D.C., 20006.)

FIGURE 1–12 (*Source:* "Economic Status of the Teaching Profession, 1970–71," *Research Report 1971–R4,* National Education Association, Research Division, Washington, 1971, p. 10.)

FIGURE 1–13 (*Source:* "Economic Status of the Teaching Profession, 1970–71," *Research Report 1971–R4,* National Education Association, Research Division, Washington, 1971, p. 11.)

2 | PLANNING A CAREER IN THE TEACHING PROFESSION

As may be concluded from reading Chapter 1, the task of preparing for a successful career in the teaching profession is far more demanding today than it was in the past. Furthermore, due to the inevitable changes that will take place in the role of teachers in tomorrow's schools, the task of maintaining a high level of success will be increasingly demanding and difficult.

Some students, unfortunately, have not given careful consideration to their decisions to become teachers, or to the basic attributes required for successful teaching, or to the means by which they can develop into the most competent teachers possible, or to the specific types of positions for which they might prepare. Some prospective teachers have decided to teach in secondary schools because, having been recently graduated, they are more familiar with this level. But if they had investigated other levels, such as early childhood education, they might have found themselves more interested in and more qualified to work with young children. Other students have decided to teach in high school largely because they feel that secondary teachers have more prestige than elementary teachers. Still others find themselves majoring in English or social studies because they are not familiar with opportunities in other areas, such as speech or hearing therapy, special education, or library science, in which they might have been interested and well qualified.

Planning for teaching involves much more than being admitted to a program of teacher education, passing the required number of courses for certification, and securing a teaching position upon graduation. A career in education is a phase of life planning which involves fundamental values of life and which is integrally related to home life and citizenship. The completion of collegiate professional training is only an initial phase in the professional life of an educator and does not ensure professional success regardless of the quality of the courses completed. The full realization of values inherent in a teaching career depends largely upon the extent to which the individual attempts to realize those values.

The Nature of Career Planning

Planning is essentially a continuous life process in which action is directed by an individual's critically reasoned values and goals. It involves the constant weighing of these values and goals.

All career planning obviously must be tentative in nature in order to adjust to changing conditions and demands. In fact, the very essence of planning is one of continuous change, modification, and adaptation. Therefore, many of the initial details of any master plan or blueprint which you may formulate for your career will change as the years pass. But a master plan will give direction to your professional growth. The details will enable you to expend energy efficiently and to gain greater realization of your goals in life.

SUGGESTED STEPS IN PLANNING A CAREER IN EDUCATION

The broad outline of steps to be followed in planning a career in education is no different from that to be followed in planning for any career. Consequently, not all your efforts will be lost if, after thoroughly exploring teaching as a profession, you come to the thoughtful conclusion that this is not the lifework for which you are best suited. Your efforts will make it easier for you to plan in terms of another occupational objective.

Importance of Values and Goals in Career Planning

An individual normally seeks to do the things that seem important to him. In other words, the things he values provide the foundation for his goals. It is important, therefore, that an individual's vocational goals be consistent with what he desires, strives for, and approves in life.

Values are the intangible bases for behavior. They constitute the foundation for the things we cherish in life. They may be expressed in such terms as freedom, equality, individualism, dignity of man, self-respect, democracy, cooperativeness, service to mankind, the golden rule, prestige, trustworthiness, dependability, thrift, and open-mindedness.

Values are acquired. They are cultural—learned through experience [118:71].

Man's behavior is governed by the values he has come to accept during the years of cumulative experiences that make up his lifetime. What he thinks, what he looks upon as "good," and what he does are controlled and restricted by the chains forged by his values: uplifting or debasing, humane or bestial—whatever his experience has made them.

Since the life experiences of no two individuals are the same, the values they hold will not be identical. On the other hand, every society has certain values which characterize it, and the individuals who have grown up in that society tend to hold those values in common. In America, respect for the uniqueness and worth of the individual, freedom, equality, and shared responsibility for the common good are examples of common basic values. Since the school is concerned with developing, strengthening, and transmitting values considered to be desirable in this society, it is important for a teacher to have a clear and functional understanding of them.

Many people have never consciously examined their basic values or tested the internal consistency of them. As a result, their behavior may seem to be inconsistent in various kinds of situations, and they may have difficulty in working effectively with others. A recent study of teacher attitudes as a function of values indicates that teachers with consistent educational values, whether they be extremely emergent or extremely traditional, were more sure of their classroom practices and displayed more approval of school practices than other teachers [23:461–462]. Since the teacher as a person is the most important single factor in the classroom, it is extremely important for him to have a clearly reasoned and consistent set of values which is in harmony with the tenets of a democratic society.

Since your values will range from mild preference to intense convictions, it will be relatively easy for you to identify your major values, such as service to mankind, and to use them as criteria for testing your career choice. It is more difficult to analyze all your values in great detail and to derive a whole pattern of criteria for testing teaching as a career. If you construct this pattern as completely as you can, you will be much more certain of your decision.

Each occupation has its unique pattern of inherent values that may be pursued by an individual who engages in that occupation. If you discover that teaching fails to meet a significant number of the tests you establish, you have an obligation to yourself and to the teaching profession to explore the possibility of preparing for some other occupation. Hence, the first and perhaps the most difficult step in planning a career in education is to answer as accurately and as completely as possible the following questions:

1. What do I value in life?
2. Why are these my values?

3. Are these values desirable?
4. Are these values internally consistent?
5. What life goals emerge from my values?
6. Can I best realize my life goals through a career in education?

Importance of Self-appraisal in Planning for Teaching

Cervantes advised, "Make it thy business to know thyself, which is the most difficult lesson in the world." His advice is certainly appropriate for anyone engaged in the process of planning a career. Furthermore, understanding oneself is essential for understanding others. Two psychologists report the following about the relationship of self-understanding to the understanding of others [60:6]:

What the teacher sees in the student, the way he feels about him, and what he derives from his dealings with him will be influenced not only by the kind of person the student is but also the kind of person the teacher is and by the kind of situation that is created when the two are together. To the extent that the student's behavior, as seen by the instructor, reflects the instructor's own perceptions and attitudes, he will be unable to understand the student unless he understands himself. Similarly, the way in which the instructor interprets or evaluates a student's attitudes or conduct will be influenced by his own values, likes, and dislikes. The greater this influence is, the more the instructor's perception of his student will be a reflection of himself rather than an objective, or unbiased, reaction. Therefore, it is essential for the instructor to take stock of his own involvement and, as far as possible, make allowance for it.

Jersild and Associates feel that understanding oneself and others involves more than an intellectual process [60:9]:

One can master the facts, principles, and laws contained in a hundred books on psychology and still understand neither oneself nor others. Self-understanding requires integrity rather than mere cleverness. It involves emotion. To know oneself, one must be

FIGURE 2–1   Major steps involved in planning a career.

1	CLARIFICATION OF Values Goals Wants		
2	ANALYSIS OF Career requirements		
3	SELF-ANALYSIS Strengths Weaknesses		
4	PLANS FOR CAREER College Intermediate Later life		

able to feel as well as think. One must be able to recognize feelings, face them, and deal with them in constructive ways; and this is something quite different from reading or talking about them with detachment.

Influence of Requirements upon Planning for Teaching

Perhaps no career imposes more varied requirements on the successful worker than does teaching. Although general competency as a citizen seems to include most of the requirements for success in many careers, it is only the first requisite in teaching. Above and beyond this requirement lie the many aspects of special expertness demanded of the teacher. The basic concern at this point is to emphasize the need for an analysis to be made of the requirements which a career as a teacher imposes. This analysis should include a stocktaking of your present qualifications. If the analysis of all your qualifications reveals certain deficiencies which you cannot or do not wish to remove, you again have warning of trouble ahead. Likewise, revelation of unusual strengths in this analysis should bear a strong implication for your future, and your plans in the field of education should involve use of these special strengths.

A subsequent section of this chapter should provide you with an understanding of the competencies you normally should have in order to be a successful teacher. An excellent statement of characteristics of the competent teacher is to be found at the end of this chapter. The changing organizational and instructional patterns and procedures discussed in Chapter 4 have implications for the competencies essential for successful teaching in the schools of tomorrow. Chapter 5 indicates some of the changes and demands that may result from the increased use of educational technology. The growing strength of the teaching profession (Chapter 6) will place even greater demand for competence upon the part of teachers.

Influence of Other Factors upon Planning for Teaching

Many other factors should be taken into consideration in order to plan a career in education wisely. Various sections of this book are designed to help you in this regard. For example, Chapter 3 should assist you in exploring the vast range of opportunities in the field of education. Should you be a nursery school or kindergarten teacher? Would you like teaching in the elementary school? Would you enjoy teaching in the emerging middle school, or the junior high school? Would you be interested in high school teaching? Could you teach on the college level? Should you do specialized teaching, i.e., teaching the gifted, the physically handicapped, the culturally different, the mentally retarded, or the emotionally disturbed? What opportunities are there for supervisory or administrative

positions, for teaching disadvantaged children, for teaching in differentiated staffing situations, for teaching overseas? Explore this wide range
of opportunities so that your abilities and interests may best be utilized
and your success and happiness in the profession may be proportionately
increased.

Attention also should be given to a number of other factors that will
affect you as a teacher. For example, teachers will be affected increasingly
with a variety of legal liabilities and responsibilities (Chapter 7). Likewise, teachers will need to be concerned with the effective solution of a
number of long-standing issues and problems in education (Chapter 8),
as well as a variety of relatively new ones that have emerged in recent
years from major social, economic, and technological changes in our
society (Chapter 9). As you continue your planning, you will discover
other factors which should be investigated and evaluated.

Further Suggested Procedures for Planning a Career in Education

In order to do a really effective job in planning for teaching, you may
wish to engage in the following major activities:

Put your plans on paper. Many people have found that the act of
writing out their plans is in itself of great help to them. The necessary
labor involved in selecting and weaving in the various ideas causes
planners to be more critical and objective. This procedure—often called
"writing the planning paper"—has been used in colleges and universities
for a number of years with considerable evidence of worthwhile results.

Many students experience difficulty in getting started in the writing
of their plans. This is understandable in view of the fact that planning is,
or at least should be, the most highly individual task that any student can
undertake. By virtue of differences in backgrounds, values absorbed,
and goals desired, each student differs from every other student. Unfortunately, our school system and our social setting are such that the average student has had little encouragement to come to grips with himself.
Furthermore, most students seem to experience difficulty in writing the
things which they have always thought about.

There is no specific method of approach to prescribe for *all* students
faced with the planning of a life career. An individual should begin his
planning in any manner which will bring the greatest benefit. Some
students, for example, start by listing their strong points; others list their
weaknesses, e.g., the things over which they worry. Some choose to list
the major decisions with which they are or will be faced and to indicate
the many aspects of their present and future life that may be affected by
these decisions. Other students choose to study critically those previous
experiences that have caused them to be the way they are today. In the
latter approach, the student does not attempt to write an autobiography
but rather attempts to isolate those aspects of his background that he
believes have a bearing upon his problem of planning a life's work.

It would seem logical for an individual to first indicate all the things that he values in life, i.e., those things which are central to his beliefs and behavior. Directly or indirectly, values are involved in every decision you make, now and in the future. You may find it helpful to group them under major headings such as the following, which are merely suggestive.

Intellectual values—such as scholarship, truth, knowledge, opportunities for self-expression, high standards of morals and ethics, clear and logical thinking

Physical and personal values—such as health and vitality, attractiveness, pleasing personality, and successful marriage and family life

Occupational values—such as service to mankind, intellectual stimulation, prestige, contacts with others, favorable working conditions, a reasonable degree of financial security, industriousness, self-sufficiency, opportunities for advancement, opportunities for creativeness, and opportunities for combining your occupation harmoniously with family life

Adjustment values—such as sense of personal worth, respect for human personality, tolerance, self-respect, independence, friendship, sense of humor, happiness, cooperativeness, and opportunities for choice and self-direction

Social values—such as social approval, stability, honesty, generosity, loyalty, kindness, fairness, justice, and impartiality

Aesthetic values—such as beauty, attractiveness of surroundings, and appreciation of cultural influences

Recreational values—such as ample time to devote to recreational activities, freedom to participate in a wide variety of activities, and stimulation to develop interests

You may also use an objective instrument such as the Allport-Vernon Scale of Values to help clarify your beliefs.

In addition to listing your values, you may wish to check to see whether they are consistent with each other and analyze each critically to determine why you hold it, as well as whether it is desirable to continue to hold it. In order to gain an adequate understanding of the origin of these values, it may be helpful to dip critically into your background. Early childhood experiences are much more important than one is inclined to suspect, so far as the formation of his values is concerned.

Any analysis of values will automatically necessitate a consideration of goals. The balance sheet that you construct of your values and goals should assist you greatly in being objective and facile in the other aspects of your planning.

Talk to others about your background, values, and goals   You doubtless have discussed your life plans at length with your parents, your public school teachers, your school friends, and various older adults in your home community; and you will probably want to consult these people again, especially your parents, as you continue with your planning.

In view of the fact that college provides a superb opportunity for anyone to extend greatly his contacts, avail yourself of this resource for planning. In your beginning course in education you will contact many other students interested in the same career possibilities that you are.

Both in and out of class you will have the opportunity to share your values, goals, and plans and to think them through critically. Participating in activities such as the Student National Education Association provides additional opportunities for engaging in intelligent, meaningful, and fruitful discussions. Seek out college instructors as well as specialists in other fields, from whom you may receive valuable aid. In short, avail yourself of every possible opportunity to analyze and appraise your background, values, and goals. It is primarily through this process that your thinking is deepened and clarified, your horizons are extended, and your planning is directed. Furthermore, the act of engaging in these experiences should enable you to gain facility in helping the pupils whom you may teach to do likewise.

Perhaps one of the most effective ways for anyone to analyze his competencies for teaching is to use various checklists or self-rating scales that have been prepared. The lists located at the end of this chapter, as well as Chapter 4, should prove to be helpful to you. In using any checklist, please keep in mind that the ratings should not be considered final and that they represent only your present competencies. You should be able to do much to improve your ratings for teaching fitness through carefully planned future experiences.

After you have rated yourself, you might wish to ask your adviser or some other competent person who knows you well to rate you on this same scale. Compare these ratings and discuss especially those that differ greatly. Your adviser or friend might be able to help you formulate plans whereby you may remove any weaknesses and increase the strengths that you have for teaching.

Obtain objective data on your specific abilities   In using any checklist, you perhaps will feel the need for objective data to support some of the relatively subjective judgments you make, especially if the appraisal of someone else differed appreciably from your own rating. You should be able to locate considerable objective data to help you appraise yourself. Data on physical health may be obtained from your college health clinic or your family physician. A speech department or clinic can give you objective data concerning your speech and hearing. A good personality test administered and interpreted by a clinician can supply emotional stability and personal adjustment data.

Practically every college and university today requires entering students to take a battery of tests. Ordinarily the registrar's office, the guidance department, or some other agency administering the entrance tests will be glad to help you obtain these results. You are almost certain to find results on your English test. English tests usually cover at least three aspects of reading: vocabulary, speed of reading, and level of comprehension. If your English scores are low, you may wish to visit a reading clinic for consultation and advice.

Many colleges encourage students to take some type of occupational-preference or interest test. Such tests attempt to indicate fields in which a particular person would likely experience happiness and success. Although the results of these tests are not conclusive, they do indicate vocational preferences or interests worthy of consideration.

Many students pursuing a specialized course in college tend to neglect their personal development along broad cultural lines. Educators generally agree that a teacher should have a well-rounded background in addition to the other requirements for teaching. Therefore, you may wish to take a test that will indicate your achievement in each of the broad fields of knowledge and plan to strengthen, either through course work or through independent study, areas in which you appear especially weak.

You may think of other kinds of test data that you will need in developing your plans. If your college does not provide the various tests for which you find a need, you can apply at the nearest testing agency. The cost is comparatively low, and the service usually includes a profile as well as an interpretation of the scores.

Please remember that objective test data have limitations. In order to ensure profitable use of the information, a careful evaluation by a qualified person of the purpose and the results of each test is an essential part of any testing program.

You may wish to develop a graphic picture of the information obtained by constructing a profile chart or psychograph of all your test results. A psychograph also would help your adviser gain a better picture of you.

Formulate your plans for the future   Planning for the future involves preparing for three rather clearly defined periods: the years in which you are still in college; the first five or ten years after graduation, during which time you are becoming adjusted to your life's work; and your later life, which extends into old age.

If you are a senior or graduate student, it is obvious that the amount of planning which you can do while still in college is fairly limited. You are faced more immediately with the need for detailed plans for the second period, the first five or ten years after graduation.

The material that follows is roughly divided into these three periods, and a few suggestions are given for your consideration.

Years in college   As indicated previously, college is an unusual environment in which you are able to take advantage of many learning opportunities that may not be present in future surroundings. For this reason your plans during the college years may differ significantly from other plans you may make.

If you feel, for example, that you need to improve your ability to work cooperatively and harmoniously with others, you can become an active member in some of the many campus activities at your disposal. You may wish to assume positions of leadership and responsibility and participate in various discussion groups to develop the characteristics of a mature thinker. There are also many opportunities on campus and in the community, such as convocations, concerts, special lectures, and forums, that will help you acquire a broad cultural education.

Other plans may include attempts to develop skills and insights for working with children. These include observing and participating in as many classroom situations as possible, working as a volunteer or paid teacher aide, taking part in camp and club activities with children, and acting as playground director or camp counselor during the summer.

Years immediately after college The years following graduation present a variety of major decisions and problems for which tentative plans should be made. There is the matter of locating a position. What type of setting would be most desirable for you—rural or urban? Near your home or a considerable distance from home? An inner city or suburban setting? In-state or out-of-state? Since certification requirements are increasing so rapidly, you should give thought to your plans for completing a master's degree.

For this period of time, consideration should be given to plans for living an interesting social, civic, cultural, and recreational life. Prospective periods of summer employment provide many opportunities for gaining valuable experience and intellectual growth. Plans also need to be made for gaining future financial security through insurance, investments, and retirement plans. Continued professional growth is essential for anyone remaining in the profession for a number of years.

Years in later life There is much merit in doing some "intelligent dreaming." Many people find added enjoyment, happiness, and security during their later years of life as a result of long-range planning.

A wide variety of cultural and recreational interests, a concern with civic and professional activities, a wise use of the increased time at your disposal, and an enlarged circle of friends can do much to promote wholesome adjustment at this time. Leisure time can become extremely boring and devasting to an individual. It takes a considerable amount of long-range planning and the development of skills, attitudes, and interests to make these years become a period of constructive fulfillment to an individual and to society.

COMPETENCIES FOR TEACHING

A prospective teacher is normally very much concerned with the competencies essential to success in teaching. Having identified these competencies, he also is concerned with the ways in which he can become the most competent teacher possible.

In recalling the many teachers you have had, you might select those who stand out as having been especially effective and analyze their characteristics carefully. As you study each of these teachers, write down the reason or reasons why you consider them outstanding. Have your friends engage in the same kind of activity. Compare and contrast your list with theirs.

In making this analysis you will probably note considerable difference in the personalities of the teachers. Some may have been quiet, gentle, and warm. Others may have been outgoing and aggressive. Whatever their differences, it is safe to conclude that there is no *one* personality which teachers must have in order to ensure success. Further study also may reveal that because of variations in situations, there is no *one* method of teaching that will ensure success. Each of your outstanding teachers probably had a distinct personality, as well as a distinct style of teaching.

The differences to be found in the characteristics of effective teachers should not be alarming to you. Nor should you be discouraged if educators tell you that they are not absolutely certain of the competencies that will ensure anyone's success in teaching. It is true that they know

What teacher competencies will be needed in order to fully develop this child's abilities for living effectively and constructively in our society? *(Photograph by Joe Di Dio, National Education Association.)*

something about the abilities required, but they hesitate to say with complete conviction that a particular individual will be a very successful teacher and that another will be unsuccessful.

One reason why it is difficult to predict teaching success is that a teacher deals with the most complex thing in the world—the human being. A successful teacher must be able to affect people in such ways that desirable changes occur in behavior. He must be able to encourage the individual to think and to make intelligent decisions; he must guide his behavior with increasing effectiveness toward constructive, democratic ends. The complexity of the interaction of the teacher with his pupils is so great that superior teaching assumes the characteristics of an art which cannot be fully analyzed. Horace Mann recognized this fact when he wrote in his *First Annual Report* in 1853, the following: "Teaching is the most difficult of all arts and the profoundest of all sciences. In its absolute perfection it would involve a complete knowledge of the whole being to be taught, and of the precise manner in which every possible application would affect it."

In planning a career in education, you should examine searchingly the competencies which generally are conducive to success in teaching. This analysis should serve as a background from which you will be able to formulate specific and long-range plans for meeting these requirements to the highest degree possible.

Identifying the Competencies for Teaching

Hundreds of studies have been made of the personal and professional characteristics of teachers in an attempt to establish which traits are the most desirable for teachers to possess and those which are definite handicaps. Several techniques have been used to identify these traits. You may wish to study these traits carefully, to analyze yourself in terms of them, and then establish specific and detailed plans for meeting as many of these requirements as possible while you are in college. It will not be possible to meet all of them at this time, since some require a lifetime of experience, study, and effort.

Studying the critical behaviors of teachers   Ryans has published the results of an extensive and rigorous scientific analysis of teacher characteristics. This study was sponsored·by the American Council on Education [107:1–416]. As an initial step in the study, teacher supervisors, college teachers, school principals, teachers, student teachers, and students in education methods courses were asked to make analytical reports on teacher behavior in specific situations which make a difference between success and failure in teaching. These reports served as a basis for the construction of a "critical incidence" blank upon which significant behavior relative to teaching might be recorded. The more than 500 critical incidents submitted by the participants in the study were reduced to the following list of generalized behaviors [107:82]:

Generalized Descriptions of Critical Behaviors of Teachers

Effective Behaviors	Ineffective Behaviors
1. Alert, appears enthusiastic.	1. Is apathetic, dull, appears bored.
2. Appears interested in pupils and classroom activities.	2. Appears uninterested in pupils and classroom activities.
3. Cheerful, optimistic.	3. Is depressed, pessimistic; appears unhappy.
4. Self-controlled, not easily upset.	4. Loses temper, is easily upset.
5. Likes fun, has a sense of humor.	5. Is overly serious, too occupied for humor.
6. Recognizes and admits own mistakes.	6. Is unaware of, or fails to admit, own mistakes.
7. Is fair, impartial, and objective in treatment of pupils.	7. Is unfair or partial in dealing with pupils.
8. Is patient.	8. Is impatient.
9. Shows understanding and sympathy in working with pupils.	9. Is short with pupils, uses sarcastic remarks, or in other ways shows lack of sympathy with pupils.
10. Is friendly and courteous in relations with pupils.	10. Is aloof and removed in relations with pupils.
11. Helps pupils with personal as well as educational problems.	11. Seems unaware of pupils' personal needs and problems.
12. Commends effort and gives praise for work well done.	12. Does not commend pupils, is disapproving, hypercritical.
13. Accepts pupils' efforts as sincere.	13. Is suspicious of pupil motives.
14. Anticipates reactions of others in social situations.	14. Does not anticipate reactions of others in social situations.
15. Encourages pupils to try to do their best.	15. Makes no effort to encourage pupils to try to do their best.
16. Classroom procedure is planned and well organized.	16. Procedure is without plan, disorganized.
17. Classroom procedure is flexible within overall plan.	17. Shows extreme rigidity of procedure, inability to depart from plan.
18. Anticipates individual needs.	18. Fails to provide for individual differences and needs of pupils.
19. Stimulates pupils through interesting and original materials and techniques.	19. Uninteresting materials and teaching techniques used.
20. Conducts clear, practical demonstrations and explanations.	20. Demonstrations and explanations are not clear and are poorly conducted.
21. Is clear and thorough in giving directions.	21. Directions are incomplete, vague.
22. Encourages pupils to work through their own problems and evaluate their accomplishments.	22. Fails to give pupils opportunity to work out own problems or evaluate their own work.
23. Disciplines in quiet, dignified, and positive manner.	23. Reprimands at length, ridicules, resorts to cruel or meaningless forms of correction.
24. Gives help willingly.	24. Fails to give help or gives it grudgingly.
25. Foresees and attempts to resolve potential difficulties.	25. Is unable to foresee and resolve potential difficulties.

Admittedly some value or subjective judgments were involved in the formulation of these descriptive statements; however, the list does tend to objectify the types of behavior that make a difference in the success or failure of teachers.

Ryans points out that there is an increasing amount of evidence that certain characteristics may contribute to the model of the teacher. Data growing out of various research in which quite different approaches and criteria have been used suggest the following list of generalizations regarding the characteristics of outstanding teachers [107:366]:

Superior intellectual abilities, above-average school achievement, good emotional adjustment, attitudes favorable to pupils, enjoyment of pupil relationships, generosity in the appraisal of the behavior and motives of other persons, strong interests in reading and literary matters, interest in music and painting, participation in social and community affairs, early experiences in caring for children and teaching (such as reading to children and taking a class for the teacher), history of teaching in family, family support of teaching as a vocation, and strong social service interests.

Questioning pupils Another technique that has been used extensively is that of questioning pupils regarding the qualities of teachers they admire. It has been found that boys and girls who have spent considerable time with a teacher are able to pass rather valid judgments regarding his competence [150:3]. A talk with some students after the first week of a school term will reveal that they have the teacher "sized up" with amazing accuracy.

Witty [152:386] analyzed approximately 12,000 letters on "The Teacher Who Has Helped Me Most" that were submitted by pupils from grades 2 to 12 all over the nation. The teacher traits mentioned most frequently by the pupils, in the order of their frequency, were the following: (1) cooperativeness, democratic attitude; (2) and (3) kindliness and consideration for the individual, patience; (4) wide variety of interests; (5) an attractive general appearance and pleasing manner; (6) fairness and impartiality; (7) sense of humor; (8) good disposition and consistent behavior; (9) interest in pupil's problems; (10) flexibility; (11) use of recognition and praise; (12) unusual proficiency in teaching a particular subject.

Witty summarized his findings by stating that "these boys and girls appear to be grateful to the school in proportion to the degree that it offers security, individual success, shared experience, and opportunities for personal and social adjustments. And these are precisely the factors which promote good learning."

Witty conducted three additional nationwide contests in an attempt to verify and expand the findings gained from the first contest. He found that the twelve traits mentioned previously were cited consistently, although their order varied from year to year [151:312].

In a somewhat similar study, Williamson asked 2,000 Colorado high school seniors to identify the most effective and the least effective teacher they had experienced during their school career and to indicate specifically why the teacher was most or least effective. Comments concerning their most effective teacher were categorized into the following six areas according to frequency of occurrence: (1) interest in the student, (2) interesting class management, (3) enthusiasm for teaching, (4) students required to work, (5) impartiality by teacher, and (6) respect for student opinion [150:4]. Their comments on their least effective teacher fell into the following categories: (1) practiced poor class management, (2) showed favoritism, (3) was uninterested in students, (4) was a poor disciplinarian, (5) knew material but could not communicate it to the students, (6) did not enjoy teaching, and (7) did not respect the student or his opinions [150:5]. Sample comments of the students, which are contained in the report of this study [150:4–7], are worth reading.

Analyzing biographies of outstanding teachers   Another method of gaining understanding of competencies for teaching is to read carefully some of the many biographies as well as fiction books that have been written on outstanding teachers. You may remember, for instance, the heartwarming story of Hilton's *Goodbye, Mr. Chips.* Biographies can be helpful in gaining an understanding of the artistic qualities that characterize outstanding teaching as well as the human factors that have rich meaning in the lives of boys and girls. Discussion of these and other books may prove profitable. What seemed to be the life values of the teachers mentioned? What did they consider the job of the teacher to be? How were they able to stimulate the interest of boys and girls and to guide their growth toward desirable ends?

Analyzing statements of competencies and research studies   Educators singly and in groups have developed lists of competencies for teaching, based upon their experiences as teachers and their observations of, and work with, other teachers. These lists often take the form of rating scales used in evaluating the work of teachers on the job and of students engaged in their student teaching. You may wish to see the scale on which your success in student teaching will be appraised and to study carefully the competencies involved. By having a clear understanding of these competencies you will be able to plan specific experiences that you should gain prior to your student teaching.

Hamachek [47:341–345] recently completed a study of the voluminous research that has been done on teacher effectiveness and considerations which enhance or restrict this effectiveness. He found that most of the research was aimed at investigating teacher effectiveness from one or more of the following dimensions of teacher personality and behavior: (1) personal characteristics, (2) instructional procedures and interaction styles, (3) perceptions of self, and (4) perceptions of others.

In summarizing the research on the personal characteristics of good or effective teachers, Hamachek states:

Effective teachers appear to be those who are, shall we say, "human" in the fullest sense of the word. They have a sense of humor, are fair, empathetic, more democratic than autocratic, and apparently are more able to relate easily and naturally to students on either a one-to-one or group basis. Their classrooms seem to reflect miniature enterprise operations in the sense that they are more open, spontaneous, and adaptable to change [47:341–342].

In discussing the instructional procedures and interaction styles of good versus poor teachers, Hamachek points out that Flanders (32) found that "classrooms in which achievement and attitudes were superior were likely to be conducted by teachers who did not blindly pursue a single behavioral-instructional path to the exclusion of other possibilities. In other words, the more successful teachers were better able to range along a continuum of interaction styles which varied from fairly active, dominative support on the one hand to a more reflective, discriminating support on the other" [47:342]. In summarizing the research on class-room behavior interaction patterns, and teaching styles, Hamachek indicates that good or effective teachers seem to reflect more of the following behaviors [47:342]:

1. Willingness to be flexible, to be direct or indirect as the situation demands.
2. Ability to perceive the world from the student's point of view.
3. Ability to "personalize" their teaching.
4. Willingness to experiment, to try out new things.

Effective communication and interaction involves more than words. *(Photograph by Joe Di Dio, National Education Association.)*

5. Skill in asking questions (as opposed to seeing self as a kind of answering service).
6. Knowledge of subject matter and related areas.
7. Provision of well-established examination procedures.
8. Provision of definite study help.
9. Reflection of an appreciative attitude (evidenced by nods, comments, smiles, etc.).
10. Use of conversational manner in teaching—informal, easy style.

The way teachers see, regard, and feel about themselves (self-perception) has an enormous impact on both their professional and personal lives. Ryans [108:1,486–1,490] found that the more emotionally stable teachers (1) more frequently named self-confidence and cheerfulness as dominant traits in themselves, (2) said they liked active contact with other people, (3) expressed interest in hobbies and handicrafts, (4) reported their childhoods to be happy experiences. After reviewing several research studies, Combs [14:70–71] concludes that good teachers typically see themselves as follows [47:342–343]:

1. Good teachers see themselves as identified with people rather than withdrawn, removed, apart from, or alienated from others.
2. Good teachers feel basically adequate rather than inadequate. They do not see themselves as generally unable to cope with problems.
3. Good teachers feel trustworthy rather than untrustworthy. They see themselves reliable, dependable individuals with the potential for coping with events as they happen.
4. Good teachers see themselves as wanted rather than unwanted. They see themselves as likable and attractive (in a personal, not physical sense) as opposed to feeling ignored and rejected.
5. Good teachers see themselves as worthy rather than unworthy. They see themselves as people of consequence, dignity, and integrity as opposed to feeling they matter little, can be overlooked and discounted.

Hamachek sketches the following interrelated generalizations about how good teachers differ from poor teachers in the way they perceive others [47:343]:

1. They seem to have generally more positive views of others—students, colleagues, and administrators.
2. They do not seem to be as prone to view others as critical, attacking people with ulterior motives; rather they are seen as potentially friendly and worthy in their own right.
3. They have a more favorable view of democratic classroom procedures.
4. They seem to have the ability and capacity to see things as they seem to others—i.e., the ability to see things from the other person's point of view.
5. They do not seem to see students as persons "you do things to" but rather as individuals capable of doing for themselves once they feel trusted, respected, and valued.

The importance of the teacher's attitude toward pupils is reflected in the research published by Rosenthal and Jacobson, titled *Pygmalion in the Classroom.* The research suggests strongly that children who are expected by their teachers to gain intellectually in fact do show greater intellectual gains after one year than do children of whom such gains are not expected [106:121]. What the teacher "said, by how and when she said it, by her facial expressions, postures, and perhaps her touch, the teacher may have communicated to the children of the experimental group that she expected improved intellectual performance. Such communications together with possible changes in teaching techniques may have helped the child learn by changing his self concept, his expectations of his own behavior, and his motivation, as well as his cognitive style and skills" [106:108]. Teachers who have low expectations of pupils tend to inhibit their progress by: (1) limiting the amount of material a pupil can learn—partly because the teacher does not try to teach him as much and partly because the teacher gives up more easily and quickly, and (2) stifling a pupil's motivation and giving him a feeling of alienation [41:52].

Teacher-competency Self-appraisal Forms

As noted previously, self-appraisal forms can prove to be helpful in appraising one's competency for teaching. Examples of these forms are to be found at the end of this chapter as well as Chapter 4. Other forms may be obtained from your teacher-placement office to use in self-appraisal.

One of the forms at the end of this chapter is concerned with the teacher's personality. Each prospective teacher should give careful attention to a study of the probable effects of his personality upon his success as a teacher. Please keep in mind that what you are as a person will be the most potent subject matter that will be in your classroom. To paraphrase Emerson, "I cannot hear what you *say,* when what you *are* thunders so loud!"

There has been some significant research completed on types of teacher personalities and their effects upon various groups of children [49:1–82]. Heil and his associates developed and applied what is called a "Manifold Interest Schedule" to over fifty public school teachers of grades 4, 5, and 6 and measured the progress of their children against the personality types of teachers identified by the schedule. It was found that children with a teacher having one type of personality made 50 per cent more academic progress than did children with a teacher having a decidedly different personality.

Another instrument called the "Children's Feeling Test," developed by Professor Heil and his associates, made it possible to identify four categories of children's personalities. One type of teacher appeared to have a deleterious effect upon children of the least well-adjusted category, whereas another type had a definitely beneficial effect upon such children.

As a result of this study, Heil and his associates concluded that the teacher's type of personality appears to have much effect on the progress of his pupils. Furthermore, it appears that the clear overriding factor in determining children's academic achievement is a positive and definite personality [49:66–68].

Some Implications for Your Planning

The school of today requires far more of teachers than did the school of yesterday. This fact is understandable when one considers the expanding function of the school in American life. In earlier days the school in this country was limited primarily to teaching boys and girls the fundamental skills of reading, writing, and arithmetic. The home, the church, and the community provided most of the other learnings essential for effective citizenship. Life was relatively simple. Today, however, life is much more complex. This is due especially to the tremendous technological advancements that have been made. Great changes have also taken place in our social, economic, and political lives. The function of the school must change and expand in order to meet the needs of youth today and tomorrow. These changes give rise to new and broader requirements for teachers.

The teacher today understands the cultural context in which all education takes place. He sees clearly the significance of industrialization, urbanization, corporativeness, economic planning, cultural lags, cultural fragmentation, the growth of a scientific attitude toward problems, and other outstanding characteristics of the contemporary American scene as they affect the lives of the people. He has the ability to understand modern problems in terms of historical conditions, to recognize the recurrent nature of many educational concerns, to use the resources of the past when faced with the problems of the present, and thus to discriminate between worthy traditional solutions and those solutions which are no longer pertinent. He understands the process whereby values are inculcated for the guidance of our conduct and judgments. He demonstrates, through his attitudes, skills, and habits, a basic understanding of democracy as a way of perpetuating the values of our culture, as a process by which each may develop his best self, as a method for solving problems, and as a process of disciplining himself for the betterment of our common lives. He possesses a critical understanding of the function of communities as agencies directing human growth and of the school as one agency by which society seeks to provide for its continued expansion as well as for the development of the individual. He sees the school as an institution which is charged with a major responsibility in determining the direction and character of this growth. He recognizes that the manner in which he goes about the teaching of boys and girls is determined by what he conceives to be the real function of education.

Educational research, during the past several years, has revealed new insights regarding human behavior and the learning process. The teacher of today needs an extensive understanding of the nature of individual development in all its various aspects so that he may recognize and anticipate the increasing needs of the student and provide the conditions which will promote his maximum growth. He is aware of the ways in which people are alike and of the ways in which they differ. He understands how the individual may become more like others and yet remain unique as he attains maturity. He comprehends thoroughly the nature of human learning, both in terms of the learner's habits, attitudes, skills, and abilities and in terms of his own role as an effective guide in the learning process. It is essential, furthermore, for him to possess expert skill in guiding the education of others toward desirable ends.

PERSONAL GROWTH TOWARD TEACHING

Much of your personal growth toward effective teaching is concerned with intangibles that are not learned in formal ways. In fact, you may get little direct help in this regard from the formal courses you take in your preparation for teaching. You do have available in your college environment, however, many resources that you may use. The amount of growth you make will depend largely upon you. Only a few areas for personal growth are discussed in this chapter, primarily for illustrative purposes.

Skill in Oral Communication

Teachers whose voice and speech are pleasing to others tend to be more effective in the classroom. Although most people have acceptable speech, almost everyone can improve his speech if he knows his own special needs. There is the true story of a young first-grade teacher who complained to her principal, "I can't underthand why tho many of my children lithp." Children are great and often unconscious imitators. It is doubly important, then for teachers to perfect their speech—not only to improve their effectiveness in communication but also to serve as an adequate model for pupils.

Each prospective teacher should make arrangements with a speech therapist for a voice and speech test. A therapist will be able to help you with suggestions about pronunciation, tone quality, pitch, speed, and enunciation.

If professional help is not available, you can record your voice on tape. Certain problems may be obvious at once. How do you like your voice? Is your voice too high or too low to be pleasant? Are your words monotonous? Are there nervous pauses and repetitions? Do you speak too fast or too slow to be distinctly understood? Do you hesitate on the pronunciation of words? Do you speak with expression appropriate to the speech? Are you sure of the correctness of your grammar? You may wish to use some form of a checklist on voice and speech to help you appraise yourself systematically.

A recording on video tape would help you check your speech as well as physical mannerisms. One of the advantages of engaging in micro-teaching activities that are also video taped is to study how you look and sound to others and how you can improve the total act of communicating and interacting with others.

Skill in Decision Making

A teacher is forced to make many decisions each day. These decisions have an effect upon the lives of his pupils and their parents, his colleagues, and other community members, as well as upon his personal and professional life.

During your college career you have many opportunities to improve your skill in decision making. It is a skill to which conscious effort should be directed. While many decisions are simply a matter of picking the things which are of greatest interest and importance at the moment, other decisions involve the making of value judgments, the careful selection of activities in the light of their real worth.

Teaching requires a high degree of skill in working with others—colleagues, pupils, parents, and other community members. Many opportunities exist within a college environment for the further development of this skill. *(Photograph by Joe Di Dio, National Education Association.)*

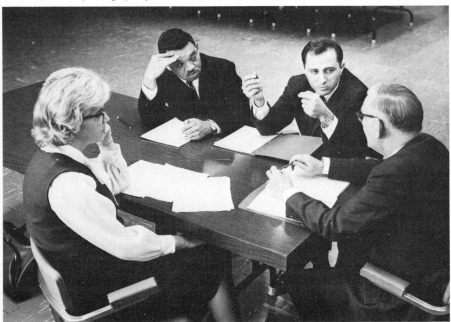

Skill in Group Participation

Much of a teacher's life involves group work with colleagues, parents, and other community members. Likewise, the teacher is concerned with helping his pupils gain skill in effective group work. In order to be truly successful in his work, therefore, a teacher must have a high degree of skill in group work. Membership in clubs, fraternities or sororities, church and welfare organizations, civic groups, sports groups, and professional societies provides opportunities for you to gain skills of good group membership.

In order to increase your effectiveness as a group participant you may find it helpful to check yourself in regard to some questions titled "Am I a Good Group Participant?" which is located at the end of this chapter.

One application of the principles of group participation can be a class discussion of some of the topics or problems found at the end of each chapter in this book. In order to get started, your instructor may temporarily assume leadership in helping your group select its subjects. After this initial step, he may wish to turn over his role to members of the group as quickly as possible so that they may gain leadership experience.

All members of the group should help decide how the group will attack the topic. Such projects as reading in the library, interviewing, bringing resource people to the classroom, writing reports, viewing films, having panel discussions, and the like may be involved. It may seem desirable for small groups to work on certain aspects of the problem and to report their findings to the entire group.

Skill in Group Leadership

There is a significant difference between being a group participant and serving as discussion group leader. Since the latter more nearly approximates the role you will play as a teacher, gain as much leadership skill as possible while in college in your course work and cocurricular activities. As a group leader keep in mind the following:

1. Help the group define the problem clearly—its nature and scope or delimitations.
2. Encourage all participants to share their thinking, information, and experience.
3. Provide opportunity for all points of view to be expressed.
4. Keep the discussion directed to the problem.
5. Help group members to clarify their thinking and to summarize their progress.
6. Utilize all resources represented in the experience of group members.
7. Strive to develop a cohesive and productive group.
8. Avoid trying to save time by telling the group the right answer.

Keep in mind that the leader is not a group instructor; he is a guide trying to arrange conditions so that each member will do creative thinking. Group discussion is not a debating society. While disagreements are to be expected, the task of the group is to find more truth than each member brings to any group meeting—a cooperative quest in which thinking is creative rather than combative.

Skill in the Effective Use of Time

You may recall Shakespeare's advice, "Let every man be master of his time. . . ." You undoubtedly recognize the wisdom of planning your personal time, and understand desirable procedures that may be used. For this reason the only points to be made are that the problem of using time effectively is ever present, that you need to check periodically to see whether or not you are using your time most profitably, that skill in the wise use of time may be gained as you work intelligently upon the problem and plan accordingly, that provision should be made for a well-balanced program of activities which takes into consideration all aspects of your personal growth, and that skill gained in the effective use of your time while in college will pay high dividends in your work as a teacher and as a citizen.

SUMMARY

As you think about yourself as a part of society, you recognize the role which planning plays in this increasingly complex and interdependent culture. You sense that an intelligent application of the process necessitates your becoming skilled not only in planning your own life, but also in helping those whom you teach to do likewise.

Several steps have been suggested for use in outlining the details of your plans for teaching. Your first responsibility is to be certain of the things in life that really seem important to you—your values. These values largely determine the things you seek to accomplish. You then examine the possibilities of a career in education to see if it holds promise of your being able to fulfill these needs and if you can meet the requirements for such a career. You then develop detailed schemes for moving from where you are to where you want to go, keeping in mind that plans are always tentative, and that modifications are made as unforeseen factors develop.

This chapter also has been concerned with competencies for teaching and with personal growth toward teaching. The results of several studies on teacher competencies have been presented so that you could compare them, note similarities, and evaluate yourself in terms of them.

No one can expect to meet all the competencies for teaching to the highest degree, either at the time of graduation or at the end of a lifetime teaching career. But with each year of experience, it is a teacher's professional obligation to move to a fuller realization of his potential. Weaknesses can be eliminated, and strengths can be made stronger; hence there is always the horizon of greater fulfillment. You may wish to study yourself in the light of those qualities that seem characteristic of effective teachers and then plan to acquire the ones you now appear to lack. The suggestions given here should point the way to many other possibilities.

Careful planning and conscientious execution of those plans will assist you in becoming a worthwhile citizen, a well-adjusted person who knows how to work with others. Such a person can become important in his own right and can justify the investment of time and energy needed to help him take his place in his chosen profession.

QUESTIONS TO CONSIDER

1. In your opinion, what values should a person have in life if he plans to teach?
2. "Values are acquired parts of an individual's life." What are some of the implications of this statement for the experiences you will plan for your pupils, and the personal influence you will attempt to exert upon your pupils?
3. In what ways do the values held in common by people in America differ from those that characterize people in an autocratic society?
4. In what ways might long-range planning have improved the lives of some of your friends?
5. Some people feel that group planning and work reduces everyone to the level of mediocrity. Is this necessarily true? If not, how can group work contribute to the development of the unique talents of an individual?
6. In addition to a thorough grounding in subject matter, what specific understandings, skills, and techniques are, in your opinion, essential to success in the teaching profession?
7. From your observations what are the most common weaknesses of beginning teachers? How can you avoid such weaknesses when you begin teaching?
8. Do you feel that your image of yourself often is reflected in how others see you? Can you present any evidence to support this point, and what are its implications for your success as a future teacher?
9. In what ways does a teacher's personality affect the progress of his pupils? Can you recall incidents that support your point of view?
10. Does a school administrator or supervisor have the right to criticize a teacher for being untidy or inappropriately dressed? If so, why?
11. What qualities of voice and speech in teachers are conducive to good discipline in the classroom?

PROBLEM SITUATION FOR INQUIRY

Louise, a 23-year-old recent college graduate, has been certified to teach in her home state. Her undergraduate studies took her five years to complete because she worked part-time to supplement the support which her widowed mother provided her.

Louise has received several job offers to teach at the secondary school level. Her long-range goal, however, is to teach at the college level. To achieve such a position would require additional work at the graduate level and would postpone much-needed income.

The problem, then, for Louise is to decide whether to accept a position at the secondary school level where she will receive a substantially lower salary over a long period of time, or to undertake graduate studies for a postponed, but more financially rewarding and more stimulating career. If you found yourself in a position similar to that of Louise, what would you do? Why?

ACTIVITIES TO PURSUE

1. Make a list of the things you really value in life. After careful study, try to arrange them in descending order according to their importance to you. Reflect upon your past experiences and try to determine why you attach importance to each of your values. Examine them carefully to see whether they are compatible with each other. Opposite this list indicate all the values you see in education as a career. Compare and contrast these two listings to determine the extent to which they seem compatible.
2. Question seriously some of your close friends regarding what they value most in life. In what ways do the values they hold differ from yours? How do you account for these differences? In what ways are their career plans being affected by their values?
3. Talk to some people who have been very successful in their careers. Question them regarding long-range plans they have followed in order to gain success. Study also the careers of some people who have not been very successful. What differences do you find in the career planning done by successful and unsuccessful people?
4. Talk with people who have retired. You will find some who are happy and well adjusted in their retirement and others who are not. Attempt to determine whether long-range planning, or the lack of it, accounts to some extent for the differences.
5. Assume that you as a teacher should be skilled in helping your pupils plan together in the effective solution of common problems. Consider some college activities in which you might engage for purposes of increasing your skill in this regard.
6. As suggested previously, collect as many objective data as possible on your special abilities for teaching. Study these data carefully, seeking help from your college instructors if needed; formulate plans for overcoming your weaknesses and building up your strengths.
7. Prepare a paper on "What I Value in Life," "What Life Means to Me," "My Philosophy of Life," or on a similar topic suggested in this chapter.
8. Interview informally a number of boys and girls about the qualities that they think teachers should have. Have them also indicate the qualities which they dislike the most in teachers. Check your findings against those listed in this chapter.
9. Draw a line vertically through the center of a piece of paper. On the left-hand side, list the factors that characterize the teacher whom you most disliked while in school. On the right-hand side, list the factors that characterize the teacher you liked best. At the bottom of the page, list the characteristics of the teacher who was of most value to you. Compare and contrast the characteristics listed for all three in an effort to determine common elements. Check your results against the findings listed in this chapter.
10. Check yourself on the "Checklist of Important Factors in the Teacher's Personality" which appears at the end of this chapter, and underline the qualities or traits in which you need to improve. Try to formulate some first steps to take in overcoming your weaknesses.
11. Consult your director of student teaching regarding competencies against which you will be evaluated in your student teaching. Secure copies of any forms that may be used, and study them carefully. Formulate specific plans for overcoming any weaknesses that may be revealed from a study of these forms.
12. Discuss with an experienced school superintendent the qualities he looks for when he is employing teachers. Also ask him to list the main weaknesses of beginning teachers.

13. Consult with the counseling services on your college campus to locate the various agencies which may be of service to you in your program of self-improvement.
14. Explore your college catalog in an effort to find those courses that may be taken to broaden your interests or help overcome a personality problem. Consider taking courses in mental hygiene, philosophy and ethics, science fields that are new to you, arts and crafts, camp counseling, folk dancing, sports, speech improvement, writing, or dramatics.
15. If possible, do some microteaching and have it recorded on video tape. Study the recording carefully to discover any improvements you might make in your speech, mannerisms, appearance, and probable affect upon others.
16. In your future group activities carefully appraise the extent to which you fulfill the characteristics of a good group member. Formulate ways to strengthen any characteristics in which you find yourself to be weak.
17. Keep an accurate record of how you spend your time during a fairly normal week of school. At the end of the week analyze the distribution of your time to see whether you are making the best use of it. You may wish to discuss the results with your friends and instructors and to plan ways of gaining more value from the free time you have available.

SELF-RATING SCALE FOR DETERMINING FITNESS FOR TEACHING

	Never	Sel-dom	Some-times	Often	Al-ways
I. Leadership ability					
1. Have you served as leader in student groups; i.e., have you held an office, taken part in programs, or led discussions?					
2. Do your fellow students respect your opinions?					
3. Do they regard you as a leader?					
4. Do your fellow students ask you for help and advice?					
5. Do you sense how others feel, i.e., whether they approve certain proposals, or like or dislike certain persons?					
6. Do you try to make others happy by listening to what they say, and by being courteous, friendly, and helpful?					
7. Do you succeed in getting others to follow your suggestions without creating friction or ill will?					
II. Health and physical fitness					
1. Do you have good health?					
2. Do you have lots of vitality? Can you stand to do hard physical tasks or nerve-racking work?					
3. Can you engage in activities which others in your group customarily do?					
4. Do you give others the impression that you are physically fit, well groomed and attractive in personal appearance?					
5. Do you keep cheerful and even-tempered even when tired or ill?					
III. Good scholarship					
1. Have you maintained a better-than-average academic record?					
2. Are you interested in the subjects you have taken or are taking?					
3. Do you enjoy studying and find it easy to concentrate when you do study?					
4. Do you express your ideas well before a class or public group?					
5. Is it easy for you to explain things so that others understand and can follow your directions?					
IV. Intellectual traits and abilities					
1. Are school subjects easy for you?					
2. Do you spend time finding out more about a topic discussed in class or covered in an assignment?					

Source: E. E. Samuelson and others, *You'd Like Teaching,* Craftsman Press, Seattle, Wash., 1946, pp. 31–35. Materials prepared and published, and permission for use granted, by Central Washington College of Education.

SELF-RATING SCALE FOR DETERMINING
FITNESS FOR TEACHING (continued)

	Never	Sel-dom	Some-times	Often	Al-ways
3. Do you read books or magazine articles on current topics?					
4. Do you like to work out ideas on your own?					
5. Do you suggest new ideas or plans which can be carried out by groups?					
V. Emotional stability					
1. Are you an even-tempered, cheerful, happy sort of person?					
2. Can you "take it" without getting angry or upset?					
3. Do you keep from worrying and feeling depressed?					
4. Are you naturally patient with and tolerant of others?					
5. Are you objectively critical of yourself?					
6. Do you see the humorous side of everyday happenings even when you yourself are involved?					
VI. Social aspirations					
1. Are you interested in the problems other people meet and do you want to help them solve them?					
2. Are you interested in finding ways by which you can help improve human living?					
3. Do you like people—especially children?					
4. Do you set high social standards for yourself and seek to reach and maintain these standards?					
5. Do you cooperate readily with other people in socially desirable activities?					
6. Are you willing to make sacrifices and endure inconveniences to reach a goal you consider worthy?					

THE CHARACTERISTICS OF THE COMPETENT TEACHER IN HARFORD COUNTY

A Statement of the Harford County Teachers' Association Bel Air, Maryland

I. **Personal Traits**
The competent teacher:
possesses adequate physical vitality.
is punctual.
is regular in attendance.

Source: "Evaluating Teaching Performance," *ERS Circular,* No. 3, pp. 26–28, American Association of School Administrators and the National Education Association, Educational Research Service, Washington, 1969.

is well groomed.

maintains appropriate emotional control.

has a sense of humor—laughs with people.

is trustworthy and conscientious.

fulfills responsibilities without constant supervision.

makes practical, common sense judgments.

uses tact.

can act in original situations without supervision.

is cooperative and a good team worker.

is receptive to constructive criticism and suggestion.

is self-confident.

is reasonable in self-evaluation.

is able to meet people on a courteous level of mutual self-respect.

II. Executive Traits

The competent teacher:

completes necessary paper work promptly and accurately.

arranges to have materials at hand when they are needed.

evaluates materials and keeps only applicable material.

organizes classroom routines so children share responsibility.

creates an atmosphere that promotes learning and discourages anti-social behavior.

recognizes each child as an individual and provides for individual differences within the framework of the school program.

assumes the responsibility for disciplinary measures unless unusual factors are involved.

makes his authority understood and accepted in a gracious manner.

transmits enthusiasm for his subject.

checks assignments efficiently.

maintains a neat, clean classroom, conducive to learning.

is willing to use professional resource people within the school system.

is in firm control of his classroom at all times.

III. Teaching Power

The competent teacher:

selects and organizes material with

definitions of aim.

compatibility with the course of study.

adaptation to pupil needs, interests, and capacities.

has intelligently prepared unit and daily lesson plans.

is aware of the importance of motivation.

uses pupil experience to enrich and give meaning to content.

uses a variety of techniques to reach desirable goals.

works to have pupils accept appropriate individual and common goals.

develops a readiness for learning.

uses pupil responses to aid his teaching.

accepts his responsibility to improve attitudes, work habits, and skills.

uses grammatically correct, precise English.

has good vocalization.

evaluates work regularly and reteaches when that is needed.

shows imagination in adapting materials for classroom use.

displays materials that stimulate children's desire to learn.

can present ideas in a clear and convincing manner.

IV. Professional Responsibility

The competent teacher:

develops a relationship with students which is warm and inspiring and yet professional.

demonstrates a high standard of ethics in accord with the HCTA Ethics for Educators.

is proud to be a teacher and lets this pride show.

supports professional organizations, regarding this as a privilege to be able to participate in activities which advance the profession.

takes personal responsibility for individual professional growth.

contributes to the advancement of education by working effectively on committees by assuming individual responsibility for improvements for schools, by having a knowledge of legislation enacted and pending relating to education.

secures support in attracting those who should and holding those who do enter the profession.

has a professional manner as shown by reasonable dignity and appropriate personal conduct.

understands and follows county and school policies and procedures.

is loyal to co-workers, principals, and other school personnel.

respects group decisions.

respects and is discreet in using professional information.

can explain an educational point of view clearly and convincingly.

maintains a spirit of mutual respect in teacher-pupil, teacher-teacher, principal-teacher, and parent-teacher relationships.

uses thoughtful observation, inquiry, and study to learn as much as possible about the community.

V. Scholarship

The competent teacher:

is a master of his chosen field of specialization.

maintains a continuing spirit of learning and understanding.

knows the psychology of learning and is aware of new trends in this field.

surveys recent educational periodicals and reads information pertinent to his work.

VI. Community Relations

The competent teacher:

is informed about local problems.

participates as a citizen in local government.

understands the strengths and the problems of the school community.

realizes that the adequate support of free public schools in the community is based upon a general understanding of and respect for the educational program.

speaks and acts in all contacts in the community to support the general understanding of and respect for the educational program.

CHECKLIST OF IMPORTANT FACTORS IN THE TEACHER'S PERSONALITY

Directions: Consider each of the ten divisions in this list separately. Read each statement under the major headings carefully and underline any of the qualities or traits which obviously are missing in the personality being rated. Before you proceed to the next division, look back over any of the statements you may have underlined; then place a check mark in the column that expressed your general opinion of the person with respect to the particular aspect of personality being considered.

Suggested Standard for Traits or Qualities	Below Average	Fair	Good	Excellent
1. *Emotional stability and mental health.* Is free from fears, remorse, humiliations, and worries about trivial things; can make a realistic inventory of his mental resources; is not supersensitive to criticism; is resourceful in self-				

Source: Howard T. Batchelder, Maurice McGlasson, and Raleigh Schorling, *Student Teaching in Secondary Schools,* McGraw-Hill Book Company, New York, 1964, pp. 9–12.

CHECKLIST OF IMPORTANT FACTORS IN THE TEACHER'S PERSONALITY (continued)

Suggested Standard for Traits or Qualities	Below Average	Fair	Good	Excellent
entertainment; is not easily irritated; is free from excessive shyness, temper tantrums, and daydreams; meets unexpected situations well; adapts readily to changing situations; exercises self-control; is free from complexes of inferiority and superiority; has control over moods, with no sudden shifts in extremes from ups to downs; can take disappointments in life in full stride.				
2. *Personal appearance.* Is dressed appropriately for the occasion; is alert and well poised; is well groomed; gives appearance of being self-possessed; exercises good taste in selection of clothes; gives impression of being refined and cultured; chooses color combinations well; keeps clothes pressed and clean.				
3. *Health and vitality.* Shows evidence of a "driving force"; is physically and mentally alert; is enthusiastic and cheerful; looks healthy; is dynamic; is wide awake to the potential possibilities in every situation; has a happy expression; has reserve energy.				
4. *Honesty, character, and integrity.* Shows a good sense of values; can be expected to do the right thing under all conditions; is trustworthy and loyal; admits mistakes; keeps his word; is fair and just in his dealings with others; fulfills obligations; is intellectually honest, maintains high standards of conduct.				
5. *Adaptability.* Accepts gracefully and understands quickly suggestions from others; accepts responsibility for making a positive contribution to a situation; is willing to inconvenience self in helping others; is challenged by new situations; is sympathetic and patient in sharing and understanding the thoughts and difficulties of others; says what must be said with diplomacy and minimum offense; responds readily to necessary routine.				
6. *Cooperation.* Can work with others for attainment of a common goal; volunteers services when they are needed; fits in where most needed; welcomes suggestions and tries to improve; places welfare of the group before self; is willing to share in the "extra" tasks; is a constructive worker on a committee.				
7. *Voice and speech.* Shows refinement and evidence of cultural background; speaks clearly and distinctly with proper degree of inflection; has well-modulated tone, controlled, and adapted to the size of the group; has an accepted and natural accent; attracts favorable attention; is easy to understand; pronounces words correctly; is free from distracting and irritating mannerisms or defects of speech.				
8. *Leadership.* Commands respect; is self-confident; shows ability in planning, organization, and execution; can				

CHECKLIST OF IMPORTANT FACTORS IN THE TEACHER'S PERSONALITY (continued)

Suggested Standard for Traits or Qualities	Below Average	Fair	Good	Excellent
persuade others to a proper course of action; can act in emergencies with decision; uses good judgment; inspires others to do their best; shows mastery of a situation; exercises initiative and originality; has the ability to put into words the thinking of a group; possesses courage to support sound convictions.				
9. *Resourcefulness.* Has suggestions for meeting a difficulty; is discerning and quick in selection of the most promising solution; can "see around a corner"; has an abundance of reserve energy upon which to draw; knows when to take action; suggests power of mental strength, and vigor.				
10. *Sociability.* Knows the rules of etiquette sufficiently to avoid embarrassing, offending, or irritating others; is unselfishly interested in others; is a stimulating conversationalist with a wide range of interests; has a sympathetic point of view; puts others at ease; seeks association with others; is tolerant of the opinions of others and of community life; wins and holds friends; is a good listener; knows when to be playful and when to be serious; creates a comfortable and pleasant atmosphere; sees the humorous element in situations; is a good sport.				

AM I A GOOD GROUP PARTICIPANT?

1. Do I propose new ideas, activities, and procedures? Or do I just sit and listen?
2. Do I ask questions? Or am I shy about admitting that I do not understand?
3. Do I share my knowledge when it will prove helpful to the problem at hand? Or do I keep it to myself?
4. Do I speak up if I feel strongly about something? Or am I shy about giving an opinion?
5. Do I try to bring together our ideas and activities? Or do I concentrate only on details under immediate discussion?
6. Do I understand the goals of the group and try to direct the discussion toward them? Or do I get off the track easily?
7. Do I ever question the practicality or the "logic" of a project, and do I evaluate afterwards? Or do I always accept unquestioningly the things we do?
8. Do I help to arrange chairs, serve refreshments, and even clean up when the session is over? Or do I prefer to be waited on?
9. Do I encourage my fellow group members to do well? Or am I indifferent to their efforts and achievements?
10. Do I prod the group to undertake worthy projects? Or am I happy with mediocre projects?
11. Am I a mediator and a peacemaker? Or do I allow ill feeling to develop?
12. Am I willing to compromise (except where basic issues such as truth and justice are involved)? Or do I remain inflexible?
13. Do I encourage others to participate and to give everyone else a fair chance to speak? Or do I sit by while some people hog the floor, and do I sometimes dominate it myself?

Source: "Am I a Good Group Participant?" *NEA Journal,* vol. 45, p. 168, National Education Association, Washington, March, 1956.

3 | OPPORTUNITIES IN EDUCATION

The teaching profession offers an enormous range of opportunities, especially for those who plan to remain in the profession. This range undoubtedly will increase as modifications are made in the organizational and instructional practices of schools, and as attempts are made to meet more adequately the educational needs of individuals of all ages. A prospective teacher's plans, therefore, should include an exploration of the many opportunities that are available.

Most educators enter the profession as teachers. As a result, you are confronted with the problem of being certain of the level and the area or areas for which you are best suited for teaching. Furthermore, the demand for teachers at some grade levels and in some subject areas is greater than in others. Teachers prepared in specialties where the demand exceeds the supply tend to receive higher salaries than do those prepared in oversupplied specialties.

No one should choose to teach a particular level or subject area solely because it holds the best promise of immediate employment. For example, it would be exceedingly unwise to prepare for elementary teaching, where the demand for teachers is stronger than it is in most high school subject areas, if you are more skilled in working with older pupils and certain that you will be happier with them.

As you read this chapter and other materials on opportunities in education and as you observe in school situations, ask yourself such questions as the following: With what age level can I work most successfully? What academic areas interest me most? Do I prefer to work with individuals rather than groups? Have I explored all the different kinds of work of educators? Would college teaching interest me? What type of work do I eventually want to do?

Population, millions

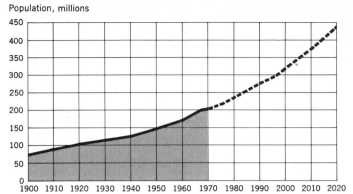

FIGURE 3–1 Part and projected increase in the United States by decades from 1900 to 2000.

General Factors Affecting Supply and Demand of Teachers

Broadly conceived, the demand for teachers consists of the total number of teaching positions to be filled in a given year. Demand is created through such factors as death, retirement, disability, dismissal, resignation, and the creation of new positions. Supply is created through the completion of certification requirements and the seeking of teaching positions. Some prospective teachers complete the requirements for certification but decide not to teach. Other teachers, who have left their positions for a different type of work, wish to return to the profession. Conditions vary from one part of the country to another.

It is estimated that the number of positions vacated by teachers who leave the profession each year is equal to approximately 8 per cent of the total number of teachers. The percentage is slightly higher for secondary than for elementary school teachers [136:25]. Of those who leave each year, approximately 30 per cent are on a leave of absence, 20 per cent retire, 13 per cent assume family responsibilities or marriage, 12 per cent enter or return to another occupation, 10 per cent return to school, 6 per cent become ill, and 3 per cent either die or become incapacitated [132:120].

The mobility of teachers represents a type of demand for teachers. Approximately 10 per cent of the total teacher population move from one year to the next. Major reasons for changing the location of employment are as follows: higher salary, improved working conditions, personal reasons, change in location of husband's work, undesirable community situation, position eliminated, marriage, disagreement with school policies or the administration, and termination of contract [132:120]. Eight out of ten of these moves are made within the state in which the teachers are located, with a majority of the moves taking place within the school system.

Some officials are unable to fill all their vacancies with qualified teachers. These positions frequently are filled with teachers who hold limited (emergency) certificates and who are not properly trained for their positions. Positions held by these emergency teachers actually constitute a demand for qualified teachers.

A number of people feel that one method of meeting the demand for teachers represented by those holding limited certificates is to lower certification standards. They likewise feel that raising certification standards will result in an increase in the number of limited certificates issued. Neither of these feelings is substantiated by facts. In general, the greatest shortages of qualified teachers occur in rural schools, inner-city schools, and in states having the lowest certification standards and lowest salaries. Most states which issue a relatively small percentage of limited certificates not only have high standards but also pay above-average salaries and maintain good teacher retirement systems.

Another factor which affects demand is the number of pupils assigned to a teacher. For example, if twenty rather than twenty-five pupils were assigned to each teacher, decidedly more teachers would be needed. Educators generally recommend no more than twenty-five pupils per teacher. However, some research reveals that, so far as academic achievement in subject matter is concerned, the results obtained in a large class may be just as good as those in a small one. On the other hand, modern education assumes that the educational process must be consciously designed to help the student (1) gain meaningful understandings, (2) develop desirable study habits, (3) speak effectively and listen critically, (4) build high ideals, and (5) gain respect and concern for others. In short, education today faces a growing responsibility for the development of habits and attitudes conducive to good adult citizenship in a local, national, and worldwide society. In order to accomplish these aims adequately, the number of pupils per teacher, especially on the elementary level, should be lowered.

Research studies do indicate that class size does have an effect upon teacher morale. In small classes teachers tend to use more new practices, give more attention to individual pupils, use a greater variety of instructional methods, and depend less on textbooks [12:35].

There are great variations throughout the United States in the pupil-teacher ratio. Generally it is lower (and therefore better) in secondary schools than in elementary schools, lower in areas where the population is sparse, and lower in areas where one-room schools are found.

There has been a definite trend toward the reduction of the number of pupils assigned to a teacher. The pupil-teacher ratio in 1929–1930 was

30.1; in 1939–1940 it was 29.1; in 1949–1950 it was 27.5; in 1969–1970 it was 22.7 [102:20]. If this very desirable downward trend continues, a sizable number of new teachers will be needed. On the other hand, this trend may be reversed as a result of the increasing resistance of the general public to the mounting costs of public education.

The number of children born each year obviously has its effect on the number of teachers needed. During the late 1920s and throughout the 1930s the birthrate in the continental United States decreased. Following World War II the birthrate increased, as indicated in Figure 3–2, but has been decreasing during the past few years. Table 3–1 indicates what may be expected in kindergarten, elementary and secondary school, and college enrollments during the next few years.

A number of factors may affect population trends. For example, the increasing concern for controlling the population may cause considerable decline in the birthrate, especially if birth control devices become more available to and adopted by the lower economic groups, where the birthrate is highest [94:25]. The size of families also may be affected by

FIGURE 3–2 Birth and death rates per 1,000 population, 1910 to 1969. The birth rate has declined more than the death rate which changes the age composition of our population. In spite of the drop in the birth rate, the population of the United States may continue to grow as the post-World War II babies become parents in the 1970s.

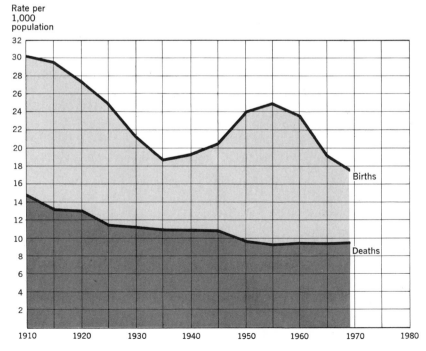

TABLE 3–1 **PROJECTIONS OF ELEMENTARY, SECONDARY, AND HIGHER EDUCATION ENROLLMENTS IN PUBLIC AND NONPUBLIC SCHOOLS 1973–1974 TO 1978–1979**

School Year	Elementary Schools and Kindergarten (K-8)	Secondary Schools (9–12)	Institutions of Higher Education	Total
1973–1974	35,500,000	16,200,000	9,357,000	61,057,000
1974–1975	35,300,000	16,500,000	9,796,000	61,596,000
1975–1976	35,100,000	16,700,000	10,222,000	62,022,000
1976–1977	35,100,000	16,800,000	10,617,000	62,517,000
1977–1978	35,200,000	16,900,000	10,971,000	63,071,000
1978–1979	35,500,000	16,800,000	11,325,000	63,625,000

Source: Kenneth A. Simon and Marie G. Fullam: *Projection of Educational Statistics to 1978–1979,* U.S. Office of Education, National Center for Educational Statistics, Washington, 1970, pp. 20–22.

economic conditions (job stability and cost of living), the increasing tendency for women to work, and the trend toward waiting to start a family.

The demand for teachers also is affected by the number of pupils who remain in school. For example, the phenomenal increase in the percentage of 14- to 17-year-olds attending secondary school has created a great demand for teachers during the past half century. The further increase in pupils attending secondary schools will make demands for additional secondary teachers. Also, as public school opportunities are extended upward to include junior college and extended downward to include kindergarten and nursery school, appreciable demands will be made for teachers qualified to teach on these levels. As evidence of the trend toward the downward extension of educational opportunities, 886,000 three- and four-year-olds were enrolled in nursery school in 1965. In 1970, the number had increased to 1,500,000 [110:2]. Undoubtedly, greater numbers of three- and four-year-olds will be enrolled in nursery schools in the 1970s.

Economic conditions affect the demands for teachers. In times of depression, fewer high-salaried positions occur outside the profession to attract teachers, more married women continue to teach, and vacancies in school systems frequently are absorbed by the remaining staff. In times of prosperity, more teachers leave the profession to accept higher-paying positions, some married women discontinue teaching, vacancies are filled by new teachers, and new positions are often created.

As the nature of the school program changes, the demand for teachers also changes. Certainly the percentage of Latin and Greek teachers is less today than it was at the time of the Latin grammar school. In recent years new demands have been made for trade-industrial-vocational subjects, special education, Afro-American studies, school librarians, and guidance counselors.

The demands for teachers also may be affected by organizational and instructional changes that may take place in the future. As you read subsequent chapters of this book, reflect upon the extent to which such factors as the use of differentiated staffing, team teaching, computer-assisted instruction, programmed learning, and vouchering may affect the numbers and kinds of teachers needed.

The attitude of society in general toward the existing proportion of men and women within the profession has an effect upon opportunities. Although teaching in the United States has been predominantly a woman's field, especially on the elementary level, the profession presents opportunities for both sexes. Young men who ultimately wish to become school principals will do well to consider the possibilities of entering the field of elementary education, where more men are especially desired.

Federal assistance to education tends to increase the demand for teachers. As a result of federal legislation during the mid-sixties, new opportunities were generated for teachers at the preschool, elementary, and college levels.

As indicated in Chapter 1, the educational needs of adults will become increasingly greater as a result of technological and social progress. Subsequent sections of this book will emphasize some of the exciting and challenging demands that will be made of teachers at all levels and in all areas of learning.

FIGURE 3–3   Past and projected number of classroom teachers in regular public and nonpublic elementary and secondary schools.

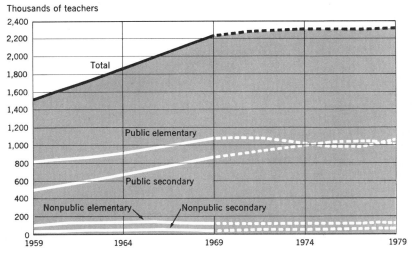

Sources of Teacher Supply

It is extremely difficult to determine accurately the total number of certified teachers who are actively seeking teaching positions. For example, some teachers who have not taught for a number of years may desire to return to the profession. Although there is no precise way of ascertaining how many teachers for any given year will fall into this category, the rate of reentry is estimated to be 3 per cent of the total number of full-time teachers [136:24]. Furthermore, some students who have completed the requirements for teaching may never seek a teaching position or may postpone accepting a teaching position for several years.

Each year, approximately 17 per cent of the elementary teacher graduates and 25 per cent of the secondary teacher graduates are not available for teaching positions. More secondary teacher graduates who major in mathematics, physical education (women's), industrial arts, music, distributive education, library science, special education, and English tend to enter teaching than those who major in agriculture, journalism, commerce, and social studies. As might be expected, non-teaching occupations draw heavily on teachers who major in such areas as business education, chemistry, agriculture, and vocational education. Approximately 5 per cent of the secondary teacher graduates continue formal study immediately following graduation, and 3 per cent become homemakers. A number of men enter military service immediately upon graduation.

In the light of the variables indicated above, perhaps the most dependable rough indication of the supply of teachers is the number of college students completing standard certification requirements. The Research Division of the National Education Association sponsors studies that provide estimates of the number who, at the end of each school year (including summer sessions), qualify for standard teaching certificates. The results of these studies are published annually. Since some changes occur from year to year in the supply and demand for teachers, a prospective teacher should consult the most recent reports available to note any trends that may be taking place. Also, he should check with his college placement officer to see whether these national data are typical of the supply-and-demand conditions in the local area which interests him.

Imbalance in the Demand and the Supply of Teachers

An analysis of Figure 3–4 will reveal that in some subject areas the number of qualified secondary teacher graduates exceeds the demand. On the other hand, in certain subjects the supply is not adequate. The excessive imbalance of teachers in the various fields and levels of teaching constitutes a serious problem in the minds of many educators. As a

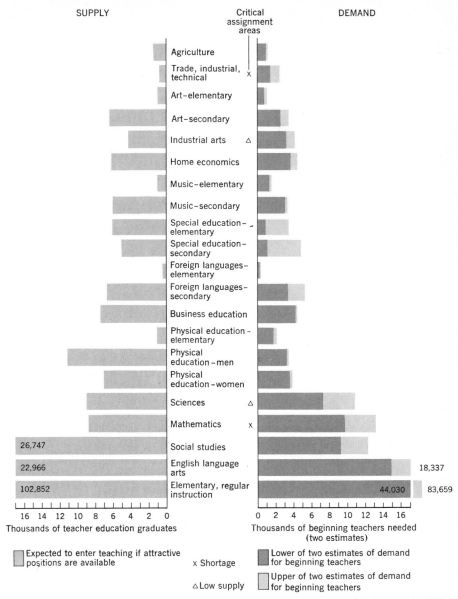

FIGURE 3–4   Supply and demand for beginning teachers according to the type of assignment for 1972. To what extent have the supply and demand conditions changed since 1972?

future professional educator you will be affected by this imbalance. How should the problem be solved? Do you feel that no planned attempt should be made to maintain a reasonable balance between the supply and demand of teachers? Do you maintain that it is undemocratic to limit, as does the medical profession, the number permitted to prepare for the profession? Do you maintain that the problem eventually will solve itself? Do you believe that, when the imbalance becomes too great, increased numbers of intelligent students preparing for secondary teaching will foresee the lack of job opportunities and therefore will not plan to teach?

Or do you feel that a definite plan should be developed to solve the problem of excessive imbalance in supply and demand? Is there no justification, so far as society is concerned, for allowing everyone to prepare for teaching who wishes to do so? Do you feel that both students and society will profit far more by guiding the less promising students into other occupations in which the probabilities of employment are much greater? Thus, many would avoid the possible bitterness of not being able to secure teaching positions and of having wasted the opportunity to prepare for something else.

A few institutions, especially in the eastern part of the United States, have attempted to limit the teacher supply by accepting only a certain number of candidates. Too often the quota plan does not give adequate attention to quality or probable fitness for teaching. Other institutions have made some attempts to control the number of graduates by raising scholastic requirements. The National Council for Accreditation of Teacher Education insists that approved colleges and universities admit to their teacher education programs only those students who have an overall grade average above that required for graduation.

In planning a career in education, it is wise to take into consideration all possible available data regarding supply and demand, especially in those areas and/or levels in which you are particularly interested. Personnel in almost all teacher education institutions today have these data available. They will be able to advise you not only in terms of the national picture but also in terms of the conditions that exist in your specific locale. Since conditions do change from time to time, it is important that you maintain close contact throughout your preparation for teaching with the teacher-employment office which your institution probably maintains.

Analysis of Opportunities in Elementary and Secondary Schools

If the school system is to meet its responsibilities to society, the demand for thoroughly competent teachers must be met through (1) filling new positions being created to accommodate increased enrollments and to continue trends toward improved staffing; (2) replacing teachers who interrupt or terminate their careers; (3) replacing teachers who have substandard professional qualifications; (4) adding teachers in order to reduce overcrowded classes to reasonable maximum size; and (5) providing adequate staffing of new educational offerings of special instructional services, and for the reorganization of instruction [136:25]. What, briefly, does each demand mean as far as your opportunities for teaching are concerned?

The number of births per year foretells the approximate size of the school population in the years to come. Since the early 1960s, the birthrate has continued to decline. With the increasing attention to the problem of worldwide overpopulation, it is reasonable to assume that it may decline further in the United States, or at least remain low. Children born in the late 1950s, prior to a significant decline in birthrate, will tend to increase high school and college enrollments until the end of the 1970s [93:25].

During the ten-year period prior to 1968–1969 the number of states providing support for kindergartens increased from twenty-two to thirty-three. It seems likely that this trend will continue. Undoubtedly more school systems will be making some provisions for three- and four-year-olds.

During the 1960s the percentage of the 14-to-17 age group attending school increased significantly. This increase will not be as great in the 1970s, since the per cent enrolled is approaching the maximum limits. The leeway for increasing the holding power of the school will tend to offset some of the decrease in the elementary school enrollment in the next few years.

FIGURE 3–5 Past and projected school age population groups. What are the implications of the projected changes in the various school-age population groups for opportunities in teaching?

80

As indicated previously, the number of positions vacated by teachers who leave the profession each year equals about 8 per cent of the total number of teachers. For the fall of 1972, for example, it was estimated that 92,200 elementary and 81,800 secondary teachers were needed to fill the positions created by teacher turnover [136:26]. Approximately 27,000 secondary teachers also were needed to fill new positions created from increased enrollments.

In addition to these two very realistic needs, others have not been met and are likely to continue. For example, in 1972 it was estimated that 234,900 elementary teachers and 166,750 secondary teachers were needed to reduce overcrowded classrooms. The problem is especially serious at the elementary school level, where both experience and mature judgment indicate that the effectiveness of the teacher falls as the 1 to 25 pupil-teacher ratio is exceeded. At the lower grade levels particularly, the immaturity of the child is such that personal attention should not be denied him. Although the number fluctuates from year to year, the U.S. Office of Education reported, in the fall of 1968, that 185,440 elementary and 131,550 secondary pupils were unable to attend normal or full-day sessions, due primarily to classroom shortages [28:22]. Unfortunately, elementary school children are less able than secondary school pupils to compensate effectively for the loss of individual attention and assistance which results from such part-time emergency measures. Any relief from these educational inequalities will demand the services of a sizable share of the graduates who annually meet elementary and secondary teacher certification requirements.

Few people would argue the fact that some teachers are not adequately prepared. There is no single answer, however, to the question "When is a person so inadequate that his removal from the classroom is justified?" Estimates of the number of teachers that fall in this category range from 10,000 to over 100,000. It could be assumed that the minimum educational requirement for qualified teachers should be the completion of the bachelor's degree, and the teachers having less than a bachelor's degree need to be upgraded or replaced. Using this criterion, it was

FIGURE 3–6   Pupils attending public elementary and secondary schools for less than a full or normal school day, according to regions, in the fall of 1969.

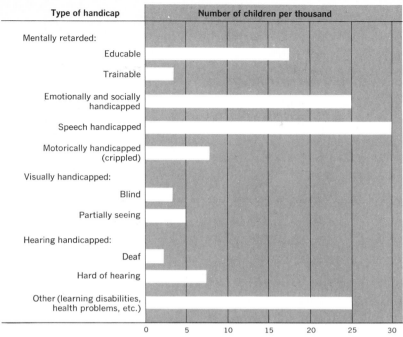

FIGURE 3-7   A general working estimate of the number of children per thousand who are sufficiently handicapped to warrant special services.

estimated that, for 1972–1973, 29,150 elementary and 6,100 secondary teachers would need to have been replaced [136:25–26]. It is gratifying to note, however, that since 1950 much improvement has been made in the level of preparation of teachers. In 1972, only 3.2 per cent of the elementary and 0.8 per cent of secondary teachers had less than a bachelor's degree [136:47].

Increasing demands are being made for the schools to provide special instructional services, enlarge the scope of educational offerings, and provide special programs for pupils having special learning needs (physically, mentally, emotionally handicapped, the educationally deprived, the culturally different, etc.). If schools are able to fulfill these functions, there will be a greater need for guidance counselors, school psychologists, librarians, social workers, vocational teachers, instructional technologists, and subject-area specialists. It is estimated that 174,150 elementary and 160,050 secondary teachers were needed in 1972 to meet this demand [136:26].

To summarize the need factors indicated above, it was estimated that, theoretically, 526,400 elementary teachers and 441,700 secondary teachers were needed in 1972 to meet the various demands. The supply of new teachers in this same year was estimated to be 148,200 elementary and 159,900 secondary teachers, resulting, theoretically, in a shortage of 378,200 elementary and 281,800 secondary teachers [136:34]. A more realistic picture of the supply and demand for teachers may be gained from studying Figure 3–8. Obviously, the demand for teachers is affected by the financial resources available to schools.

The growing surplus of teachers is resulting primarily from increases in higher education enrollments, and in the percentage of college students preparing for teaching. The increases in college enrollments are expected to increase until 1980. The annual percentage of college graduates prepared to teach has increased from 26.7 per cent in 1950 to 36.2 per cent in 1971. Between 1961 and 1971 the annual supply of graduates prepared to teach increased from 129,188 to 305,711. By 1978 it is estimated that the annual number of graduates prepared to teach will be 397,000 [46:84].

The expected large surpluses of teachers in the future should not be confused with the total number of vacancies that will occur each year. In addition to former teachers reentering the profession, the 1970s promise employment for more than 100,000 qualified beginning teachers each year, which does not differ greatly from the total annual demand during the 1960s [131:72–73]. The situation does mean in general that there will be greater competition for the available positions and that school officials will be in a position to employ only the best qualified of the beginning teachers. Careful and comprehensive planning should increase one's chances of securing a position upon completion of the requirements for teaching.

FIGURE 3–8 Supply of beginning teachers expressed as a per cent of normal demand, 1952 to 1979, according to present trends. The surplus would disappear if society wanted high-quality education enough to pay for it.

Per cent of demand

Subject Combinations for Teaching
in the Secondary Schools

Beginning secondary school teachers frequently are asked to teach in two or more subject areas. Even in large school systems teachers may teach in more than one subject area. Teachers in special subject areas such as agriculture, business subjects, fine arts, home economics, industrial arts, and music are more likely than other secondary teachers to teach in one subject area only.

The ease with which a prospective teacher obtains his initial appointment will depend to some degree on the extent to which the subject combination he selects is in demand. A combination that is seldom in demand, such as foreign languages and physical education, is little better than a single subject, while foreign languages with English is demanded more frequently.

Fortunately the combination of subjects tends to follow definite patterns. Unrelated combinations, such as fine arts, agriculture, physics, and English, asked by employing officials in the past, are disappearing. Small secondary schools are revising programs of study so that various courses are offered in alternate years. Many small schools are reducing the number of highly specialized subjects that are offered. Furthermore, the trend toward school consolidation, which increases the enrollment and the size of the faculty of each school, means that teachers may be assigned more nearly according to their preparation.

Many studies have been made of the combination of subjects taught by secondary teachers. Your college teacher-placement officer probably makes an annual study of the subject combinations requested by employing officials. Although almost every possible combination may be found, there are certain ones that occur more often than others. There is considerable demand for such combinations as commerce and social science and/or English; English and social science, foreign languages, or speech; mathematics and general science, social science, or English; music and English; and men's physical education and social science.

The demand for various subject combinations fluctuates from year to year and varies in different sections of the United States. For example, in some states the secondary school candidates are heavily concentrated in certain fields, while in other states they are more widely distributed. Considerable variation in the demand for subject areas may exist between school districts. Your local teacher-placement officer may be of great help in selecting the combination of subjects that seems most desirable for you and most consistent with your abilities and interests.

Opportunities for Teaching on the College Level

A number of individuals value the opportunities that college teaching provides for writing, conducting research, and engaging in other scholarly pursuits. Some value highly the prestige that college instructors have, compared with that of public school teachers.

In some college departments, especially in the subject matter areas, a few highly selected graduates are encouraged to study immediately for higher degrees. The students usually are granted assistantships that entail some teaching, supervision of laboratories, or the like, while they continue their studies. The assistantships pay a relatively small amount of money but may provide fee exemptions for college work taken by the student. Others may receive scholarships or continue their educations at their own expense. You may wish to investigate possibilities along these lines.

A large percentage of college teachers began their teaching careers in public schools. They pursued graduate work during their summer vacations or returned for full-time study to complete their degrees. Usually they have found their public school experiences to be of great value in their college teaching. A number of years of successful elementary or secondary teaching experience is a prerequisite for securing a position for teaching education courses.

Opportunities for college teaching will be affected by the extent to which college enrollments increase. For a number of years the percentage of the group of college students 18 to 21 years old has increased approximately 1 per cent a year. This percentage recently has increased to $1\frac{1}{2}$ per

FIGURE 3–9 Past and projected instructional staff positions for resident degree-credit courses in public and private colleges and universities.

cent and may increase even more in the future. From 1950 to 1969 the percentage of high school graduates going on to college increased from 43 to 66 per cent [142:1]. Since the peak number of births in the United States occurred in 1957, the peak number of freshmen will not reach our colleges and universities until 1975. It is estimated that a peak college enrollment of 13,751,000 will occur in 1982 [142:5]—in contrast to a reported enrollment of 7,377,000 for the fall of 1970 [67:67]. In viewing these mounting numbers, several pertinent questions arise [137:11]:

1. Will junior colleges continue to be the most rapidly growing division of higher education?
2. Will the universities concentrate to a greater extent upon graduate instruction?
3. Will nonpublic institutions push their admission requirements higher, with the intent of holding enrollments at approximately the present figure?
4. Will the public universities restrict classes of entering freshmen to the top percentiles of high school graduating classes?
5. Can the small nonpublic colleges survive in the competition for really competent teachers?
6. Will there be, in fact, an open college door for all who seek admission in the years ahead?
7. Will external degree programs, which enable students to earn a college degree largely outside the confines of traditional university settings, become more prevalent?

In addition to the number of students that may be involved, another variable to be considered is the load of each teacher. It has been estimated that the nationwide student-teacher ratio in all higher-education institutions is approximately 14 to 1, although the range is great from institution to institution. In order to extend the utilization of faculty members, efforts are being made to [137:11]:

1. Thrust greater responsibility upon the individual student for his own learning.
2. Eliminate nonessential and overlapping courses, and stem the tendency toward fragmentation of subject matter into highly specialized courses.
3. Experiment further with variation in class size.
4. Make joint use of teachers by two or more institutions.
5. Use mechanical and electronic devices, including television.
6. Use nonprofessional personnel to perform nonprofessional tasks.
7. Reevaluate the committee system as a part of administrative procedure.
8. Improve the general climate and overall working conditions on the campus.
9. Clarify further the role of the college teacher as a citizen in the community.

It has been estimated that an additional 118,000 full-time instructional staff members will be needed in institutions of higher education during the six-year period 1973–1974 through 1979–1980 [121:73]. This estimate does not include a 6 per cent replacement rate for those (5 per cent) who leave employment in institutions of higher education and those (1 per cent) who die or retire. In addition to the instructional staff, it has been estimated that 24,000 additional professional staff members will be needed between 1973–1974 and 1979–1980 for general administration and service support duties. This figure does not include the number needed for replacement of staff leaving the profession [121:73]. The extent to which meeting these needs becomes a reality depends largely upon the extent to which the public is willing to finance higher education.

It is estimated that, between 1970 and 1980, the number of junior colleges will increase from 800 to 1,200 and will enroll approximately 4,000,000 students in 1980 [10:119]. Opportunities for teaching in junior colleges, therefore, may be reasonably good for those possessing at least a master's degree. Generally the doctoral degree is desired for teaching in four-year institutions and in graduate schools.

Opportunities in Other Areas of Education

Unfortunately most people limit their concept of the opportunities in the field of education mainly to teaching in the public or private school classroom. It is true that over 80 per cent of those engaged in public school work are regular classroom teachers. On the other hand, there are specialized kinds of instruction and services to be rendered, such as counseling and guidance; research analysis; teaching speech and hearing therapy and remedial reading; teaching the mentally retarded, physically handicapped, partially seeing, hard-of-hearing, emotionally disturbed, the gifted and the culturally disadvantaged; serving as librarian; and teaching driver education and distributive education courses. Attention already has been called to the large number of superintendents, principals, supervisors, and others involved in administrative services.

It would be exceedingly interesting to analyze all the different kinds of work demanding the services of educators and to note the number involved in each. Unfortunately these data are not available. The following listing of the more common educational opportunities may be of interest to you. In no sense is the list complete.

FIGURE 3–10   Number of professional employees per 1,000 students.

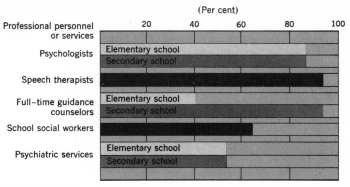

FIGURE 3–11   Per cent of public school systems, enrolling 25,000 or more pupils, having various types of special professional personnel.

I.   Preschools—nursery and kindergarten
    A.   Teachers
    B.   Supervisors
    C.   Consultant in child growth and development
    D.   Research worker in child growth and development
    E.   Director of a private nursery or kindergarten
    F.   Director of day care centers
    G.   Director of Head Start projects
    H.   Director of follow-through programs
II.   Elementary schools
    A.   Teacher for separate grades or combined grades
    B.   Teacher of special subjects such as art, music, or physical education
    C.   Teacher of a subject such as arithmetic or geography in a departmentalized school, or in a team-teaching situation
    D.   Teacher of physically handicapped, partially seeing, or hard-of-hearing children
    E.   Teacher of exceptional children—talented, mentally retarded, or emotionally disturbed, or disadvantaged
    F.   Supervising teacher in a laboratory or experimental school
    G.   General or special subject supervisor
    H.   Assistant principal
    I.   Principal
    J.   Librarian
    K.   Speech correctionist and/or hearing therapist
    L.   Visiting teacher
    M.   Child psychologist or counselor
    N.   School nurse
    O.   Curriculum consultant
    P.   Guidance counselor
III.   Secondary schools
    A.   Teacher of subjects such as English, foreign language, social studies, or music
    B.   Teaching of special subjects such as art, home economics, industrial arts and trades, music, physical education, driver education, speech and hearing therapy, Afro-American studies
    C.   Teacher of disadvantaged children
    D.   Supervising teacher in a laboratory or experimental school

   E. Department head of a subject area
   F. Assistant principal
   G. Principal
   H. Supervisor of a subject area
   I. Curriculum consultant
   J. Athletic coach
   K. Guidance counselor
   L. Librarian
   M. Visiting teacher
IV. Administrative and special services
   A. Superintendent
   B. Assistant superintendent—usually assigned a specific phase of work such as finance, personnel, or instruction
   C. Business manager (supplies, purchasing, etc.)
   D. School secretary
   E. Research director
   F. Attendance officer
   G. Director of audio-visual materials
   H. Director of school and community relations
   I. School psychologist
   J. School psychometrist
   K. Vocational counselor and placement officer
   L. School statistician
   M. Clerical assistant
   N. Cafeteria manager
   O. Dietitian
   P. School physician or dentist
   Q. School nurse or health officer
   R. Adult education director
V. Junior colleges
   A. Teacher of different fields (English, mathematics, science, etc.)
   B. Personnel director
   C. President or dean
   D. Admissions officer
   E. Registrar
   F. Business manager
   G. Health service officer
   H. Director of minority group education
   I. Director of vocational, technical education
   J. Director of continuing education
VI. College or university positions
   A. Teacher of a subject field
   B. Assistant to dean
   C. Dean of a separate college such as liberal arts, education, engineering, agriculture, law, medicine, fine arts, pharmacy, social service, dentistry
   D. Dean of continuing education
   E. Dean of students
   F. President
   G. Director of programs for minority groups
   H. Chairman of a department
   I. Alumni secretary
   J. Director of public relations
   K. Registrar
   L. Director of counseling

      M. Business manager
      N. Research worker
      O. Director of research
      P. Secretary and/or accountant
      Q. Field worker for recruiting students
      R. Field worker for carrying services of university to the people
      S. Placement director
      T. Health service personnel

VII. Professional organizations such as the National Education Association, the American Federation of Teachers, the National Association for Afro-American Education, as well as state education associations
      A. Director
      B. Executive secretary
      C. Research worker
      D. Field worker
      E. Writer
      F. Director of publications

VIII. State departments of education
      A. State superintendent of instruction
      B. Director of curriculum
      C. Director of guidance
      D. Director of special education
      E. Special field worker

IX. Educational directors or consultants for noneducational agencies
      A. Publisher of newspapers, magazines, films
      B. Manufacturing firms—job training, recreation, testing, etc.
      C. Religious associations
      D. Chambers of commerce
      E. Aviation companies
      F. Service agencies, such as state tuberculosis association
      G. Minority groups

X. Municipal, private, religious, and civic agencies
      A. City recreation director
      B. Boy and girl camps—director, instructor
      C. Director of youth organization
          1. Boy Scouts and Girl Scouts
          2. 4-H club
          3. YMCA and YWCA
      D. Teacher in a hospital
      E. Teacher in a church or Bible school
      F. Director of minority groups

XI. Federal agencies
      A. U.S. Office of Education
          1. International education (Teacher Exchange)
          2. Teacher Corps
      B. Department of Defense
          1. Dependent schools overseas
          2. Military service
      C. Department of Interior—Bureau of Indian Affairs
      D. Department of State (Peace Corps)
      E. UNESCO

XII. Foreign countries
      A. Teacher
      B. Conductor of tours

C. Consultant
D. Research worker
E. Defense Department appointments, military government

It should be pointed out that many of the different kinds of educational work listed above do not exist in the small schools. Furthermore, successful teaching experience normally is required for many of the positions not involving classroom teaching.

In forecasting the future, Shane [119:29–32] feels that between 1970 and 1980 a number of new assignments and specialties will materialize. The basic role of the teacher may change noticeably, to the extent that it should be more accurate to term him a "learning clinician." He explains that [119:31–32]:

In the school of the future, senior learning clinicians will be responsible for coordinating the services needed for approximately 200 to 300 children. In different instructional units (an evolution of the "team" concept) we will find paraprofessionals, teaching interns, and other learning clinicians with complementary backgrounds. Some will be well-informed in counseling, others in media, engineering, languages, evaluation, systems analysis, simulation, game theory, and individual-need analysis.

But on the whole, the learning clinician will probably not be appreciably more specialized in subject matter disciplines than he was in the 1960's except for being skilled in using educational technology. He will do more *coordinating* and *directing* of individual

The Peace Corps provides an opportunity to render service while getting travel and teaching experience. Here Judith Roberts of San Carlos, California, is shown teaching English at the College of Education in Bangkok, Thailand. *(Photograph from ACTION/Peace Corps.)*

inquiry and will engage in less 1968-style group instruction. He will be highly concerned with providing and maintaining an effective environment, skilled in interpersonal transactions, and able to work with persons of different ages and learning styles.

Ten years from now, faculties will include:

Culture analysts , who make use of our growing insights into how a subculture shapes the learning style and behavior of its members.

Media specialists, who tailor-make local educational aids, who evaluate hardware and software and their use, and who are adept in the information sciences of automated-information storage and retrieval, and computer programming.

Information-input specialists, who make a career of keeping faculty and administration aware of implications for education in broad social, economic and political trends.

Curriculum-input specialists, who from day to day make necessary corrections and additions to memory bank tapes on which individualized instructional materials are stored.

Biochemical therapist/pharmacists, whose services increase as biochemical therapy and memory improvement chemicals are introduced more widely.

Early childhood specialists, who work in the nonschool, preschool, and minischool programs and in the preprimary continuum.

Developmental specialists, who determine the groups in which children and youth work and who make recommendations regarding ways of improving pupil learning.

Community-contact personnel, who specialize in maintaining good communication, in reducing misunderstanding or abrasions, and in placing into the life of the community the increased contributions that the schools of the 1970's will be making.

A prospective teacher should not confine his exploration of educational opportunities to the school system of the United States. New educational opportunities are continuing to develop in the business world. Industries, businesses, and labor unions all over the country need educational directors, would be glad to employ them if they were available, and would give them opportunities to make very significant contributions to education in general. The field of educational radio and television is expanding rapidly. Textbook publishers and some of the giant industries (Xerox, General Electric, Raytheon, IBM) have been uniting for the purpose of preparing instructional materials. The need for "educational engineers" is great. Also, as will be discussed later, the whole field of adult education is barely getting started in this country. There is room for thousands of new jobs in that field for men and women with sound general training, creative imagination, and drive.

For the more adventurous person, the opportunities to work in even the most remote areas of the world continue to increase. For example, over 1,000 new teachers are needed each year in the American Dependent Schools Overseas. The Peace Corps offers many opportunities to teach in a number of underdeveloped countries. You may wish to check upon the requirements and opportunities for working in schools in outlying states and areas of the United States and in schools and programs sponsored by the United States government, such as the American Dependent Schools Overseas, Teacher Exchange, Information Services, and Agency for International Development.

Preparation in the teaching profession certainly presents many

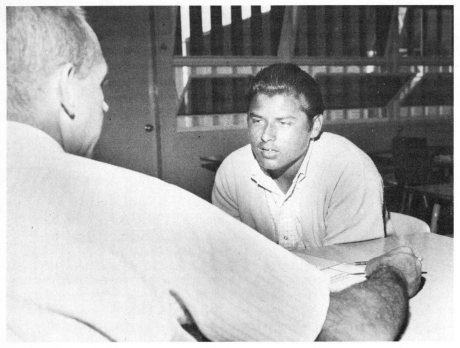

An increasing number of industries, businesses, and community agencies feel the need for educators who can counsel, and who can plan educational programs for their personnel. *(Photograph by Joe Di Dio, National Education Association.)*

different opportunities, and you can engage in the type of activity of special interest to you. If you are willing to prepare yourself well for a particular type of work, the chances of reaching your goal are good.

SUMMARY

The teaching profession is, by a wide margin, the largest of all the professions. It provides a great variety of opportunities for anyone who wishes to prepare for, and remain in, the profession for a number of years. Most people enter the profession as public school teachers.

Many factors affect the supply and demand for teachers. In periods of economic depression the supply tends to become greater than in times of economic prosperity. Birthrates, pupil-teacher ratios, turnover, and expansion or contraction of educational services rendered by the school affect significantly the demand for teachers.

Since the birthrate has been decreasing, elementary school enrollments are expected to decline during the 1970s, and secondary school enrollments are expected to increase. Birthrates and the number of births alone do not determine entirely the demand for new teachers. Undoubtedly there will continue to be considerable downward extension of schooling during the 1970s, for which demands will be made for well-qualified early childhood teachers. The holding power of the secondary schools undoubtedly will continue to increase, although the rate may not be as great as during the 1960s. The expansion of specialized kinds of instruction and services, the changes in organizational and instructional patterns that will take place in the foreseeable future, and the increasing need for educators in business, industry, and continuing education will generate additional opportunities for teachers.

A dramatic increase in enrollments is projected for junior colleges and four-year colleges and universities, with the peak of enrollments being reached in 1982. This increase, in addition to the normal replacement rate of 6 per cent of the total instructional staff, should generate a number of opportunities for those interested in teaching at the college level—assuming that the general public will be willing to increase its financial support for higher education.

QUESTIONS TO CONSIDER

1. Many educators feel that more men should be attracted into public school teaching, especially into the elementary schools. Do you agree or disagree? What are your reasons? By what means could this end be accomplished?
2. For what reasons should educational opportunities be extended downward at public expense? How far down should these opportunities be extended? Why?
3. For what reasons can you expect the number of fourteen- to seventeen-year-olds attending secondary schools to continue to increase?
4. What major and minor teaching combinations are in greatest demand in the area where you plan to teach? Least demand?
5. What suggestions would you make for solving the problem of excessive imbalance of teachers in the various fields and levels of teaching?
6. What sacrifices are made by pupils when they are forced to attend excessively large classes or half-day sessions?
7. As you review Chapter 1, what new opportunities do you foresee for educators?
8. What advantages and disadvantages do you see in teaching on the college level?
9. How might the growth of junior colleges affect the opportunities of secondary school teachers?
10. If you had to change your subject area or level of teaching, what would you choose? Why?
11. What are some of the opportunities that exist in adult education?
12. In your opinion, what are the frontier opportunities for teachers in industry, business, and overseas programs?

PROBLEM SITUATION FOR INQUIRY

Mr. Harris is the principal of the elementary school in the small community of Oakwood. He has held his position for six years and has developed close relationships with the faculty and the community. Harris has an ideal situation. The students are well-behaved; there is an active PTA group in the school; he is respected in the community; and he gets strong support from the district superintendent. In essence, both Harris and his family are very happy in Oakwood.

The school board of North Crest, a wealthy suburban area, recently contacted Mr. Harris and offered him a position as principal of the North Crest Junior High School. Mr. Harris was flattered with the offer, but he requested some time to consider it before making a decision. Upon investigating the North Crest situation, he discovered many problems. He found that the students are rebellious and unconcerned about their education, and that discipline problems in the school are numerous. Principals who have previously served in the school have found it impossible to handle this large group of uninhibited youngsters. Parents are often too caught up in the community social activities to be concerned with the education of their children. These students have everything they want materially. They get bored, and try to grow up too soon.

The principalship at North Crest pays a salary of $18,000, which is considerably more than Harris's present salary in Oakwood. The new job would mean leaving the pleasant community of Oakwood in which he has a secure position. However, the new job, in addition to providing a larger salary, would offer a tremendous professional challenge. If you were Mr. Harris, what would you do? Why?

ACTIVITIES TO PURSUE

1. Plan a number of visits to more than one school, observing various elementary and secondary school classes. Attempt to make, or further verify, an original decision regarding the subject areas and/or the level you may wish to teach.
2. Plan some leadership experiences with children of different age levels to make, or further verify, an original decision regarding elementary or secondary teacher preparation. Experience as a camp counselor, playground supervisor, boy or girl scout director, and the like should prove very valuable to you.
3. Consult your local superintendent to see if you might serve as an assistant in a school between the time public schools open in the fall and the time your college courses begin; or at some other convenient time. Attempt to gain broad experience both in the classroom and around the school. Study these experiences in terms of your fitness for teaching, the level on which you should teach, and learning significant for future courses in education.
4. Question a number of teachers whom you respect, especially those teaching on the elementary level, regarding the advantages and disadvantages of preparing for teaching in the subject areas and/or levels which they represent.
5. Visit some inner-city schools to see if teaching in such schools might interest and challenge you.
6. Consult the adviser and the teacher-placement official in your college concerning the probable supply and demand for teachers when you expect to graduate. Secure from educational literature as much data on this problem as possible.
7. If you do not plan to teach in the locale where you are attending school, secure data on teacher supply and demand for the area in which you expect to begin your work.
8. Examine the organizational setup of a large city school system to discover the different kinds of positions involved. Talk with those individuals who hold positions that may interest you. Discuss such matters as qualifications, duties, advantages, and disadvantages of the work.
9. Discuss with your college adviser any occupational plans other than teaching that you may have in the field of education. Consider specific implications that these plans may have in your preparation for teaching.

FIGURE 3–1 (*Source:* Data from *Statistical Abstract of the United States,* U.S. Department of Commerce, Bureau of the Census, Washington, 1971, p. 7.)

FIGURE 3–2 (*Source:* Data from *Statistical Abstract of the United States,* U.S. Department of Commerce, Bureau of the Census, Washington, 1971, pp. 50 and 55.)

FIGURE 3–3 (*Source:* Kenneth A. Simon and Marie G. Fullam, *Projections of Educational Statistics to 1979–80,* U.S. Office of Education, National Center for Educational Statistics, Washington, 1971, p. 6.)

FIGURE 3–4 (*Source:* "Teacher Supply and Demand in Public Schools," *Research Report 1972–R8,* National Education Association, Research Division, Washington, 1972, p. 38).

FIGURE 3–5 (*Source:* Kenneth A. Simon and Marie G. Fullam, *Projections of Educational Statistics to 1979–80,* U.S. Office of Education, National Center for Educational Statistics, Washington, 1971, p. 8.)

FIGURE 3–6 (*Source:* Data from Richard H. Barr and Betty J. Foster, *Statistics of Public Elementary and Secondary Day Schools, Fall, 1969,* U.S. Office of Education, National Center for Educational Statistics, Washington, 1970, p. 22.)

FIGURE 3–7 (*Source:* Data adapted from Samuel Kirk, "Educating the Handicapped," *Contemporary Issues in American Education,* U.S. Office of Education, Washington, 1965, p. 89.)

FIGURE 3–8 (*Source:* Adapted from William S. Graybeal, "Teacher Surplus and Teacher Shortage," *Phi Delta Kappan,* vol. 53, no. 2, Phi Delta Kappa, Bloomington, Ind., October, 1971, p. 83.)

FIGURE 3–9 (*Source:* Kenneth A. Simon and Marie G. Fullam, *Projections of Educational Statistics to 1979–80,* U.S. Office of Education, National Center for Educational Statistics, Washington, 1971, p. 6.)

FIGURE 3–10 (*Source:* "Pupil-Staff Ratios, 1966–67," *NEA Research Bulletin,* vol. 46, no. 1, National Education Association, Research Division, Washington, March, 1968, p. 21.)

FIGURE 3–11 (*Source:* "Public School Programs and Practices," *NEA Research Bulletin,* vol. 45, no. 4, National Education Association, Research Division, Washington, December, 1967, p. 106.)

4 | THE CHANGING ROLE OF THE TEACHER

What duties and responsibilities are expected of teachers in the classroom? What does the community expect of teachers? What organizational changes are taking place that may affect instructional procedures and practices? The answers to these questions provide a major part of the framework for a teacher's professional and personal life.

This chapter will review briefly a few of the major classroom and community responsibilities of teachers, and then examine in some detail the newer organizational and instructional procedures that are bringing some dramatic changes now and promising more in the future.

MAJOR CLASSROOM RESPONSIBILITIES OF TEACHERS

It is unlikely that any two classroom teachers would have identical responsibilities. There are great gaps between what an elementary teacher does in a one-room rural school and what a senior English teacher does in a large metropolitan high school. Likewise, conditions in public schools and communities differ considerably throughout the United States and may well change tremendously in the future. As a result, teachers' working lives vary in significant ways. Still, there are some responsibilities that are common to the work of all teachers.

Instruction

A teacher is expected to have a thorough understanding of the subject matter and skills to be taught in his area. His main responsibility is to assist in the development of adaptable, rational, creative, and cooperative individuals who are capable of coping with the world in which they live, who are prepared to be productive citizens in the world of tomorrow, and who possess an awareness of moral, spiritual, and social values [13:13].

Elementary teachers generally have gone about the task of educating children by staying with one particular group for the greater part of the day. They have planned their lessons before and after school or during released periods when the students may be receiving instruction from itinerant specialists in music, art, or physical education.

In secondary school, teachers generally have met several different classes in each day; the variety of subjects taught by each teacher has usually been greater in small schools than in large ones. In their attempts to provide for the needs and interests of a burgeoning school population, secondary schools have added many subjects. In fact, curriculum workers view with alarm the tendency to change the secondary school program merely by adding courses. The trend they prefer to encourage is toward reducing these numbers. Curriculum workers have suggested removing courses which are outmoded or inappropriate, combining the common learning experiences of pupils in a given school around areas of living which draw upon many subjects and resources.

In attempting to assure reasonable teaching loads in member schools, the North Central Association of Colleges and Secondary Schools has recommended as one of its school accrediting policies that each teacher be assigned at least one conference and preparation period daily [91:14]. In schools operating on a six- or seven-period day, this would mean that a teacher should be assigned no more than five classes and/or study halls. In schools using eight or more periods, a teacher should be assigned not more than six classes and/or study halls.

Of course, the number of classes is only one aspect of a teacher's load. Other factors to be considered include the subject being taught, class size, length of period, administrative or supervisory duties, assignments in extraclass activities, counseling duties, and length of school day. In addition, recent innovations in teaching, such as television and other

FIGURE 4–1   How elementary and secondary school teachers divide an average work week. Noncompensated school-related activities include lesson preparation, grading papers, making reports, attending meetings, etc.

electronic aids, flexible scheduling, ungraded classrooms, team teaching, and the use of programmed material with or without machines, tend to make the "number of classes taught" a less accurate description of a teacher's day.

Student Guidance and Counseling

A major goal of education is to develop students who are capable of and dedicated to a lifetime of learning. This means helping students define their most pressing needs and interests and problems; helping them understand themselves better; and helping them understand their families, their friends, their whole community. Out of this will emerge certain specific objectives the youngsters will consider important to achieve. The teacher's function is to guide students in formulating and appraising their objectives in terms of their value to the learners and to the community. The teacher guides the students in planning ways and means of arriving at those objectives.

In order for learning to be relevant, pupils must be able to relate the facts they have discovered to their everyday lives. This requires numerous deliberate applications and the development of generalizations which make sense to the learners—which they can use to gain better control over their future behavior. Research seems to indicate that on tests of academic achievement requiring analysis, synthesis, evaluation, and application of knowledge, the more informal group processes described here obtain better results than more formal lectures and recitations [122:20]. These are important considerations that apply in the teaching of all grades and all subjects.

The modern classroom teacher, using standardized test results, careful observations, and records of past performances, gains insight into each student's level of ability. The teacher places those of somewhat similar abilities together for certain learning experiences. However, these groupings are flexible, and as students grow in their abilities, they move from one group to another. Through careful observation, teachers are often able to select groups with similar interests. Group interests may be used to solve mutual problems or to act as a motivating force for further learning. Grouping is only one of many teaching techniques which the modern teacher uses to individualize instruction. Ungraded classrooms and flexible scheduling enable teachers to group pupils in terms of their individual needs, interests, and abilities.

Some students will need the attention of specialists who can help them with academic or emotional maladjustments; the teacher who knows the individual abilities, strengths, and weaknesses of the pupils will obviously be in a better position to render a service to students. Teachers, whose assignments make it necessary to be responsible for large numbers of students, find the teacher-guidance role more difficult.

Elementary teachers in self-contained or modified self-contained class-rooms have a distinct advantage over most secondary teachers.

Maintaining Discipline

The traditional concept of discipline centers around order in the class-room, techniques of maintaining that order, and means of punishment. The modern concept is based on certain principles which have grown out of the findings of psychology and the viewpoints of such educators as Dewey and Kilpatrick. Sheviakov and Redl [120:9–16] listed some democratic principles which guide discipline practices in a modern conception of education:

1. Teachers use positive ways of guidance which communicate this belief in the value of each personality, rather than negative ways which undermine self-confidence and self-esteem.
2. Teachers consider each incident when discipline or order has broken down in relation to the particular persons involved, their needs and their life histories.
3. Our schools provide a climate in which mutual respect and trust are possible.
4. Teachers build understanding and communication between individuals and groups.
5. Teachers help children to understand the reasons for standards and rules and to foresee the consequences of their own behavior.
6. Schools provide for children's growth in self-government through which they share increasingly in planning their own activities.
7. Teachers study children's behavior scientifically, searching for causes and formulating hunches and hypotheses about how changes may be made.
8. Teachers help young people to understand the reasons for their own and others' behavior and to develop more effective ways of meeting common conflicts.

These principles suggest self-discipline, the internalized behavior that Kilpatrick talked about—control from within rather than control from without. The teacher assumes vastly different duties in carrying out this modern concept of discipline. Instead of assuming the authoritarian, dictatorial role, the teacher takes the part of guide and director of the learning experiences which will provide opportunities to develop self-discipline. Planning with the students and evaluating these plans becomes an important teaching technique. Children help to build their own rules and regulations within which they will operate. Prevention of behavior problems is given keen consideration by both teachers and students. Teachers help children to channel their energies and initiative into socially acceptable behavior.

Pupils learn the democratic way of life by living it. Since self-discipline is a cornerstone of the democratic way of life, the learning experiences which the school provides must foster law and order from within each individual.

In an introductory course in education, it would be premature to include an extensive discussion of the teacher's role in fostering self-discipline within students. In order to gain an adequate comprehension of this extremely important responsibility, it is essential for a prospective teacher to establish a broad base of understanding in such areas as psychology and sociology.

Evaluating Pupil Progress

Ideally throughout each learning experience, teachers and pupils take stock of their progress to see whether their goals are being attained or whether their objectives need revising. They appraise their procedures and decide whether they are the best that can be used and whether they are being used well. They take inventory of available resources to determine whether their selection and use have been adequate and wise. These aspects of evaluation may require written reports, committee minutes, anecdotes, checklists, questionnaires, rating scales, personal documents such as diaries, projective techniques, and a variety of tests. Some of the tests will be formal and standardized, whereas others will be informal teacher-constructed instruments, both essay and objective. In either case, the administering, scoring, and interpreting of the tests will be among each teacher's important functions. Beginning teachers can receive valuable help in constructing their own evaluative instruments by turning to teacher or administrator colleagues.

Reporting to Parents

The teacher is expected to keep parents informed about the progress of his pupils. If he does this systematically and regularly, it can prove to be one of the most fruitful avenues for bringing together the public and the schools. This should involve reviewing and summarizing the information available about each youngster, going over his activities and anecdotal records, looking into his cumulative record, observing test results of various sorts, and, finally, making an appraisal of each. This should be done in terms of each student's individual growth and development toward the stated objectives.

Unfortunately, instructional practices do not often reflect a strong goal orientation, because considered thought regarding purpose is seldom evident. Therefore, evaluation of individual student progress in terms of specific goals sought does not often take place. If this were not the case, evaluation would more often focus upon the individual and his progress—where he started and where he is now—in contrast to some other reference point. Expectations and standards would, of course, vary considerably.

Evaluation involves a negative experience for too large a number of students. It does not have to be this way. Evaluation and subsequent reporting to parents can be oriented in a positive direction: these are the ends toward which we (students and faculty) are directing our energies; this is where the student was at the beginning of instruction; here is where he is now; and, finally, here is what *we* are doing to help him achieve stated objectives. Notice the emphasis upon the individual and the supportive role of the teacher in working with students.

It is unfortunate that in most schools, particularly secondary schools, a student's accomplishment usually is determined by comparing him with other members of his class, and he is graded in terms of where he stands "on the curve." In other instances, a larger group may be used—perhaps, all the students in the school or school system at a given grade or age level. And in still other cases the reference point may be the teacher's expectation of what a student in a specific grade or subject area ought to be able to do.

All the conventional systems of grading and reporting to parents have serious limitations. Many of them fail to inform adequately, and a few actually misinform. Parents, prospective employers, college officials, even the students and the teachers are frequently confused and misled by "A-B-C" grade reports. Where numerical percentages are used, the situation is even worse. Grouping plans further complicate the picture. Does an "A" in an accelerated group mean the same as an "A" in a slow-learning section?

The most common methods of reporting to parents are report cards, parent conferences, and letters to parents. The usual parts of a report card include letter grades [104:75], attendance and tardiness records, and a checklist section on personal characteristics. In a few schools, usually on the elementary level, letter grades have been eliminated. However, even in most schools which have abandoned or supplemented the traditional report card, grades remain a part of the total evaluation of pupil progress. In view of the current emphasis on preparation for college and on college entrance requirements, it is probable that such grades will continue to be an important phase of pupil appraisal on the secondary level.

It is interesting to note that while secondary schools continue to emphasize grades, colleges and universities are now reducing such emphasis. Pass-fail grading, once an innovation in higher education, is now quite common. About two-thirds of the institutions of higher education now use some form of pass-fail grading.

Parent-teacher conferences have gained in frequency, particularly at the elementary level, and to some extent at the secondary level. Research indicates that a preference exists at the elementary school level for reporting through a combination of cards and parent conferences [105:81–82]. It is obvious that parent-teacher conferences are more easily arranged in an elementary school than in a secondary school. In an elementary school such a plan involves perhaps twenty-five to thirty-five conferences with parents. In a secondary school such a plan involves conferences with 100 to 200 parents for each report period. The latter

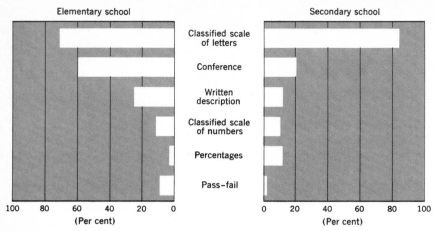

FIGURE 4–2   Methods used by public-school teachers to report pupil progress to parents.

plan is practically impossible, and other patterns have been suggested, such as parent conferences with the homeroom teacher or designated counselors. At any rate the problem is a major one at the secondary level.

Some schools have experimented with letters to parents. However, such letters are time-consuming and frequently become almost as formalized as report cards.

In the final analysis, by far the most common type of reporting remains the report card, with many schools combining it with parent-teacher conferences, and a few using letters to parents. In most schools these reports are made either four times or five times a year. In reporting to parents, new procedures and new instruments are urgently needed.

Cocurricular Responsibilities

Most secondary and some elementary teachers have some responsibilities for cocurricular activities. Class plays, yearbook production, student government, and class organizations are typical examples of student activities which are popular with students and are capable of producing real and significant values to them.

The trend in school systems throughout the country is for teachers to receive extra compensation for cocurricular activities that demand portions of their time outside the classroom. This is justifiable, since these responsibilities are not shared equally by all teachers. However, the value a teacher may receive in experiencing a healthy new relationship with students may well outweigh any financial compensation that may be provided.

Professional Responsibilities

Classroom teachers have many other duties of a miscellaneous nature which call for careful attention. There will be letters and professional inquiries which must be answered. Teachers are occasionally asked to answer questionnaires from other educators who are conducting research. Teachers must keep current in their own field, and one way is to plan a regular time for the reading of professional books, journals, and other materials. Some teachers spend time and effort in educational experiments and writing of their own. These things take time, but they are rewarding in terms of professional growth. New teachers will be able to receive help from experienced educators when they wish to gain information about acceptable ways of systematizing the various routine teacher tasks. However, the matter of keeping professionally alert and growing through reading and study is a highly individual matter that requires personal commitment and dedication.

Teacher Evaluation

Every teacher should feel an obligation to review systematically the quality of his teaching. Through frequent self-analysis and appraisal a teacher gains insight with regard to ways in which his teaching may be improved.

In a very practical and informative booklet titled *Are You a Good Teacher?* Alexander [2] has prepared a list of twenty indicators of the quality of teaching. This list is located at the end of this chapter for you to use in planning your career, and for checking yourself periodically after you begin teaching.

The quality of each teacher's work will be appraised by his superior, usually the principal, and this appraisal may be casual or very formal. According to a study made by the Research Division of the National Education Association [69:12–18], written ratings or evaluations are required in three-fourths of the schools for teachers not on tenure and in two-thirds for teachers who are on tenure. Beginning teachers are evaluated more often than are experienced teachers. Usually the appraisal is made as a result of observing the teacher in the classroom. Other methods of evaluating a teacher may include "gathering impressions from pupils, study of pupil achievement records and office records on each teacher, and noting what parents and other teachers say about the teacher being evaluated" [69:13].

A nationwide sample survey of public-school classroom teachers [133:70–72] indicated that most teachers think they should be evaluated. Three-fourths of the teachers felt that both probationary and tenure teachers should be evaluated regularly, and another 15 per cent felt that

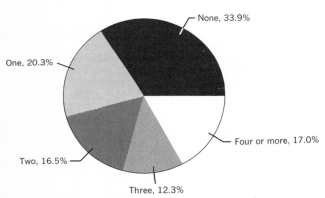

FIGURE 4–3   The results of a study of the number of times teachers were observed in their classroom work for five minutes or more, as reported by teachers.

only probationary teachers should be evaluated. The teachers agreed almost unanimously that the school principal should be responsible for teacher evaluation. The overwhelming reason why teachers wish to be evaluated is in order to improve their teaching competence.

Relationships with Other School Personnel

Teachers have considerable freedom in fulfilling their classroom responsibilities, but they are expected to abide by and operate within the framework of school board policies in the areas of curriculum organization, teaching techniques, standard report forms, and professional behavior. In most school systems the administrator who is responsible for overseeing the detailed work of each teacher is the building principal.

The principal is responsible to the superintendent for the total educational program in his building. He works closely with the teachers, pupils, and patrons within his district. He is responsible for administering the building and school program and activities, as well as for working with teachers and other staff members to improve the instructional program. Larger school systems may employ special supervisors whose major responsibility is the improvement of classroom instruction.

All teachers have a responsibility to work cooperatively with department heads, various kinds of special teachers, teachers of the same grade or subject, health and social workers, business staff members, and custodians and clerical workers. Successful school programs depend upon all these people working enthusiastically and cooperatively.

A teacher's professional responsibilities are not limited to those things which happen in the classroom with students. School programs must gradually, but constantly, change and improve, and this improvement is the result of teachers, administrators, and other staff members setting goals and working toward attaining them. This process requires faculty meetings, committee meetings, discussions, reports, and problem-solving sessions. Every teacher is expected to help further the school's progress toward important goals by extraclass professional activities.

COMMUNITY RESPONSIBILITIES OF TEACHERS

Teachers are expected by the community to show interest in their pupils, to be able to work effectively with them, and to be competent in their subject matter and other assignments. Additionally, teachers are expected to demonstrate certain attitudes, understandings, and behavior patterns which the community has come to associate with teachers. There is more to being a teacher than classroom instruction. A teacher's contribution is considered to be a public service paid for at public expense and influenced very decidedly by what the community wants. Despite changing views on the subject, teachers are still expected to set examples, in action and appearance, for those with whom they work and live. Teachers are considered leaders in the business of helping people grow and learn, and of helping whole communities become better places in which to live.

Community Participation

Beginning teachers can expect to have many opportunities to assume a very active role in community affairs. Educators are eagerly sought participants in most community organizations. Religious groups, social clubs, cultural and recreational groups, and health and social-welfare organizations are usually represented by one or more professional edu-

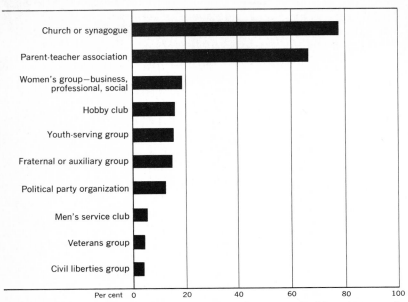

FIGURE 4–4 Percentage of teachers having membership in certain civic and community organizations.

cators. The frequency with which teachers participate in these organizations varies greatly from community to community.

Traditionally, teachers have exhibited community awareness and concern by voting. In the 1968 national election approximately 90 per cent of all teachers voted as compared to a national average of 61 per cent [101:65]. However, only a very small percentage of teachers are ever candidates for public office. In the past teachers have been discouraged from exercising their political rights and responsibilities, including such rights as campaigning for and serving in public office, because of the effect which such service might have on their tenure rights, retirement, or other job status. It is undoubtedly true that many teachers have chosen not to run for political office because it might jeopardize their teaching position. We may expect to see the number of teachers seeking public office grow. The National Education Association has taken a very strong stand [75:79] affirming the educator's right to run for and serve in public office without losing any personal or professional rights.

What is expected of any teacher depends in part upon the community where he is employed. In small schools, teachers usually have personal relationships with a relatively large percentage of the total school population. Teachers in small communities come in contact with and are known and appraised by large percentages of the people. Teachers in such communities might anticipate less liberal attitudes than those they would find in large cities. The situation may be quite different in large urban areas where a teacher may work in one section and live in another. In such instances, it is possible for the teacher to be known by a very small percentage of the total community population.

Personal Conduct

Parents often expect teachers to be better examples for children than parents themselves are. In some communities teachers are expected not to smoke or drink alcoholic beverages in public places. Few communities frown upon such activities when practiced in moderation in private homes and parties. The teacher in many communities enjoys as much freedom in personal matters as any other professional person. As our nation adopts a more permissive attitude toward individuality in dress and behavior, teachers will share in this freedom, but will do well not to take extreme positions in controversial changes in taste.

Public Relations

The classroom teacher helps shape public attitude toward the school. As Frasier points out [33:10]:

Good teaching is the best public relations for a school. The teacher's reputation in a community is determined largely by the children and their parents. If the teacher is doing a good job, the children are happy and bring home a positive attitude toward the teacher and the school, to their parents who transmit this feeling to their friends. When a citizen says, "We have a fine school system," he usually means that he is pleased with the type of teaching his children or his neighbor's children are receiving.

The school today needs the understanding and positive support of the public more than ever before. Many teachers engage in a variety of school and community activities that promote lay interest and participation in the schools. Teachers must be conscious of their own responsibility for developing good community relationships.

A checklist titled *How Well Are You Doing in Public Relations?* is located at the end of the chapter. It will give you a good idea of the many ways in which teachers can promote positive relations between schools and communities. You may wish to use this checklist periodically after you begin teaching.

CHANGING ORGANIZATIONAL AND INSTRUCTIONAL PATTERNS AND PROCEDURES

Changes are being called for and are taking place at all levels of the educational enterprise. Nurtured by widespread concern for instructional improvement, a search has been going on for means to make the nation's schools even better. Reforms are taking place in organizational patterns, subject content, and teaching methods.

Convincing evidence has mounted to indicate that an educational reform has begun. Throughout the country educators are formulating fresh, new approaches to learning. Education has become a field in which creativity is prized. We know that innovation includes the act of recombining old ideas into new programs as well as injecting new ideas and concepts into past practices or originating entirely new practices.

Since the late 1950s, programs designed especially for gifted pupils have been developed, guidance services have been expanded dramatically, and emphasis has been placed on new approaches in mathematics, science, modern foreign languages, and the social sciences. Educators have been trying innovative methods and formulating fresh programs to provide quality educational programs for children coming from socially and economically deprived backgrounds. Special consideration has been given to finding ways to improve the educational opportunity for minority groups. Prekindergarten educational opportunities, summer programs, and work-study projects are common today. More education and better instruction are accepted as imperative for contemporary and future living. Educators are in the forefront of the social force which is searching for solutions to the problems of environmental decay.

In 1959, the National Academy of Sciences held an important meeting at Woods Hole, Massachusetts. The conference director, Jerome Bruner [8], kindled a flame for curriculum reform in a book, *The Process of Education*, which reported the views of those attending the meeting. Bruner called for new methods of viewing content and argued convincingly for emphasis on developing understanding, as opposed to only acquiring facts, in teaching. Since 1959, curriculum reform has been going on in all the subject disciplines. Academicians have joined teachers in finding improved ways of organizing content with an emphasis on developing critical-thinking skills. What was taught a decade ago may not be taught next year. National curriculum projects in most all the disciplines have sought to organize knowledge in a sequential order and to give attention to nurturing the student's desire to learn.

As new programs have been developed, many teachers have taken additional college work or participated in workshops designed to prepare them to work in these new programs. The federal government, as well as various philanthropic foundations, have pumped vast sums of money into projects for the reeducation of teachers. With the contemporary interest in school improvement and the production of new knowledge, the modern teacher is faced with the constant problem of keeping abreast of emerging trends and new developments in the disciplines.

In 1959, the National Education Association authorized the inauguration of the NEA Project on Instructional Programs in the Public Schools. By 1963, a three-volume report of the project had been prepared.

This NEA Project wove together proposals related to content and methods of organization. Not only were recommendations made concerning what should be taught, but recommendations were set forth calling for a change in the teacher's methods of instruction and in the school's organization. Further, a series of recommendations were made for educators to consider as they planned for instruction in the years ahead. This NEA report gave attention to both expanding societal objectives for education and suggested means to achieve them. Emphasis was put on suggesting means for individualizing instruction.

While the development of improved curricular programs has been underway, attention also has been given to fresh approaches in organization for instruction. J. Lloyd Trump called for team teaching, flexible scheduling, and an improved utilization of the schools' professional and material resources. Working as director of the Commission on the Experimental Study of the Utilization of the Staff in the Secondary School, Trump stimulated studies in 100 schools of the proposals later advanced in his book *Guide to Better Schools: Focus on Change* [144]. The outcome of the Trump studies was that ways were sought to further professionalize teaching and to develop means to individualize instruction. Efforts were made to take advantage of new techniques and instructional devices resulting from our advancing technology.

In 1957, Robert Anderson, who directed the SUPRAD (School and University Program for Research and Development) project at Harvard University, pioneered the concept of team teaching at the elementary school level. His efforts received national recognition and resulted in a decided trend toward the use of team teaching in elementary schools.

Exploring New Uses of Manpower

Much of the effort to improve the quality of schools has centered upon organizational structure and the manner in which educational manpower is utilized in the teaching-learning process. Options other than the typical one-teacher-per-twenty-five students in a self-contained elementary classroom are possible. Likewise, instruction at the secondary level need not be characterized by traditional one teacher/five period teaching assignment. It is possible to conceive roles which are neither self-contained nor departmentalized.

The innovations discussed in the sections that follow involve various attempts being made to more effectively utilize manpower resources in our schools. Although much of the experimentation in instruction is being done by individual teaching, increased strength is provided if more than one person is involved in working on program improvement. Work that is shared appears lighter, and obstacles may more easily be overcome when several people work cooperatively on a given problem. The modern teacher no longer has to work in the isolation of a single classroom but may work with others in planning and providing instruction. The contemporary professional is engaged in the continuous process of evaluation and in searching for improved methods. Education has become a developing field, seeking original solutions to the complex problems associated with individual development.

Teacher Aides

Teacher aides, or paraprofessionals, have been used in order to increase the effectiveness of the school. By employing housewives or other nonprofessional personnel to handle noneducational tasks, the school frees the teacher to do what he was trained to do: teach. When the teacher has help for nonteaching chores and can devote his attention and time to instruction, learning products are maximized.

A national survey of the use and payment of teacher aides in public schools [130:37–39] revealed that most of the teacher aides are paid for their services, although a significant number work on a voluntary basis. The ten most widespread duties of the teacher aides receiving pay, listed in descending order of frequency, were: duplicating tests and other material; helping with classroom housekeeping; typing class materials, tests, etc.; setting up A-V equipment and other instructional materials; helping with children's clothing; supervising the playground; correcting tests, homework, workbooks, etc.; reading aloud and story telling; assisting in the school library; and collecting money from pupils [130:38].

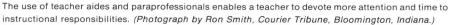

The use of teacher aides and paraprofessionals enables a teacher to devote more attention and time to instructional responsibilities. *(Photograph by Ron Smith, Courier Tribune, Bloomington, Indiana.)*

The use of teacher aides, or paraprofessionals, is often associated with team teaching. Just as frequent, however, is the assignment of aides to teachers performing more traditional roles, i.e., self-contained or departmental roles. Always the attempt is to seek ways in which maximum use of the teacher's professional skills can be realized and the quality of education received by students enhanced. Although the teacher aide concept was introduced in Bay City, Michigan, in 1952, little progress has been made until very recently in defining the role of such personnel.

Team Teaching

During the past decade, one of the most significant developments has been the trend toward team teaching. An alternative to the traditional self-contained and/or departmental role, professional faculty work together in teaching teams, each group being responsible for the education of a large group of students.

Just as the team approach has been used in medical clinics and business organizations, a team-teaching situation allows schools to take advantage of the individual talents, interests, and special training of teachers. While there are almost as many definitions of team teaching as there are schools that practice it, the keys to team teaching are variability, individualization, and team planning.

Most team-teaching programs feature variability or flexibility in numbers, space, and time as well as teacher variability. The objective of these variations is to provide a total school environment which encourages and accommodates individualized instruction. In a team-teaching situation teachers will work with large student groups, small groups, and individuals. Room size will vary with group size. Flexibility in length of instructional periods can be arranged to suit the needs of individuals or groups. Most experienced educators will contend that teaming must include regular team planning sessions to be successful.

Beggs [5:29–37] points out that the variety of applications of the team concept is infinite. However, some of the advantages cited for teaming are generally agreed upon. Team teaching allows one teacher to profit from the judgment and advice of his colleague(s) since all the team members plan together and work with the same pupils toward commonly designated objectives. Team teaching provides the opportunity for each member of the team to contribute his particular strengths to the team's instruction. Teaming is intended to narrow the range of the teacher's preparation for daily class meetings. Thus, it is assumed the teacher's preparation can be sharper and more effective.

In practice the many organizational plans vary tremendously. Two teachers at a grade level may decide to "team," planning together and sharing some aspects of teaching their own classes. A teacher may have the part-time or full-time assistance of a teacher aide in order to teach fifty to sixty students. Two teachers and one aide might have the responsibility for seventy-five to one hundred students. An aide may be assigned to a team of seven teachers. Special teachers may be assigned to assist a team of classroom teachers as the need arises. All the primary grade teachers may constitute a teaching team with self-contained classes in the intermediate grades, or there also may be an intermediate team. Many of these same plans are used at the secondary level, although most secondary team plans are intradisciplinary, while elementary and middle school programs are often interdisciplinary.

Team leadership varies as does the organization. Teams of teachers may have equal rank, status, and responsibility. This was very typical of early attempts at teaming. Teams may also have differentiated rank, status, and responsibility. In this case the leadership of the team may revolve on a time basis or need basis. The leadership may be permanent, with the leader receiving a higher salary as an indication of greater responsibility. This type of leadership is usually associated with differentiated staffing, described in detail in the next section.

Typically noncertified workers may assist a team by handling all the "nonteaching" chores, such as typing, duplicating, collecting lunch money, taking attendance, etc. In many cases aides work with one or more students in a small group following the directions of the professional teacher. Aides are frequently utilized in the library or instructional materials center to help students locate and use materials.

Beginning teachers may be assigned to a teaching team led by one or more experienced teachers. With the addition of one or more student teachers, interns, and one or more aides, the adult/pupil ratio may be reduced effectively.

There are disadvantages to teaming. Not all teachers can participate effectively within a team. Many teachers are unable and unwilling to be exposed to the full view of their peers. Some teachers are unable to cope with the free exchange of ideas, suggestions, and criticisms which is necessary for a team to improve its methods of functioning.

Not all school systems adopting team teaching have provided the time for teachers to meet on a regular basis to plan, coordinate, and evaluate their efforts, and this has proven a costly error. Teaming which provides teachers with group planning periods during the student's school day is admittedly expensive, but worth it when one considers the alternative, which is the ineffective functioning of a team effort because the importance of adequate planning time was not considered.

Many team-teaching programs have failed for lack of a well-planned and well-executed public information program. Community dissatisfaction, brought on by misinformation and lack of information may doom any program to failure before it has had a chance to succeed. It also bears mentioning here that probably more consideration should be given to communicating the efforts of a team (or any innovative group) to its colleagues. Sometimes those not participating in a new effort feel resentment or reservation, which might be forestalled through some sensitive briefing.

Early advocates of teaming felt that teacher time would be saved as the special strengths, capabilities, and talents of each teacher were used, and as large groups freed several teachers for planning or study. In practice it has been found that unless there is an unusually high percentage of time devoted to large group instruction, there is no time saved at all. Even with time saved by the use of paraprofessionals, the increased need for team planning and the consideration given to meeting individual student needs require more time than is needed in non-teaming plans.

Teaming demands particular teacher characteristics. A team teacher needs self-confidence and the willingness to give and receive constructive criticism. He needs to be able to work closely and cooperatively with others. He needs to be committed to improving the broad education of students and be willing to share responsibility for the decisions of the team. The isolation and security provided by a closed classroom door is removed in teaming. The teacher who faces the prospect of teaming should examine his own feelings and attitudes before he accepts such a position.

Differentiated Staffing

The differentiated staff concept is a natural outgrowth and a refinement of the team-teaching movement that has evolved over the past several years. Whereas most members of teaching teams had similar backgrounds (all members of the primary team were elementary majors, or all members of the high school mathematics team were mathematics majors) as well as identical teaching responsibilities, differentiated staffing emphasizes (as the name itself implies) varying background as well as responsibility in the team operation. An illustration would perhaps be helpful.

Differentiated staffing patterns allows for the many interests, abilities, and ambitions of teachers, the diversity of tasks associated with the teaching act, as well as recognizing the need for auxiliary personnel to relieve teachers of nonprofessional responsibilities. Attention to individual differences among teachers is long overdue.

The first major attempt to implement the differentiated concept took place in Temple City, California, in the fall of 1969. In addition to a desire to improve educational opportunity so that each student might more effectively develop his individual capabilities, two other factors influenced the specific changeover to differentiated staffing: (1) the desire of teachers to have a share in decision making; and (2) the desire of teachers to "shoot for top positions" without going into supervision/administration. As a result, the Temple City Model developed as indicated in Figure 4–5. In the differentiated staff model, as described by

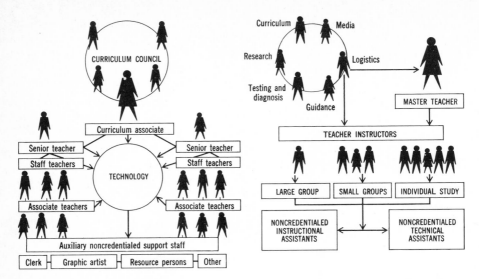

FIGURE 4–5 Two patterns for differentiated staffing. How do these patterns change the organizational structure of the school?

Olivero and Buffie [87:189–225], the master teacher is a districtwide curriculum and research specialist. His job is to keep abreast of all research in new methods, material, and content in a given field and to work with senior teachers in devising pilot projects to test new ideas. Having the equivalent of a doctorate, he teaches 25 per cent of the time and is employed for twelve months at a salary two to three times the salary of a beginning teacher [18:10–12].

A senior teacher serves as a team leader. He is an acknowledged master practitioner, a learning engineer, and a skilled diagnostician of the learning process. He devotes about 50 per cent of his time to teaching. He is responsible for program, for the employment and evaluation of paraprofessionals as well as for student teachers and/or interns, and shares with the principal the responsibility for selection and evaluation of professional colleagues. He possesses a master's degree, or its equivalent. He serves as a member of his school's Academic Senate. Earning about twice as much as a beginning teacher, senior teachers, like master teachers, do *not* have tenure. They may, however, have tenure as staff teachers.

Staff teachers are full-time classroom teachers. They comprise the bulk of the faculty. They are employed for a nine-month year and are paid according to the regular salary scale. Staff teachers must be effective in small, medium, and large group instruction. The bachelor's degree is a minimum requirement.

Associate teachers may be student or probationary teachers, or teaching interns. Their salaries fall below the range of full-time classroom teachers. Auxiliary support personnel include instructional aides and clerks. Aides work with students and teachers in resource centers, learning laboratories, and libraries. A system survey revealed that approximately one-third of the teachers' time was devoted to supervising study activities and other nonteaching tasks. Such activities are now directed by competent paraprofessionals.

The principal, whose noncertified assistant (called a "manager") reconciles the budget, orders supplies and equipment, schedules the buses, runs the cafeteria, etc., is the educational leader of the school. A catalyst, he also chairs the Academic Senate but has only one vote and no veto power.

The Academic Senate, a five-member body of four senior teachers and the principal, is the primary decision-making body in the school. All decisions affecting the school and its policies are made by this group.

Comparable decision making at the district level is made by the Academic Coordinating Council. Master teachers sit on this council, which is chaired by the superintendent. Again, he has but one vote and no veto power.

Early results of this pioneering effort reported in the spring of 1971 were very promising: 93 per cent of the students polled felt they were getting a better education; 83 per cent of the staff indicated that differentiated staffing provided a more effective way of improving instruction [128:153]. Interestingly enough only 50 per cent of the parents favored the program. Superintendent Rand commented that teachers "respond and blossom" under differentiated staffing. An evaluation of this Ford Foundation sponsored effort by the California State Department of Education's Division of Finance disclosed that: (1) staffing costs are no more under this plan; (2) capital outlays for specially constructed buildings may be a little more; and (3) flexible scheduling and supporting services costs depend upon the quality of the services provided.

Like its predecessor, team teaching, it is not likely that any single pattern of differentiated staffing will emerge in the immediate future. Because of the benefits that can be derived, we may expect a considerable amount of exploration with this concept. Dwight Allen [18:4–5] believes that differentiated staffing can produce many positive benefits. Among them:

1. When positions are identified delineating what needs to be done and are assigned on the basis of competence, there will be a basis of salary differentiation on which school boards, administrators, and teachers can agree.
2. Good teachers, who deserve as much money as administrators, will be able to afford a career in classroom teaching.
3. There will be a place for those teachers for whom no amount of money can make up for the lack of job satisfaction.
4. There will be a place for talented teachers who want only limited professional responsibility (e.g., the teaching housewife).
5. Teachers will be able to take postgraduate courses to make themselves more

competent in their specific jobs instead of taking courses on an indiscriminate units-equal-dollars basis.

6. Longevity, with all its educationally crippling effects, would cease to be a criterion for promotion.
7. Inservice teacher training could be an internal program aimed at solving problems at hand rather than problems perceived by someone once or twice removed from the school's student population.
8. Evaluation could be based on real knowledge from intimate contact and cooperation between teaching professionals.
9. Many existing problems in negotiating salaries and existing differences between professional teachers and administrators should disappear in a staff wherein status derives from performance and competence.
10. Young talent would be encouraged to grow.
11. The school would regain some control over apportioning dollars now committed to perpetuating the median rise in salary costs brought about by tenure, longevity, and automatic promotion practices.
12. Colleges could begin to focus on training teachers to handle specific responsibilities and specific teaching skills.
13. Counseling and interpersonal student-teacher relationships could be established at more profound levels of personal choice and personal relevance.
14. The best talent would be free to seek the best alternative teaching techniques, learning modes, and innovations in general through persistent liaison with colleges, universities, and other schools.

Given the changing relationship between supply and demand for teachers as well as the conservative nature of the profession, differentiated staffing is destined to become one of the hottest issues of the seventies. It poses a direct threat to two well-entrenched traditions—the self-contained classroom and the single-salary schedule.

Flexible and Modular Scheduling

Flexible or modular scheduling is widely associated with secondary schools. This scheduling concept dictates that the frequency, duration, and instructional group size be varied depending on the particular requirements of the content. Traditional class periods are replaced by modules of 15, 20, or 30 minutes. Some classes meet fewer than five times a week. And some of the time pupils are in classes of 7 to 15 pupils; at other times they are in classes of 40 to 150 or more. In addition, pupils in schools utilizing a flexible or modular schedule usually spend part of their day working individually.

In a flexible or modular schedule, the size of each class is determined by the instructional purpose. When the teacher wants to present content, test, or use audio-visual aids, large groups are mandated. When the teacher wants pupils to discuss, verify, question, or react, small groups are scheduled. The large classes usually last no more than 40 minutes, but the small-group classes are likely to last 90 minutes. Some laboratory sessions last for several hours.

Flexible or modular scheduling encourages the use of team teaching. In some schools teachers work mostly with large groups, and in others teachers work almost entirely with small groups. This allows teachers to specialize in those aspects of instruction they can do best.

Figure 4–6 shows a flexible scheduled school. In the flexible organization, the cycle is normally a week in length. In other words, the schedule does not repeat itself for five days. In the traditionally scheduled school, the cycle is the day. Each day's activities are the same as each other day's program.

Flexible or modular scheduling has two prime objectives. First, it is intended to provide the organizational means for teachers to individualize instruction. Pupils can meet with teachers during independent study time. Also, pupils can work for blocks of time on their own or with other pupils on particular problems or projects. Pupils can be excused from content presentations when these are not contributing to their intellectual growth. In this type of scheduling, pupils can become active in discussing, verifying, and working at task-oriented projects and activities. Second, flexible scheduling allows the teacher to use both human and time resources to the advantage of pupils. If one teacher likes to and can present content better than another teacher, then the teacher with this competency can work with more pupils in this way than the traditional schedule allows. If the teacher works best in small groups, then he can spend his time working with pupils in this way.

People learn from activity—from working, discussing, constructing, and experimenting. The flexible schedule provides the opportunity for pupils to be far more active in the learning process than does a traditionally scheduled school. Teachers in the flexible-scheduled school conserve time by giving content presentations once, to a large group of pupils, rather than repeating the presentation to smaller groups. The

FIGURE 4–6   A flexible or modular secondary school schedule.

	Module	Monday	Tuesday	Wednesday	Thursday	Friday
8.30	1	Mathematics	Music	Mathematics	Mathematics	Mathematics
	2	Mathematics	English	English	Mathematics	Music
	3	English	English	English	English	Music
	4	Social studies	Independent study	Physical education	Independent study	Physical education
	5	Social studies	Independent study	Science	Independent study	Science
	6	Social studies	Independent study	Science	Independent study	Science
	7		Lunch	Lunch	Lunch	Lunch
	8	Lunch	Science	Health	Lunch	Independent study
	9	Science	Science	Independent study	Science	Independent study
	10	Typing	Independent study	Independent study	Science	Independent study
	11	Typing	Independent study	Independent study	Science	Independent study
	12		Independent study	Independent study	Music	Typing
	13	Independent study	Social studies	Independent study	Music	Typing
	14	study	Mathematics	Social studies	Social Studies	English
3.30	15		Mathematics	Social studies	Social Studies	English

teacher's time, conserved by taking out the repetition, is used to buy the opportunity for teachers to work with individuals and with small pupil-centered groups.

Many schools using modular scheduling have developed some type of multimedia package—a course designed by the faculty. Students move through this course at individual rates. The "learning packages" are often housed in the library or laboratory.

Flexible scheduling often incorporates the concept of unscheduled or "free" student time. This requires stations or facilities in the building where students can go to relax without disturbing those who are studying. Unscheduled time is credited with creating most of the problems of modular scheduling. Vandalism, skipping, and general time-wasting are not uncommon. These problems can be attacked successfully if the school deals with the individual student violator and refrains from reacting as though all students are guilty.

Flexible schedules are often developed with the use of computers. Schedule determination is just one of the uses of the computer in modern education. Test score analyses, population studies, and other applications of computer technology are being used to provide educators with data with which more intelligent decisions can be made about pupils and the school's program. As computers become more widely available and as educators become more sophisticated in their use, flexible scheduling may become the means of providing a highly personalized, rich, and individual learning program for each student.

Nongraded Schools

The nongraded school concept refers in part to the absence of specific grade levels, such as grades 6, 7, 8, etc. It is an attempt to eliminate, reduce, or at least minimize the effects of grade-level designations. A major purpose is to encourage teachers to view children as individuals and to abandon the idea of a predetermined lockstep curriculum that is relatively the same for all students. Still another purpose is to remove the unnecessary restrictions on depth, breadth, and rate of children's learning. As with other innovations, the motivation is to help the individual pupil achieve this maximum potential. To achieve this purpose, end expectations must vary for each student, and program accommodations must be made so that a student's progress will be continuous.

Nongradedness is said to meet the needs of individual students more effectively than the graded school does. However, examples of nongraded secondary schools that are fully implemented are rare. It has not been unusual for freshmen to take senior subjects nor for upper classmen to take freshmen or sophomore courses. Is this nongradedness? The answer is no. Eliminating or ignoring grade-level designations is not enough.

Grade level
in which
plan is used

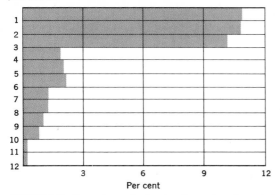

FIGURE 4-7   Percentage of school systems at each grade level using a nongraded form of organization.

The curriculum must be ungraded. Teachers and faculties who want to ungrade their programs must individualize their program and break away from the idea of covering a predetermined sequence of learning. This is a genuine obstacle in most subject-matter centered high schools staffed by specialists.

Melbourne (Florida) High School has been a pioneer in developing a nongraded program. Pupils in the Melbourne High School are not bound by curriculum guides and texts, but they are able to go into a subject with as much breadth or depth as they are able to handle. Teachers work individually with pupils to chart a course of study. Heavy emphasis is put on independent study, where pupils work on their own or with a few others.

Schools using the nongraded organization necessarily must have a wealth of instructional materials, far more than is usually found in the typical school. There is a greater need for resources in the way of specialists and librarians to assist the teacher as he encourages students to use a variety of learning sources.

Multigrade Grouping

Certain elementary schools which wish to capitalize on the advantages of a plan that minimizes the importance of grade levels and emphasizes individualization have chosen to adopt a program that is known as multigrade grouping. In a multigrade plan the students in each class represent an equal number of first-, second-, third-graders and third-, fourth-, and fifth-graders, or some similar combination. The children of different grade levels are deliberately placed together on a random-selection basis to encourage the teachers and parents to see the students as individuals and not as fourth-graders, second-graders, etc.

Multigrading can be seen as an initial, but substantial, first step toward the development of a nongraded program. Children in a multigraded plan retain the grade-level designations for record-keeping and report purposes. However, the groupings within the classroom are not on the basis of grade levels.

Multiage Grouping

Another way of organizing the elementary school to encourage greater personalization of instruction is multiage grouping. This plan calls for classrooms in which children whose ages span three years are placed together on a random-selection, heterogeneous basis with no attempt being made to put students together on the basis of ability or achievement. The age groupings may overlap. There might be one or more classes of seven-, eight-, and nine-year-olds and one or more of nine-, ten-, and eleven-year-olds. This pattern allows administrators greater flexibility in moving students from group to group. The student can easily remain a member of a group for two to three years, and move on to another group which will contain some students of his own age-group. One basic hypothesis of this plan is that a student should have the opportunity, sometime in his school career, to be a member of the youngest, the middle, and the oldest age group in the room.

A multiage grouping plan undoubtedly comes the closest to approaching nongradedness of any grouping plan that has gained prominence.

Independent Study

While secondary schools have made relatively little progress in developing nongraded programs, their success in offering students the opportunity through independent study to develop unique talents and interests has been more substantial. Nongraded in philosophy, such activity frequently involves the development of instructional materials centers.

Independent study is difficult to describe because it takes so many forms. However, there are basic guidelines which can be used in preparing and facilitating independent study.

1. The entire faculty and staff should understand the rationale, even though particular people may have no special responsibility for the program. The understanding is necessary for the program to be supported. All teachers, administrators, and counselors should be able to explain and support the project to parents and students. Early

In the privacy of a study carrel, this little girl pursues her independent study project. *(Photograph by Ben Spiegel, National Education Association.)*

and deep involvement of students, parents, and other community members in the rationale of independent study is crucial to its success.

2. Motivation must be developed. Individual, small-group, and large-group activities should be provided as a way of stimulating student interest and involvement.

3. Independent study must be taught. Secondary students are often inclined to be overly dependent upon teachers for guidance and supervision. The teacher's objective should be to become less directive as the student's responsibility and self-direction grows. However, it is a teaching assignment and becomes part of the teacher load.

4. The amount of time each student spends in independent study will vary.

5. Materials, equipment, personnel, and facilities to support the program must be provided. This calls for programmed material, audio-visual hardware and software, work rooms, and instructional assistants to man workrooms and maintain records.

6. Evaluation procedures must be developed which reflect the individual student and program goals.

Other Individualization Plans

New, specific systems of individualized instruction are being developed through the cooperation of local school districts, universities, federal research centers, and private industry. These plans are designed:

Absorbed in the world of sound. In what ways can recordings be used to provide effective learning experiences for students? *(Photograph by Esther Bubley, National Education Association.)*

1. To allow pupils to work at their own rate.
2. To encourage initiative and independence.
3. To increase the pupils' problem-solving abilities.
4. To encourage self-evaluation.

Individually Prescribed Instruction was developed in the Pittsburgh area schools and by the fall of 1970 was serving 75,000 pupils in 264 schools throughout the country. IPI, a federally supported program, developed most of its own curriculum within the framework of detailed objectives, organization of techniques and materials to attain the objectives, individual pretesting for diagnosis and prescription, daily evaluation and guidance of each student, and constant curriculum evaluation and revision. Proponents of IPI contend that students of all school ages are working independently at different levels of achievement with little or no supervision.

Project PLAN—Program for Learning in Accordance with Needs is a project, similar to IPI, which was developed by Westinghouse Learning

Corporation and American Institutes for Research, and is the nation's second most extensive project to systematically individualize instruction. Unlike IPI, PLAN uses a computer, not to teach, but to make information available on the daily progress of each student.

Both the PLAN and IPI projects are expensive. The costs vary, but the minimum might be as much as an extra $100 per pupil per year. Some IPI projects have run well above that figure. Until the cost can be reduced, the projects will not be expanded rapidly.

The Dual Progress Plan

The Dual Progress Plan [127:221] was started in schools in Ossining and Long Beach, New York. The theoretical base of this upper-elementary plan consists of four principal elements: (1) the concept of cultural imperatives versus cultural electives; (2) the dual progress of students based on the language arts and social studies; (3) a thorough curriculum reorganization; and (4) changes in preservice teacher education.

Children in grades 3 through 6 retain their grade-level designation in language arts, social studies, and physical education but progress through mathematics, science, music, art, recreation, and health as quickly as their interests and achievements allow. One-half the day is spent with a homeroom teacher in the basic group subjects (language arts, social studies, physical education); the other half is spent with specialists.

Middle Schools

One current innovation which may eventually have great impact on educational planning, and which certainly seems to challenge conventional organizational patterns, is the emerging middle school program.

The middle school is defined as "a program planned for a range of older children, preadolescents and early adolescents that builds upon the elementary school programs for earlier childhood and in turn is built upon by the high school's program for adolescence" [3:5].

Current literature on the middle school is limited in quantity, and with very few exceptions, limited in its theoretical perspective of the function of middle school education. Most writers see the middle school as a transitional unit between elementary-school childhood education and high-school adolescent education.

Much of the debate concerning the middle school centers on the proper grade levels to be grouped together. This argument presupposes that grade-level designations are the sole appropriate ways of providing horizontal and vertical grouping of students. "The realities of child development defy the rigorous ordering of children's abilities and attainments into conventional graded structure." [43:3]. Boys and girls from 10 to 14 have social, physical, emotional, and mental ranges that make grade-level designations impractical in accommodating their developmental patterns. It would seem that successful middle school programs would tend to emphasize the individuality of students and deemphasize lockstep curriculum offerings.

The middle school organization is growing despite its minimal and frequently inconsistent rationale. Some boards of education are attempting to remedy overcrowding by placing students in middle schools on the basis of availability of space. Integration is a factor in some cities. Population shifts within cities have created abandoned buildings which have been converted to middle schools. The pressure to restore the four-year senior high school has prompted some middle school organization.

There are valid, educationally defensible reasons for establishing middle school programs and these reasons primarily have to do with current understanding of the growth and development of children 10- to 14-years old. The emerging adolescent:

1. is characterized by an increasing awareness of himself and his own physical and intellectual identity.
2. seeks answers about his own personal development and his relations to peer groups.
3. has an exceptional need to understand his own culture.
4. has a heightened interest in self-understanding induced by his own dramatic physical, mental, and emotional changes.

Prekindergarten Programs

Prekindergarten education, long popular in European countries as a means of providing daytime child care for working mothers, is now being developed in the United States for a variety of reasons. Most of the reasons are closely related to the fact that there are pockets of poverty in an otherwise affluent American society, and children who grow up in the socially and economically lowest levels do not come to school with the skills and ideas that seem to be essential for formal learning. Slum homes do not provide their children with the opportunity to develop the language skills which lead to other school-valued behaviors. Since many of the slum children come from racial minorities, a high proportion of the failure-prone children are nonwhite, and the school becomes a place of failure which reinforces racial prejudice and despair.

Prekindergarten programs for deprived children are generally based on the theory that education must start at a very early age in order to minimize the lack of home orientation to formal learning. There are also those who advocate a radical change in current programs. Slum children have a viable culture, and the schools should recognize this culture and use it in the classroom.

The Year-round School

With communities showing their impatience toward the rising cost of education, old year-round school plans are being dusted off and reexamined, and new ones are being developed. Some educator groups are turning to the year-round school as a means of providing an answer to the demands of the knowledge explosion. Whatever the reason, year-round schools are seen as a way of adding school facilities and manpower without creating new classrooms.

There is no single year-round plan. There are scores of them. They can be grouped into three basic types: the extended school year, or 11-month plan; the four-quarter plan; and the three-semester plan. Each plan has dozens of combinations.

The extended school year usually calls for a strong summer school program offered on a voluntary basis. This plan calls for little interference with regular programming.

The three-semester plan divides the calendar year into three parts. Students may elect to go two of the three semesters.

The four-quarter plan, with all its variations, is the most familiar year-round program. The school year is divided into four quarters of twelve weeks each with one week of vacation between quarters. Students attend school three quarters and vacation one quarter, giving them approximately 16 weeks of vacation per year. Teachers usually may elect to teach one, two, or three quarters of each year. Some may elect to teach four quarters occasionally.

A very interesting experiment in the use of a year-round school calendar was initiated June 30, 1970, at Romeoville, Illinois, which is a fast-growing community located 35 miles southwest of Chicago. This plan, a compulsory education system for all students in the district, calls for a 45-day (nine week) learning session followed by a 15-day (three week) student vacation [141:42]. The students are scheduled into four groups and are staggered so that only three groups attend school at any one time—reducing the enrollment at any particular time by one-fourth. Although the so-called "45–15 Plan" presents some problems for teachers, school administrators, students, and parents, it holds the promise of being used more extensively.

There are various sources of opposition to the year-round school. The vacation issue creates the most opposition. Year-round schools necessitate that some students take winter, fall, or spring vacations, rather than the traditional summer vacation, or of taking periodically short vacations throughout the year.

Additional opposition is created when it is discovered that year-round schools do not offer immediate cost savings. Year-round schools may mean better educational opportunities for students and may save a community some money by requiring fewer facilities and making better use of manpower; however, year-round schools usually are more expensive to operate on a short-term basis, since the savings in building costs are not readily apparent.

SUMMARY

Although no two teachers will have identical responsibilities, there are some major responsibilities that are common to the work of all teachers —instruction, student guidance, maintaining discipline, evaluating pupil progress, reporting to parents, cocurricular activities, professional growth, teacher evaluation, and working effectively with other school personnel. In addition to these responsibilities, as well as many others that could have been indicated, the school community expects teachers to show interest in their pupils, to work effectively with the pupils, and to be competent in their subject matter and other assignments. They also are expected to demonstrate attitudes, understandings, and behavior patterns which the community generally has come to associate with teachers. They normally are expected to participate in various community activities, depending in part upon the types of communities in which they are located. They often are expected to serve as better examples for children than parents themselves choose to be. Teaching is an intimate social work. It is a powerful molding force. It is small wonder that those who hire teachers should scrutinize them carefully and set certain standards which they feel must be upheld. Such concern should be interpreted as a tribute and a challenge—a tribute to the significant role of teachers and a challenge to lead the community and all its people to a higher level of living.

Changes are being made in organizational and instructional patterns and procedures. Throughout the country educators are formulating fresh, new approaches to learning. Although the change throughout the nation has not been spectacular, we can expect, in the years to come, greater use of teacher aides, team teaching, differentiated staffing, flexible scheduling, nongraded classrooms, multiage grouping, independent study, and year-round school calendars. It is highly probable that the middle school will tend to replace the junior high school, and that prekindergarten programs will become accepted as an integral part of our public school system. These innovative practices undoubtedly will change the role of the teacher and hopefully will provide more efficient use of educational manpower resources.

QUESTIONS TO CONSIDER

1. In what ways does the work of a teacher in a large school differ from the work of a teacher in a small school?

2.   How might teachers be relieved of some of the time-consuming routine duties, so that they might have more time to devote to the truly professional aspects of teaching?
3.   In your opinion how should the progress of pupils be evaluated?
4.   What do you consider to be the best way(s) of reporting the progress of pupils to their parents?
5.   Some parents (and teachers) feel that the school provides too many cocurricular activities. How do you account for this feeling? What position will you take? Why?
6.   It is frequently pointed out that most teachers who lose their jobs do so not because of lack of knowledge in their teaching fields but because of lack of ability in working with others. To what extent do you feel this statement is correct and why?
7.   If teachers are to be considered "professionals," to what extent are parents justified in expecting teachers to be better examples for pupils than the parents choose to be?
8.   In what ways may a teacher be able to serve as a public relations agent for his school?
9.   How is the role of the teacher affected in the use of each of the following practices:
     a.   Teacher aides
     b.   Team teaching
     c.   Differentiated staffing
     d.   Flexible or modular scheduling
     e.   Nongraded school
     f.   Independent study
10. What advantages and disadvantages do you see in the middle school?
11. What are the arguments for and against providing prekindergarten experiences for children?
12. What are the pros and cons of year-round public schools?

PROBLEM SITUATION FOR INQUIRY

Sally Smith, an attractive first-year high school English teacher, was furious. She had just left the principal's office after receiving a lecture regarding her personal appearance in the classroom. The chief complaint, no matter how Dr. Thompson had disguised it, was that her skirts were too short and her hairdos too exotic. The principal had not criticized her teaching methods. In fact, he told her that the extra help she was giving some of the slower readers after school was commendable.

Just what *was* wrong about wearing clothes that were in style? The girls in her classes seemed pleased that they had such a "cool" teacher. And if the boys took more than an academic look at her, they kept their thoughts to themselves.

Dr. Thompson had argued that any normal, red-blooded American boy might be "turned on" by the "accentuated" dress of a very attractive young lady, and that the boys might pay more attention to her physical appearance than to what she was teaching.

But was there evidence that the boys were not learning English? Had they done worse on the departmental exams? Had anyone made a pass at her, or come up with a wolf whistle, or tried to date her?

Dr. Thompson had indicated that he was concerned over what the boys and girls might say to their parents—not that such talk would be malicious. Quite the opposite. Student comments would probably be favorable, but what would the parents think of a school which had a dress code enforced by the students which was being violated by one of the teachers?

Sally was in a real dilemma. She liked teaching at Jefferson. She liked the students, the other faculty members, and her teaching assignments. In fact, she thought she liked Dr. Thompson until this incident occurred. But she also enjoyed her freedom to wear what she pleased and to look as she pleased. She could see no harm being done. If you were Sally, what would you do? Why?

ACTIVITIES TO PURSUE

1. Spend as much time as you can for two or three days in succession observing the same teacher and class in school. Make a careful record of the duties the teacher performs. Try to identify those responsibilities which are most important. Examine those selected to determine whether they are of the mechanical or the leadership and human relations type.
2. Compare the daily schedule of classes of a small high school with that of a large high school. What differences do you observe in the number and variety of offerings? Consider both the regular curriculum and the cocurricular activities. How do the educational opportunities for pupils in the two schools compare in terms of available offerings? Which areas of teaching and learning appeal to you most? Why?
3. Become acquainted with a social or religious organization which serves children or youth in your community. Make several observations of the group at work. What relationships do you observe between the youngsters and the adult leaders of the group? Between the adult leaders and the parents of the youngsters? What similarities do you find between this situation and teaching in the public schools?
4. Discuss the problems of discipline with various teachers. Try to ascertain the principles that guide them as they deal with the various kinds of discipline problems.
5. Visit a number of modern classrooms and note improvements in the construction of school plants and equipment. Discuss with your colleagues how these improvements may help the teacher in meeting the educational needs of pupils today.
6. Through the use of the checklist "How Well Are You Doing in Public Relations?" appraise one or more of your former teachers to see how well each fulfilled his public relations function.
7. If possible, spend some time observing in schools that are using team teaching, differentiated staffing, flexible or modular scheduling, teaching machines, nongraded classrooms, and individually prescribed instruction. Talk with the teachers as well as students about the advantages and disadvantages of these innovative practices.

TWENTY SELF-RATING QUESTIONS FOR TEACHERS

(These are among the characteristics of teachers the YOUTH-POLL students said they most needed and admired. Give yourself 5 points for every "yes" answer. Score 75 and you're pretty good.)

_____ Do I really care and let my students know?

_____ Do I really listen to my students and hear what they say?

_____ Am I there when my students need me—after class, after school, at home by the telephone?

_____ Do students bring their personal problems to me?

_____ Do I know all my students' names?

_____ Am I there to make any student feel important, rather than just to make myself feel powerful?

_____ Can I tell when a student is "up tight" and respond to his feelings?

_____ Do I know my subject matter well enough to welcome all questions in class?

_____ Do I get my students to think instead of merely parroting back what I say?

_____ Is there an orderly climate for learning in my classroom?

_____ Do I emphasize learning more than discipline?

_____ Do I spend time with the slow learners who really need it, rather than "copping out" by concentrating on just the bright ones?

_____ Do I keep my students from getting bored or going to sleep in my class?

_____ Do all my students participate?

_____ Do I work my students and myself hard enough so we both end the year with a sense of accomplishment rather than merely a feeling of relief?

_____ Do I grade on learning, rather than on a like-dislike basis?

_____ Can I admit my own mistakes openly?

_____ Can we still be friends if one of my students disagrees with me and proves me wrong?

_____ Do students learn from my tests, instead of merely memorizing and then forgetting?

_____ Would my students have characterized me on YOUTH-POLL as their best teacher?

Source: Gordan A. Sabine, *How Students Rate Their Schools and Teachers.* National Education Association, National Association of Secondary School Principals, Washington, 1971, pp. 75–76.

TWENTY INDICATORS OF THE QUALITY OF TEACHING

	Indicating a high quality of teaching	Indicating a low quality of teaching
Work with individual pupils:		
Assignments	Varied for individuals	Uniform for all
Pupil-teacher relations	Friendly; personalized	Very formal or very flip-pant
Pupil-teacher conferences	Frequent, to help pupils	For disciplinary purposes only
Pupils' work	Carefully reviewed, promptly returned	Carelessly handled; errors not checked
Planning and preparations:		
Daily continuity	Each day built on one before	Work unrelated from day to day
Teacher's knowledge	Well-informed teacher supplements books pupils use	Unable to answer simple questions
Lesson plans	Plans on blackboard or otherwise obvious	No evidence of plans

Source: William M. Alexander, *Are You a Good Teacher?* Holt, Rinehart and Winston, Inc., New York, 1959, p. 26.

TWENTY INDICATORS OF THE QUALITY OF TEACHING (continued)

	Indicating a high quality of teaching	Indicating a low quality of teaching
Advance arrangements	Necessary materials at hand	Necessary materials lacking
Use of teaching aids:		
Use of books	Pupils know how to use books	Pupils unacquainted with special features of books they use
Use of library tools	Pupils use effectively card catalog, reference guides, other tools	Pupils unable to get information in the library on their own
Use of audio-visual aids	Aids carefully related to work of class	Little advance explanation or follow-up of aids used
Use of field trips	To introduce or supplement class study	Used as holiday from class
Involvement of pupils in varied learning experiences:		
Types of experiences	Many different types used	Experiences mostly of one type
Pupil-teacher planning	As their maturities permit, pupils help in planning	Pupil participation or reaction not sought
Responsibilities of pupils	To prepare their own work and to help class as a whole	Only to prepare own assignments
Techniques of motivation	Work made interesting and important to pupils	Threats and criticisms only
Active leadership of the teacher:		
Use of pupil leaders	To give leadership experiences under supervision	To rest the teacher
Use of play or entertainment experiences	To provide a balanced program under teacher guidance	Also to rest the teacher
Active leadership of the teacher:		
Handling behavior problems	Disturbers promptly and consistently dealt with	Inconsistent leniency, harshness
Discussion	Genuine and general participation	Drags or dominated by a few

HOW WELL ARE YOU DOING IN PUBLIC RELATIONS?

Note: When you become a teacher you should check yourself periodically on this checklist. You will be doing very well if you can answer "yes" to all the following questions:

Do you believe that public relations activities should foster lay participation in the educational program? _____

Do you really enjoy talking and working with children? _____

Source: Glen E. Robinson and Evelyn S. Bianchi, "What Does PR Mean to the Teacher?" *NEA Journal,* vol. 48, no. 4, p. 14, National Education Association, Washington, April, 1959.

Do you really enjoy talking and working with adults? _____
Are you genuinely proud to be a teacher? _____
Do you believe that good public relations are your responsibility? _____
Do you regularly visit your pupils' homes? _____
Do you ever send newsletters home to parents? _____
Do you ever send notes to parents concerning things other than problem behavior? _____
Do you ever send home complimentary notes concerning your pupils who are not outstanding students? _____

Do you encourage your pupils' parents to visit you and the school? _____
Do you schedule regular conferences with parents? _____
Do your contacts with critical parents tend to placate them rather than increase their irritation? _____
Do you have a room-parent organization? _____
Does your school have a parent-teacher organization? _____
Do you regularly attend parent-teacher-organization meetings? _____
Does your school foster parent participation in planning class work and activities? _____
If so, do you personally take advantage of this policy to involve parents in your classroom planning activities? _____
Do you ever enlist the help of parents in the performance of routine clerical tasks? _____
Would you recognize the parents of most of your pupils if you met them on the street? _____
Do you encourage your classes to invite laymen to share their experiences with the class? _____
Do you make an effort to bring school matters of public interest to the attention of appropriate officials or news media? _____
Do your classroom activities ever involve community problems and contacts with laymen? _____
Do you willingly accept invitations to address groups of laymen, either on school matters or on other subjects? _____
Do you take an active part in church, political, civic, or fraternal organizations in your community? _____
Do your personal actions reflect credit upon your profession? _____
Do your remarks in the community tend to present a constructive view of teaching and of your local school situation? _____

FIGURE CREDITS

FIGURE 4-1. (*Source:* "The American Public-School Teacher, 1965-66," *Research Report 1967-R4,* National Education Association, Research Division, Washington, 1967, p. 27.)

FIGURE 4-2. (*Source:* "School Marks and Reporting to Parents," *NEA Research Bulletin,* vol. 48, no. 3, National Education Association, Research Division, Washington, October, 1970, p. 77.)

FIGURE 4-3. (*Source:* "Methods of Evaluating Teachers," *NEA Research Bulletin,* vol. 43, no. 1, National Education Association, Research Division, Washington, February, 1965, p. 14.)

FIGURE 4-4. (*Source:* Data from "The American Public-School Teacher, 1970-71," NEA Research Bulletin, vol. 50, no. 1, National Education Association, Research Division, Washington, 1972, p. 7.)

FIGURE 4-5. (*Source:* James L. Olivero, "The Meaning and Application of Differentiated Staffing in Teaching," *Phi Delta Kappan,* vol. 52, no. 1, Phi Delta Kappa, Bloomington, Indiana, September, 1970, pp. 38-39.)

FIGURE 4-7. (*Source:* "Grade Organization and Nongrading Programs," *NEA Research Bulletin,* vol. 54, no. 4, National Education Association, Research Division, Washington, December, 1967, p. 119.)

5 | EDUCATIONAL TECHNOLOGY, CHANGE, AND TRANSITION

Education at all levels stands on the threshold of a major technological revolution, and this revolution will affect more than the length of the school day or school year; it could transform the schools tremendously. New technology could bring about demands for a reexamination of the teaching-learning process, new visions of schools and of school construction, and totally new concepts of the role of the professional educator.

Research and careful observation have revealed that students have different learning styles; some students learn by reading, others by listening, and most by both reading and listening. Books and other visuals are needed for reading. Audio equipment is needed to develop listening skills. A combination of sight and sound materials help with reading and listening. Despite the relatively undeveloped current state of the art of technology, it can be said that the next decade will undoubtedly bring the development and deployment of expensive and inexpensive teaching tools that will encourage radical changes in education.

The aim of this new technology is not primarily to replace the teacher but to give the teacher and the student the necessary tools that will add new dimensions to learning. These new tools will allow the teacher to set up a support system of technological aids which can encourage exciting new ways of organizing for learning.

The newer technological resources now available are largely a by-product of the large expenditures that have been made for defense and for the exploration of space. Education is now in a position to profit from the research and experiences that private industry and the government have had in these areas of exploration [138:1].

It is obvious that ideas for advancement in educational technology will come from many sources. Schools will learn to make better use of the technology they currently have available and will strive to make use of new equipment and materials as they are produced. In this section we

The use of a wide variety of audio-visual material enables teachers to provide more effective learning experiences for students. *(Photograph by Joe Di Dio, National Education Association.)*

will examine some of the well-established technological innovations as well as the technology of the future.

Programmed Learning

The classroom teacher has often devised special practice materials for pupils or has selected appropriate exercises from available workbooks for pupils needing additional work. This is not new, nor is recognition of the fact that pupils need to know the immediate results of their work in order to make corrections and proceed effectively. Textbooks and workbooks with answers in the backs of the books are not new either. Having such material already prepared in a systematic way, based on principles coming from the experimental laboratories and available to the pupil to use independently, is new in the sense that machine-type instruction has now been put to wide use. Allowing students to proceed at their own pace for drill work or even original instruction from programmed material frees the teacher to do what he can do best in person: guide the educational growth of pupils.

The teaching machine, a mechanical device introduced a decade ago, is used to help the pupil learn. The machine, however, is of value only in terms of the program it contains. The learning program, housed in the teaching machine, divides organized information into small parts or frames. A user of a learning program goes from one to another related but more advanced piece of information. Immediately the pupil knows whether he has mastered the information being studied, because the learning program gives feedback on what was previously learned.

The promise of programmed learning through the use of teaching machines is greater for the future than is its current ability to help teachers. Too few programs have been developed, and to date the content of most teaching-machine programs has placed too much emphasis on factual materials.

The Computer

As a result of Project PX, one of the best kept secrets of World War II, the modern electronic computer was born. It now became possible for man to go to the moon and beyond and to envision major breakthroughs and achievements in virtually every field of human endeavor.

Data processing, well established in business and industry since the first computer was put on the market in 1950, has begun to make its appearance on the educational scene. In addition to the use of data processing in school business offices and for class scheduling, computers are now being used as instructional tools.

An important function of educational computers of the future will be information retrieval. "An information retrieval (IR) system can be defined as a man-machine system combining human intelligence and electronic and photocopying equipment for the purpose of gathering, classifying and storing factual and textual material, and for retrieving and disseminating this information upon demand" [9:61].

Computer-based IR systems will be used in automating libraries and eliminating all cumbersome record filing. Students, teachers, administrators, counselors, as well as librarians, will eventually use IR systems in carrying a wide variety of administrative and learning tasks.

Stanford University opened the first computerized elementary school classroom at Palo Alto, California, in 1966, where first-grade students were aided in reading and in mathematics through the use of the computer. The Stanford music department has had favorable results in using the computer to teach pitch to singers. A professor at Florida State University has developed a computer-assisted instruction course to teach introductory college physics. Personnel at the University of Connecticut have developed a means of computer analysis of English compositions.

Other projects are attempting computer production of braille materials from print for blind children. These are merely a few of the examples of the vast amount of exploration that is taking place in computer technology [15:1–3].

The "talking typewriter" is the name given to a multisensory (sight, sound, touch), multimedia, fully synchronized computer-based learning system. It is designed to teach reading, writing, spelling, speech, and other language arts skills. Information is presented both by sight and sound. It has been used effectively with seriously handicapped students in special classes [21:31].

Computer-assisted instruction, whether in music, mathematics, science, reading, foreign language, or whatever, is based on the theory that a well-programmed computer can provide individualized and flexible instruction. Slow or fast students can move from one topic to another through materials that can be independently controlled for each student. The theoretical limits of the computer's ability to teach are defined only by the limits of man's creativity. However, there is one dramatic disadvantage to computer-assisted instruction that promises to limit the spread of this activity. The costs are exceedingly high. Computer hardware, installation, service, programming, and operations are costing millions today at the experimental stages. It will take, conservatively, hundreds of millions of dollars to allow all students to benefit from the advantages described for computer-assisted instruction. It is for this reason that, despite all the national publicity about computer-assisted instruction (CAI), very few teachers are actually involved with this very creative and innovative effort. Computer instruction, where it is utilized, usually takes place in large school systems, more often in the Northeast and Midwest than in the Southeast and West. Mathematics is by far the most popular subject for computer programming [85:158].

Educational Television

Educational television (ETV) was widely proclaimed a decade ago as a panacea for education. It is apparent now that ETV is far from the total answer to educational problems, although its use is an accepted part of educational technology throughout the country and is especially strong in certain areas. "ETV enjoys a phenomenally high adoption rate in Michigan" [139:2]. ETV is so widespread throughout the nation that there are efforts to coordinate the study of its problems on a national scale. Some educators and students complain about poor programming. Hardware problems (e.g., no back-up equipment, not enough receivers, inadequate sound) have interfered with many projects. Poor coordination of content and schedules has reduced the effectiveness of many ETV projects.

ETV is a potentially good tool. Millions of dollars are being spent annually to provide better programs, to improve equipment, to train classroom teachers and television teachers, and to make good programs more accessible.

The many studies of ETV indicate that it is an effective teaching tool. When ETV is compared to face-to-face instruction, the achievement of students proves to be just as good [139:2]. In certain circumstances ETV is more effective. Some science classes use television to enlarge and project exhibits under a microscope that could not be seen by a regular class. Television is being used, on an experimental basis, in conjunction with computers. The student requests information from a central resource area, dialing the computer through a telephone network, and receives his information almost instantly on an individual television screen.

The educational potential of television has been realized most successfully by "Sesame Street." A federally supported project, this children's program, aimed primarily at preschoolers, has been shown throughout the country. A year-long study of preschool age children in many different types of environments was conducted by Educational Testing Service, an independent agency. Not only did "Sesame Street" reach its intended audience (7 million out of a potential viewing group of 12 million), but teaching and learning were effective, as represented by pre- and post-test scores relating to thirty specified objectives [113:2].

Closed circuit television is spreading in use throughout the country. Currently it is being used at all levels of education, but especially in secondary schools and in colleges and universities. Transmitting stations are set up in a single school or within a school system, and they usually link the transmission point with several classrooms. With some programs on video tape, the teacher can select the ideal time for the presentation rather than being forced to change his entire schedule to accommodate the television schedule. It is also possible to use the services of one teacher to serve students in several classrooms. Some classrooms and auditoriums are equipped with devices that enable the viewing students to relay questions to the teacher.

Satellite television programming may be used in Alaska, the first state to make such an attempt. A huge state, covering the areas of Texas, California, and Montana combined, Alaska has less than 300,000 people and is the only state without educational television. A satellite located 20,000 miles above the equator, beaming live television signals, could be used to provide commercial radio and television, telephone, computer and data-processing services, as well as educational television [58:37].

Still another variation is the use of Cable TV (CATV) in which TV programs may be transmitted from a local station over coaxial cables to classrooms, homes, hospitals, libraries, and the like [58:38]. School systems may utilize much of their own equipment; i.e., closed-circuit television cameras and video tape recorders, in developing programs to transmit over Cable TV.

The most extensive working relationship established between a local CATV operator and a school system is to be found in Long Island, New York [58:38–39]. An area educational service center SCOPE (Suffolk County Organization for the Promotion of Education) has produced a variety of special programs. To name but a few: (1) "Let's Talk Cents"—a video tape dealing with school budgets; (2) video taping of over 35 educational conferences, workshops, seminars; (3) 100 free films were video taped and sent to CATV for local showing; (4) special video taped production relating to drugs and narcotics; (5) production of student-made films, the best of which will be video taped and shown over CATV; (6) production of 20 slide-tape sets of field trips in the community.

Other Media

It may be decades before all teachers have the assistance of a computer to aid in teaching; however, scarcely any teacher will be expected in the 1970s to rely solely on textbooks, chalkboards, and simple visual aids as teaching tools. Most beginning teachers can expect to have available a wide variety of educational films and filmstrips, audio tapes and records, individualized equipment for science instruction, special-purpose equipment for reading instruction, overhead and special purpose projectors, and even closed circuit television in addition to the more commonplace instructional television. Furthermore, it can be assumed that current audio-visual software and hardware will be redesigned and modified and adapted to specific learning strategies.

The electronic laboratory is an example of technology that has undergone much change since it was first introduced. Electronic laboratories are to be found in most secondary schools and in some elementary schools. Originally it was a simple system, which allowed a pupil to hear taped presentations and then called for him to make a response. The electronic learning laboratories were designed to be used most frequently in foreign language instruction but were also used for instruction in reading, speech, shorthand, and other areas.

The purpose of the electronic laboratory was to enable the student to go through selected content at his own pace. It provided him the opportunity to play back what he had heard previously. The repetition reinforced what he had learned.

An interesting adaptation of the electronic laboratory concept is the electronic and class piano. These spinet-sized pianos are powered electronically and connected to a teacher's console piano. Using headsets, the students hear only their own playing or instructions from the teacher. The teacher can instruct students individually, in groups, or by class. The electronic piano can be used to supplement voice training or can be used for regular keyboard instruction. The pianos never require tuning.

Students in primary school and adult education can use them. Their potential for individualized instruction is very appealing.

Many schools, especially at the secondary level, are now using a multimedia, package-approach to instruction. Learning packages prepared by teachers include sight and sound media. A science package, for example, might contain slides, 8-mm film loops or a 16-mm film, audio-tapes and/or filmstrips. The student would use the package as often as needed in a library type carrel. Such instructional packages are becoming commonplace in science, humanities, foreign language, and social studies departments. These electronic packages are only as good as the content of the programs housed within them and that content depends upon the availability of materials and the initiative, industry, and creative planning of teachers.

To aid students and faculty in gaining immediate access to a wide variety of audio and video type materials, attempts are being made to develop and implement a plan called Dial Access Information Retrieval System. Utilizing a coaxial television cable system connecting a main center with various terminals located in individual schools, electronic switching systems will be used to bring together the student and whatever material he is seeking.

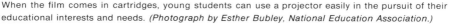
When the film comes in cartridges, young students can use a projector easily in the pursuit of their educational interests and needs. *(Photograph by Esther Bubley, National Education Association.)*

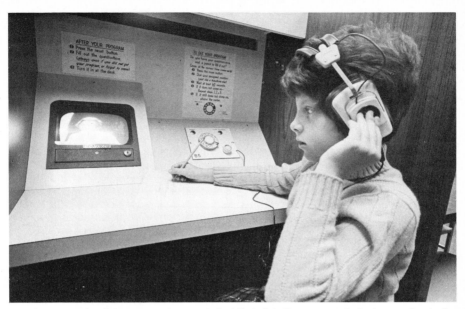

In order to use the dial-access system, a student first dials the program desired, according to the number listed in a card file. He then views and listens to the content presentation. This type of technology may be used for presentation of any programmed material for enrichment, reinforcement, or for make-up purposes, by means of which the student is able to study at his own rate and level of sophistication. *(Photograph by Esther Bubley, National Education Association.)*

Manufacturers have placed a major emphasis on developing and marketing equipment and materials, hardware and software, that can be operated and used by students of all ages with a minimum of damage and breakdown. The cassette tape recorder, which avoids the frustration of fumbling with delicate tapes and can be loaded and unloaded by very young students, offers great advantages to classroom teachers. Storage is simple, and damage can be reduced to a minimum.

Other recent developments in communication media include the use of portable video tape recorders. At the moment the recorders are used chiefly for improving professional performance, particularly that of the beginning teacher. Video-tape playbacks of the teacher-in-action can be analyzed for a variety of purposes. The potential advantages of this medium for aiding students in performance-oriented activities are great.

Rapid progress is being made in the development and use of video tape cassettes. In the foreseeable future, television sets in homes and in schools will be equipped to use cassettes. There is an enormous potential use of these cassettes for independent study, not only for the education of youth but also in the area of continuing education.

SCHOOLS IN TRANSITION

Change in American education comes on a broken front. For example, while some schools are attempting to move from an 8–4 plan to a 6–3–3 organization, other schools are developing highly-sophisticated middle schools. Still other school districts are concentrating on the development of educational parks which will put all district schools on one site. Although the self-contained classroom still is the predominant organizational pattern in elementary schools, many educators are advocating nongraded, multiage groups, and other responsible professionals are pointing toward differentiated staffing as the best means of deploying educational manpower.

New buildings of revolutionary design are being erected in some districts—buildings designed for flexibility in space and number of students per group, and equipped to utilize the latest technological advancement. However, most new school construction has not departed radically from the familiar egg-crate design that has characterized school buildings for the past century.

The effects of desegregation attempts, urban blight, overpopulation, and demands for community control of the schools are being felt by a majority of school systems. These are important examples of the many social forces that are generating questions about the purposes of education and questions about educational practice. While few school systems are faced with all these problems, no school is completely isolated from them and the changes they foster.

Although the innovations described in this as well as in the previous chapter seem impressive, the extent to which these innovations have affected the mainstream of the educational enterprise is limited. For example, Fred T. Wilhelms, Executive Secretary of the Association for Supervision and Curriculum Development, reported in 1968 that efforts toward team teaching, despite the warnings of Anderson and Trump regarding role clarification and responsibility, had more often than not been reduced to nothing more than departmentalized teaching [98:19]. He noted further that the Trump Plan (large group, small group, independent study) had seldom been achieved in its entirety. Despite widespread development of public educational television, evidence of increased achievement on the part of students simply has not been forthcoming.

In their book, *Behind the Classroom Door*, Goodlad and Klein [44] report upon a study they had made of 67 schools in 13 states in which they evaluated 150 K–4 classrooms against 10 reasonable expectations concerning educational innovations. Among other things, these researchers hoped to find: (1) clear-cut educational objectives; (2) a wide assortment of instructional materials; (3) individualized instruction; (4)

flexible standards for evaluating and reporting student programs; and (5) expanded curricula drawing from projects in mathematics, science, and the social studies. They found that many, if not most, of the highly recommended and publicized educational innovations of the 1960s had not reached the classroom. Teachers and principals understand little regarding such innovative practices. Supporting Wilhelm's observations, they found that team teaching was too often just departmentalization; nongrading was a form of homogeneous grouping; new content was being taught by the same old methods. Teachers still focused on content—as a goal. Covering "x" amount of material, rather than helping students achieve educational objectives which are carefully specified, still appeared to be the central thrust of an "education." Lectures, recitations, textbooks, and workbooks continued to characterize instruction, which was still group-oriented rather than being individualized [57:121].

The Problem of Change

The question may be asked, "Why have these exciting innovative practices and technological advancements not penetrated our educational structure to a greater extent than seems to be the case?" Undoubtedly there are a number of reasons, one of which is the fact that most individuals tend to resist change. Change tends to threaten or upset our sense of security. It necessitates adaptation, adjustment, and creative thought. It is so much more comfortable to continue operating in terms of well-established patterns. Although change is an inevitable component of life, few of us have been educated in such a manner which allows us to live comfortably and creatively with change—and especially with the accelerating rate of change that characterizes life in today's world.

A number of educators are concerned about the effects of rapid change upon the mental and emotional health of people—and teachers are people. In commenting upon "the premature arrival of tomorrow," Shane states that [116:191–192]:

The pressure of increasing knowledge and a growing awareness on the part of the thoughtful human that he must assume personal responsibility for the futures that are being created can be a severe strain on the individual's mental and emotional health. But perhaps an even more unsettling problem which deserves study is what the rate of change in our lives today is doing to people—especially in industrially advanced areas such as the U.S. where many new techno-, bio-, psycho-, and sociofutures are rapidly taking shape.

Let us look with care at the significance of change—at the same time keeping in mind its manifold possibilities and problems for the curriculum developer.

Suppose that one of our remote ancestors lived 50,000 years ago in the Yantze River Valley, or in the once-fertile Lake Chad area, or in a Swiss lake village cluster, or in the Dordogone Valley caves of France. If his offspring, and their children through the centuries, had lived to be 60 to 65 years old they would represent an unbroken genetic chain of 799 forebears; a chain in which a man who is 60 years old today would be the eight hundredth living link.

In the last three decades of the 800th man's life, more changes have taken place than occurred during the previous 799½ lifetimes!

Julius Caesar probably would have been able to understand rather quickly the lives and artifacts as they existed in the 799th man's world of 1910. However Caesar and the 799th man both would be at a loss to understand computers, the uses of atomic power, or the sophisticated technologies that are involved when man travels in space.

From an historical point of view, it seems reasonable to say that for the first time in the history of the human race man has been propelled from yesterday into tomorrow with no familiar "today" during which to become acclimated to change. We have encountered the future so rapidly, and with such violent changes in the ordered familiar patterns of our way of life, that we are suffering from what Toffler aptly called ". . . the dizzying disorientation brought on by the premature arrival of the future."

The fact that half of the biotechnical changes of the last 50,000 years have come about in the past 30 is especially important because of what this transition has done to people. Many of the changes have rendered useless the "maps" of the cultural terrain with which most persons over 30 years of age were provided by their upbringing prior to 1950.

The "dizzying disorientation" referred to by Toffler in his book *Future Shock* [143] is certainly reflected in our reactions to educational innovation. Too frequently changes in organizational structure and the use of technology may be considered to be panaceas for something that seems to be wrong or inadequate. As a result, efforts may be made to lengthen the school year; start school earlier; replace the junior high school with the middle school; go to large group/small group/independent study patterns of instruction; try educational television; experiment with programmed materials or adopt a modern mathematics series. Yet the gap between expectations and reality remains alarmingly wide. Why?

Innovative efforts, by accident or design, have not generally centered upon people and the changing of their behavior or their roles. And the result is that relatively little success has been achieved. People are the key to change. Only people can make decisions and determine purposes. And the matter of purpose could well be the missing element in the whole enterprise.

Consider questions related to the affective/cognitive domains, or priorities related to matters of process and content. Many people believe today that the way students feel is as important as what they know or can do: how do they feel about themselves (self-concept); how do they feel and behave toward others (humanism)?

Programs focusing upon cognitive development, when viewed in its knowledge (content) and basic skill dimensions, result in certain types of programming. To predetermine a given amount and kind of content to be learned by all is a position quite different from that associated with a view that content is a means to an end, that different kinds of content can be used to help students develop an understanding of generalizations, principles, broad understandings common to all areas or topics under study.

A "basic skill" oriented program is very different from one which

FIGURE 5–1   Per cent of elementary and secondary schools throughout the United States using newer techniques of instruction.

stresses rational development and creative thought; one which envisions tomorrow as being a quite unpredictable world—complex, and demanding of people who will deal rationally and creatively with problems unknown and undreamed of today. Such process considerations may well be expanded to include such considerations as self-evaluation and the development of personal responsibility and self-discipline for much of one's own learning.

Is it any wonder that when some form of technology, or some new organizational scheme, is put into effect, it may be dropped later? This usually occurs when there is no central purpose to sustain the effort when the going gets rough. Commitment to purpose is a primary motivating force. Significant and lasting change is *not* likely to take place without dealing with this question. Goodlad and Klein's research is very alarming in this regard, for it is all too evident that little attention, or even recognition, is given to the question—of what is worth learning and for what purpose. For the most part, education still consists of covering material, of establishing fixed standards for all, of moving through material toward those standards at a fixed rate for all.

Most of the new ideas and innovative materials have merit—*when* used to help students achieve particular kinds of purposes or objectives. Programmed learning is excellent when skill development and understanding of certain kinds of content are central to the effort. If goals related to rational development through inquiry and creative thought or something related to humanism are a concern, then programmed learning materials are not apt to be very appropriate. Ideas and materials used for inappropriate purposes result in little payoff.

Another major factor, which certainly is related to the first, is the lack of any real concern or commitment to the process of evaluation. Unless educational objectives are specified in clear-cut terms, it is virtually impossible to assess the extent to which progress is being made in achieving the objectives. All of us need to receive feedback, in reasonably objective terms, that what we are doing makes a difference, that it is worth all the time and energy that faculty and students are putting forth. Should such data not be forthcoming, then people predictably will not continue to exert much energy or try to improve.

Evaluation is also the process by which accountability can be established. The typical American teacher receives little, if any, professional criticism at any point in his professional career. Student teachers typically complain that they do not get constructive criticism from either their cooperating teachers or college supervisors; beginning and/or experienced teachers frequently indicate that they receive little of value from supervisors, consultants, etc.. As a result of ineffective supervisory practices, some of these supervisory positions, particularly in large cities, are being eliminated. Too much time and effort have been devoted to establishing and maintaining a happy social atmosphere, while tough-minded, hard-nosed assessment, which should be an integral part of one's professional activities, has been avoided.

There are growing signs that accountability can no longer be avoided. National assessment, bitterly opposed by virtually all professional organizations in the early and middle sixties, has finally become a reality. The first results began to emerge as the decade of the seventies got underway.

Interest in performance contracting is growing—a situation in which school systems contract with *business* regarding certain aspects of the school's program, i.e., reading and/or mathematics. Business *guarantees* student progress or else full payment for services rendered need not be forthcoming. Some school boards are moving toward performance contracting, which was initially funded by the federal government.

The use of educational vouchers—a situation whereby parents can enroll their children in a school of their choice by submitting a voucher to the school so that reimbursement for services rendered may be made—is still another attempt to establish some form of accountability. Should state and/or federal support of private schools become a factor, perhaps via an educational voucher system, then an alternative to public education could for the first time be universally available to the American public.

The American public is becoming increasingly sympathetic to the idea of alternative choices as is indicated by the growing number of private schools. In addition, so-called "free schools" are growing in number, particularly in Boston and San Francisco. These schools, inspired by the development of the British Infant Schools and the ideas of Jean Piaget, with their emphasis upon creativity and the development of self, numbered in the hundreds at the start of the seventies. Should events such as these show continued success, then accountability will become a reality of life with which educators must contend.

The topics of national assessment, performance contracting, and vouchering will be discussed in greater detail in a later section of this book. They are mentioned at this point primarily to indicate changes that are taking place in the American educational scene at a time when there might seem to be considerable resistance upon the part of many teachers to change, to innovate in terms of clear-cut purposes, to evaluate in terms of well-conceived performance objectives, to be genuinely concerned with the relevance and quality of education for youth today. If you read about the historical development of American schools, you will find that such institutions as the Latin Grammar Schools and the Academy declined when those institutions failed to be responsive to change. To what extent might some of our public schools be facing the same destiny as those earlier institutions?

Tomorrow's Schools

Changes in the schools of the future are certain to take place. How extensive such changes will be is difficult to predict. These changes undoubtedly will reflect technological advances, organizational change, and new curricular emphases. The current emphasis on research, interest in innovative programs, and the development of new practices will make the schools significantly different, even from the most modern of today. As Locke points out [66:44]:

The most encouraging sign is that educational research is finally beginning to lead instead of follow educational experimentation. Almost all of the classroom innovations introduced in the United States after World War II—the use of audiovisual materials, language labs, educational television, and even flexible scheduling—were developed without the benefit of research into the processes of learning. Some of these ideas succeeded, but not because they rested on a foundation of research; rather because they happened to match some obvious needs. The first instructional innovation to be developed by people with a background in educational psychology and research was programmed instruction, which for that reason has more potential than many of the early developments.

Although an accurate picture of tomorrow's schools cannot be seen in detail, some obvious trends are in evidence. As examples, the school of the future will be characterized by its focus on the individual. Group teaching methods will tend to give way to personalized teaching. The teacher will become more sensitive to variations among learners, and to the educational needs of multi-ethnic groups. And the teacher's role will change. In the school of the future the teacher will tend to become a diagnostician, prescriber, and resource person, instead of a group teacher. Paraprofessionals, flexible schedules, and independent study will result in the self-contained classroom becoming less self-contained. These trends are apparent today.

School facilities will be vastly different. More space in schools will be fashioned into laboratories and individual work stations. Less space will be used for classrooms, as pupils spend increased time working on their own and meeting in small groups. Large lecture rooms will be outfitted for presentations by teachers. In these areas the appeals will be made to the pupil's sense of sight, as well as to his sense of hearing. The

FIGURE 5–2 The Valley Winds Elementary School in suburban St. Louis is an example of the innovations being made in the designing of school buildings. The school building is shaped like a snail's shell with classrooms radiating from a central core. It is air-conditioned, is carpeted throughout, and has giant-sized classrooms to accommodate the ungraded curriculum.

community beyond the walls of the school will offer educational facilities.

The largest area in the school will be the instructional materials center. Here all the advances of technology will be harnessed for aiding pupils. For example, dial-access systems, whereby pupils can retrieve information through a screen and earphone set, will be housed in the instructional materials center. Rich storehouses of books and booklets will be available in every school, and study carrels, small stations giving privacy on three sides, will be used by pupils as they accumulate understandings and develop skills. The length of the class period, the school day, and the school year will be varied and suited to the individual student's learning pattern. A major emphasis will be placed on developing independent learners instead of students overly dependent on teachers. Group processes will be familiar to pupils at all levels of the educational system.

New ways of financing American public education will be required in order to capitalize fully on the advantages possible through selective use of technology for well-defined purposes. Greater participation by the federal government seems likely, and such activity will necessitate a reordering of national priorities and commitment.

More and more, content will be viewed as a means to an end. A better balance between content *and* process—unique, discovery, and problem-solving activities particularly—will emerge. Independent learning and self-evaluation will also be stressed. Content emphases will focus upon broad understandings, generalizations, principles, and properties, in contrast to discrete information so often stressed today.

Public education undoubtedly will be extended past the twelfth year into post-high school vocational and junior or community/regional college programs. Programs for children below kindergarten age will be common. It is quite possible that children will start school around age three and continue studying regularly the rest of their lives.

Conditions of teaching will change substantially. In addition to increases in compensation and in insurance and retirement benefits, teachers will have more and better tools with which to work. Accompanying these improvements will be a demand for continuing in-service education. The teacher of the future will be a more highly trained and skilled professional than today's teacher. Focus in teacher education programs will be upon developing carefully specified competencies. Such competencies may quite predictably be used at some point in the future as a basis for certification. Performance-based teacher certification is already being developed in sixteen states [85:158].

Though problems of learning will continue to exist, special education classes for the retarded may gradually disappear. Although their potentialities are only beginning to be realized, developments in chemistry and biochemistry will not only extend and influence our understanding of the learning process and the mind of man but may be used to control certain hereditary deficiencies of children.

The constant for the future will be change. The continuing quest will be for improvement. Added resources for education, society's demand for fully educated people, and a developing profession will be the means for shaping the new schools of the future.

SUMMARY

Education at all levels stands on the threshold of major technological changes that could transform educational practices, school organization, and the role of the teacher. Undoubtedly in the schools of the future, extensive use will be made of programmed learning, computer-associated instruction, computer class scheduling, closed-circuit television, cable television, cassette tape recorders, video-tape cassettes, dial-access information retrieval systems, electronic laboratories, and multimedia learning packages.

The function of this new technology is not primarily to replace the teacher, but to give the teacher and the student the necessary tools that will add new dimensions to learning. It is highly probable in the years to come that much of the kind of learning taking place in schools today will be accomplished by the students in their homes. Time spent in school will be directed more toward humanizing types of experiences—gaining skill in working together, communicating, inquiring, discovering, valuing, and developing a consistent and reasoned point of view toward life. As a result, the role of the teacher will become more truly professional—calling for a high degree of expertise in guiding the educational growth of each student.

Change in educational practices takes place on a broken front. Teachers in some school systems already are exploring the use of a number of technological resources. Many other teachers prefer to be unaffected by the possible use of these resources. With the normal human penchant for the status quo and a fondness of the "good old days," it is not at all disquieting to perceive that the educational process of change should be painfully slow. At the same time, the general public is concerned with quality education, as well as with the mounting costs of public education. Questions are being raised about educational assessment and accountability. Industry is evidencing interest in applying its expertise in the use of technology to the field of education. Undoubtedly these forces will stimulate more educators to explore the applications of technology to their work.

The rash of innovative and inventive measures for improving our educational scene during the past several years at times may have appeared to be sporadic, frenzied, disorganized, and discouraging. But this seems to be characteristic of change. The important thing is that educators are beginning to sift through the realizations of how best to proceed, and priorities are beginning to emerge.

The rapidity of change in the future will be many times that found in the past fifteen crowded years. Sharply differing instructional practices will become more evident as even newer technologies develop. Faculty deployment will become more varied and imaginative as significant attempts are made to provide greater opportunities for the teacher to help shape educational change and future planning.

The key to a better tomorrow is people—not technology, not organizational patterns. Technology and new organizational patterns are only means to an end. The question of "What shall be the proper ends of education?" will always be determined by people—and teachers play a key role in answering this question. Goal orientation with a strong philosophical base for all activity, together with the use of new technological aids, should produce an unexcelled educational era.

QUESTIONS TO CONSIDER

1. Within the next ten years, what uses of technology in the field of education do you foresee, and how might these uses affect your role as a professional educator?
2. In what ways should the technological expertise of business and industry be used in the field of education? What role should the professional educator play in this involvement?
3. What changes in educational practices and school organization do you foresee resulting from extended use of the computer?
4. What impact might the extensive use of video tapes have upon educational practices in public schools? In what ways might the use of video tapes enhance adult education?
5. How do you account for the slow rate of change in educational practices? What might be the consequences if teachers refuse to change their instructional practices?
6. In what ways do you feel that teaching within the next decade will become even more interesting and challenging?

PROBLEM SITUATION FOR INQUIRY

Miss Crone is a middle-aged high school social studies teacher. From the beginning of her teaching career, she has required students to submit written outlines and answers to questions for each chapter in the textbook which she, without examining any of the work, merely records in her gradebook. Students are graded on the basis of short-answer objective tests which she has used from year to year without change. The students invariably take a free ride on both counts, for the homework is copyable and the tests are public domain. Her discussion in class frequently involves a recounting of the events of the weekend, which are spent at her home. She feels that the students really like her as a teacher, and she points with pride at the high grades most of her students receive.

The manner in which Miss Crone conducts her classes is well known to parents. They hesitate to criticize her teaching, since they like the high grades their sons and daughters receive from her. Miss Crone is several years away from compulsory retirement, and teaching is her sole means of support.

Miss Crone steadfastly refuses to have anything to do with the innovative practices which many of her colleagues are using. Every time the principal or other teachers have encouraged her to change, she has rebuked them with the statement that "There is no substitute for good, solid academic instruction. All of that stuff is just a passing fad. I'll have no part of it, and I'll stand on the high grades my students make."

If you were chairman of the social studies department (or the principal) in this school, what would you do? Why?

ACTIVITIES TO PURSUE

1. Spend some time in schools that have performance contracts. Try to determine how teachers and students feel with regard to this practice. How do the roles of both teachers and students change under such circumstances?
2. Examine various types of teaching machines and programmed learning materials. What strengths and weaknesses do you see in the use of these materials?
3. Interview some teachers who have used instructional television. What advantages and disadvantages do they see in the use of this medium of instruction?
4. Talk with some school administrators and teachers regarding problems involved in changing instructional practices and procedures. Try to determine what they consider to be the basic reasons for teacher resistance to change.
5. If possible, visit a school in which considerable use is being made of educational technology. Compare and contrast the role of the teacher in this kind of setting with that of a more conventional setting.

FIGURE CREDITS

FIGURE 5–1. (*Source:* Data from "Use of New Techniques in Instruction," *NEA Research Bulletin*, vol. 49, no. 3, National Education Association, Research Division, Washington, October, 1971, p. 83.)

FIGURE 5–2. (*Source: Shaver and Company, Architects, Salina, Kansas.*)

6 | THE TEACHING PROFESSION: ITS STATUS, ORGANIZATIONS, PUBLICATIONS, AND CODE OF ETHICS

What constitutes a profession? To what extent is teaching a profession? In what ways does it differ from other professions? What is the importance of the Code of Ethics of the Education Profession? What different organizations exist in the teaching profession? In what ways may these organizations benefit the individual teacher? Through what organizations can the individual teacher contribute most to the profession?

It is only as individual teachers and groups of teachers give serious consideration to questions such as these that the teaching profession can continue to advance and to assume its deserved role among the great professions.

TEACHING AS A PROFESSION

Anyone who becomes a teacher becomes a member of a profession, with responsibility for improving the status of that chosen profession. A professional person may find it difficult at times to differentiate among his professional services in teaching, his personal life, and his work in the activities of the profession itself. Perhaps this sense of dedication is one of the distinguishing characteristics of a professional person. In this chapter teachers in preparation are asked to think carefully about their role in the profession and its organizations.

Characteristics of a Profession

What constitutes a profession? Many scholars and many scholarly groups have given careful thought to formulating an answer to this question. The professions have studied themselves in attempts to enlighten their own members and the public concerning the characteristics and role of a profession. Although these various statements have differed in many details, there seems to be consensus concerning some of the major practices descriptive of a profession.

A profession requires that its members:

1. Commit themselves to the ideal of service to mankind rather than to personal gain.
2. Undergo relatively long periods of professional preparation to learn the concepts and principles of the specialized knowledge which earns the profession its high status.
3. Meet established qualifications for admission and keep up-to-date through in-service growth.
4. Establish and adhere to a code of ethics regarding membership, conduct, and practice.
5. Demand a high order of intellectual activity.
6. Form organizations to improve the standards of the profession, the services of the profession, self-discipline in the profession, and the economic well-being of its members.
7. Provide opportunities for advancement, specialization, and independence.
8. Regard the profession as a life career and consider membership in the profession as permanent.

Certainly there are differences among the requirements and characteristics of manual labor, skilled labor, the subprofessions, and the professions. However, in many cases it is not a simple task to differentiate between the subprofessions and the professions. The professions of medicine, law, and the ministry have long been recognized. But what of the additional groups that have sought recognition as professions—nurses, teachers, engineers, journalists, and many others? And what of recent patterns of differentiated staffing in which para-professionals and interns are used as supporting personnel in a teaching team? Does this approach to the use of various types of personnel in the total teaching situation more clearly delineate the professional person or does it further confuse the description? In addition, critics of the teaching profession sometimes charge that many teachers want to be prepared as technicians but want to be recognized and paid as professionals. Although it is obvious that at present teaching is considered a profession, it is only fair to point out that this status is challenged by many persons.

Status of Teaching as a Profession

It is true that the requirements for entrance into the teaching profession have not always been as high as those for some other professions. It is also true that in the profession of teaching there are some members who have not lived up to desirable levels of conduct and service. Furthermore, many persons have used teaching as a stepping-stone to other professions. Finally, there are major differences between teaching and the other professions. However, these aspects of teaching and teachers do not deny to teaching its status as a profession.

FIGURE 6–1.   Change in the level of preparation of public school teachers. How may this distribution change in the future?

In what ways does teaching differ from other professions? These differences lie in the control, support, size, and the ratio of the sexes [53:66–70]. The legal control of education belongs to the public, not to the profession itself. Thus, the members of the teaching profession must work constantly to inform the public and must participate extensively in public concerns. Public school teachers are paid from tax money, which presents certain limitations and problems not inherent in other professions. Until very recent years the need for large numbers of teachers has affected the policies of recruitment and selectivity within the profession. Furthermore, the fact that women outnumber men in the teaching profession differentiates it sharply from law, medicine, and the ministry. Nevertheless, these differences should not prevent teaching from being accorded professional status.

Because of these differences between teaching and other professions, it has been said that teaching can never achieve professional autonomy; i.e., it can never become a self-managing profession. To achieve a high degree of autonomy, the members of the profession need to be clearly and firmly in charge of those aspects which are characterized as professional concerns. As Stinnett [125:12] points out, the profession should be responsible:

for determining the standards and seeing to their enforcement, for selection and admission to teacher education programs, for guidance, screening, and retention during preparation, for accreditation of teacher education institutions, for licensure and revocation of licensure, for professional growth, for working conditions, for protecting its members against unjust and capricious treatment, and for disciplining its members for unethical and unprofessional conduct.

In other words, professional autonomy means control by the profession of those standards on which it guarantees the competence of each member admitted to practice and permitted to continue in practice and through which it defines the conditions under which members will work. Perhaps the most outstanding thrust has been made through the work of the National Commission on Teacher Education and Professional Standards. This very important commission will be discussed later in this chapter.

It has been pointed out that the goal of professional autonomy is in direct conflict with our national tradition of local control of education and that "The professionalization of teachers and local, lay control of education are on a collision course" [109:333]. The 1968 Ocean Hill-Brownsville controversy in New York City is cited as an early example of this conflict. However, national opinion, according to a Louis Harris poll, apparently supports by a substantial majority the point of view that "teachers should have a bigger voice in the educational system" [79:3]. This is especially important in education today with the growing emphasis on accountability. "The teaching profession must have certain responsibilities delegated to it by the public if it is to contribute significantly to the improvement of education and to be accountable for what happens in the schools" [45:3].

What are the conditions and characteristics which support teaching as a profession? Among them are the following:

1. Most teachers are working for the sake of giving service to mankind rather than for great personal gain.
2. Teachers are required by law to complete certain requirements for certification and entrance into the profession, and these requirements are constantly being strengthened.
3. Teaching requires careful skills and understandings.
4. Teachers have professional publications to help them keep up-to-date.
5. Teachers attend summer school, extension classes, workshops, conventions, and institutes and engage in a wide variety of other in-service activities.
6. Teaching is well regarded as a life career.
7. Teachers have their standards and ethics operating through national, state, and local education associations.

Prestige of Teachers

Occupations differ in regard to the respect or prestige generally assigned to them by members of a community. The prestige of teachers remains consistently high. For example, George Gallup, Director of the American Institute of Public Opinion, found through identical surveys that the prestige of the teaching profession had risen between 1953 and 1962 in a list of professions from a rank of seventh to a rank of third. In 1967 educators ranked fifth in a list of seventeen major professions and occupations in which the "American public places its esteem and confidence" according to a Louis Harris national poll [78:3]. They were preceded by doctors, bankers, scientists, and military leaders. They outranked such personnel as corporate heads, psychiatrists, U.S. Supreme Court Justices, local retailers, clergy, congressmen, and federal government leaders. Another Gallup poll in 1968 indicated that 62 per cent of American adults would advise young people today to take up teaching as a lifetime career. In describing the teaching profession, the people interviewed used such words as "rewarding," "creative," and "challenging" [37:B18].

What about parents' views toward teaching as a profession? Another Gallup poll in 1969 found that three-fourths of American parents would like to have their children take up teaching as a career. There were only minute differences between the opinions of white and nonwhite parents, Protestant and Roman Catholic parents, and parents thirty years of age or older. Parents under thirty years of age and Jewish parents held somewhat less positive opinions, 65 and 63 per cent respectively [34:51].

Perhaps a number of factors have contributed to this continuing high prestige of teachers. As previously indicated, the complexity of our technological and social world has placed an increasingly higher premium upon the need for education, and teachers are the chief instruments for obtaining this education. Research studies indicate that members of professions requiring extended and rigorous preparation tend to have greater prestige than those of whom little training is required. The number of years required to become a teacher has increased significantly. There is considerable evidence to support the fact that the holding power of a profession increases as the standards for entrance increase. Also, teachers are assuming an increasing role as political citizens in the life of the community, state, and nation [123:264–271]. They may feel certain that the amount of respect and prestige accorded teachers will continue to rise as professional standards, salaries, quality of members in the profession, and importance of education in everyone's life continue to rise.

FIGURE 6–2. Willingness of teachers to teach again if they were to be given the chance to start over. Teaching appears to be growing in attractiveness for both men and women. To what extent would similar results apply to other professions?

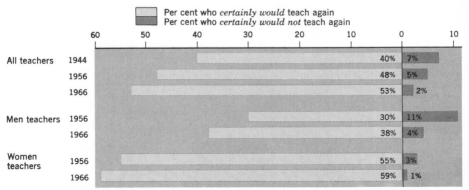

Number in the Profession

In 1970–1971, there were more than 2,000,000 public school teachers, more than 230,000 nonpublic school teachers, approximately 13,000 superintendents, more than 121,000 principals and supervisors [67:67], and more than 97,000 other instructional personnel [27:35]. More than 830,000 faculty members were employed in public and nonpublic colleges and universities in the United States [67:67]. In addition there were many thousands employed as staff members in professional organizations, in government offices of education, and in private agencies with educational programs. The sheer size of educational endeavors in this country can be effectively summarized as follows: "If we add to the full-time students at all levels, the teachers, principals, and instructional specialists, and the cooks, bus drivers, and custodians, and the people engaged in selling or producing something for the schools, the total is 30 per cent of this country's population" [63:2].

There are conflicting forces at work and conflicting types of evidence which make it difficult to predict whether or not the number in the profession will increase substantially in the next few years. The tremendously increased number of people 5 to 17 years of age between 1950 and 1960 will move into the adult group and will then be having children. There is a growing tendency to include kindergartens, nursery schools, and junior colleges in our free public school systems, and this will increase enrollment. Also, increasing numbers of boys and girls are continuing their high school studies rather than dropping out of school. New demands for comprehensively trained personnel are being heard in many fields of instruction, and those for educational services are equally urgent. There are needs for trained counselors, specialists in remedial

FIGURE 6–3. Differences in the age distribution of men and women teachers in public schools. What changes in these distributions may take place in the future?

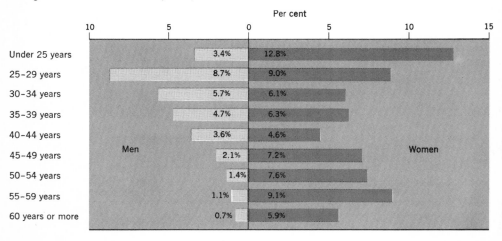

reading and speech, and instructors of the handicapped and the culturally disadvantaged, as well as for teachers in other areas not commonly present in our school systems. Further demands are being made in the field of adult education, since the educational needs of adults will continue to increase. Thus, the services of the school may well extend in many different directions.

On the other hand, the financial stringency facing many school systems at the beginning of the decade may force a hold-the-line policy in terms of numbers of professional persons employed. Thus, there may be increased class sizes in some school systems, cutbacks in special services and programs offered, and efforts to use professional personnel more efficiently in professional tasks.

Distribution of Men and Women

Unlike European countries, where teaching has been considered a man's work, the United States has far more women than men teaching in its public schools. From 1880 to 1920 the percentage of men teachers in public schools decreased from 43 to 14 per cent. In the 20 years that followed, the percentage of men rose to 23, but during World War II it declined to 15 per cent of the total. Since then there has been a steady increase; in 1970, it had reached 32.4 per cent of all public school teachers, including 15.4 per cent of elementary teachers and 53.5 per cent of secondary teachers [27:35].

Considerable effort is being made to attract more men into public school teaching, especially into the elementary schools. Teachers and the public generally feel that more men are needed in classroom teaching. The adoption of single-salary schedules has provided added incentive for men to consider teaching on the lower level, where the opportunities are

FIGURE 6–4. During a half century of time, the percentage of men teachers in public schools has increased significantly, especially in the secondary schools.

great. Higher salaries for all public school teachers should encourage more men to enter the profession on all levels.

PROFESSIONAL ORGANIZATIONS AND PUBLICATIONS

Many years and the efforts of countless people have been involved in the development of the teaching profession in America. During this time the profession has developed a system of purposes, refined its procedures, set standards relating to training, and reduced to a definite code certain important elements in the behavior of its members.

One of the important conditions of professionalism is membership in various organizations. By sharing ideas and experiences with others through these organizations, teachers can improve the general level of their performance and exert their collective influence in bringing about more desirable conditions for work. A great portion of the improvements in education has resulted from the work of these organizations. In this world of special-interest groups, there is a very real need for teacher organizations.

In considering the services and characteristics of professional organizations, the Educational Policies Commission of the National Education Association, for many years, suggested that they should aim to do the following [95:54]:

1. Encourage members to cherish education's distinctive knowledge and insight
2. Aid in disseminating information and understanding throughout the profession
3. Promote research, support research, encourage research by members, and foster the application of research findings
4. Help improve teacher education
5. Safeguard teachers' basic freedoms
6. Meet members' personal needs
7. Improve teaching loads and school environment
8. Seek adequate salary provisions
9. Promote professional ethics
10. Inform the public
11. Take positions on issues affecting education
12. Cooperate in counseling the public
13. Influence public policy
14. Cooperate with interested lay groups

Since the organizations for teachers are considerable in number and vary in scope of membership, purpose, and procedure, a few of the more important ones should be discussed.

Local Education Association

Local associations provide opportunities for teachers to consider matters that are of concern to the immediate community and teacher group.

Through the association, teachers are able to participate in the formulation of local school policies, to keep the community informed regarding educational matters, and to influence the policies of their state and national associations. Outside of large cities, local units are frequently formed on a countywide basis. Local groups usually are represented in their respective state associations and participate in the election of state association officials.

Local teacher organizations differ considerably in form. They may include all the school personnel within a school system, or there may be separate organizations for classroom teachers and for administrators. The number as well as the nature of the meetings held each year varies. Frequently, the organizations are very strong, and the members are vitally concerned with problems common to the group. Various subgroups may be working on such problems as reporting to parents, textbook selection, curriculum reorganization, evaluation of teachers and programs, and professional negotiations. Participation in these groups usually provides an excellent opportunity for professional stimulation and constructive work with colleagues.

State Education Association

Educational workers are also organized at the state level. A journal is published, usually monthly, to keep teachers in the state informed on problems, trends, and events in education. Meetings of the total membership are arranged usually once or twice a year. Public schools may be dismissed for about two days, so that public school educators may attend the state convention. The state educational meetings generally are held in the capital city or in selected regional cities. Participation of many teachers and administrators is required in order to make these conventions successful and to carry on the activities of the association throughout the year. However, in many states less teacher enthusiasm for this type meeting is being exhibited, and there may well be major changes in plans for state meetings within the next few years.

The typical state education association has a headquarters building and a competent central office staff, a comprehensive organizational plan, and a constitution and bylaws. Often significant experimentation and research are centered there, and the results are communicated to the entire professional body. State teacher associations frequently know of important job opportunities within the state, and some provide placement services. Some state associations also provide for members a program of term life insurance at rates lower than normally available to an individual.

Most state organizations provide legal protection for individual teacher members against unfair or unjust practices which may arise in local situations. Few individual teachers would be able to wield much influence or stand the expense involved if such a problem should need to be carried far in the courts. It is reassuring for teachers to know that there is an organization ready and able to fight for their cause.

Since the central legal responsibility for education rests with the separate states in America, the state organization usually recommends minimum standards for teacher certification, school facilities, instructional programs, and the like. Some of the most significant laws relating to education in several states are created and promoted by the state education associations. Securing favorable legislation and improving conditions in the schools are primary functions of state education associations.

National Education Association

Medical men have the American Medical Association to represent them. Lawyers have the American Bar Association. One of the organizations which teachers have to represent them is the National Education Association of the United States, usually referred to as the NEA, which is the oldest teacher organization in the United States. It began in 1857 when forty-three educational leaders from twelve states and the District of Columbia met in Philadelphia to establish the National Teachers Association for the purpose of elevating the character and advancing the interests of the teaching profession and promoting the cause of popular education. From 1870 to 1906 the organization was known as the National Educational Association, and the present name was adopted when the association was chartered by the Congress of the United States.

The association grew slowly at first. After World War I, teachers sought a more active role in the national organization. This was achieved through a reorganization of the association, whose control was then vested in a representative assembly made up of elected delegates from state and local teacher organizations that held membership in the NEA. At about the same time, a building in Washington, D.C., was secured to house the national headquarters. The NEA has grown in membership and influence to such a point that it approaches the status of being the official spokesman of the public school people of America (a claim likely to be disputed by the American Federation of Teachers). More than half of the public school teachers in the United States belong to the NEA. In 1970 the Association was made up of more than 1,100,000 members, and through affiliation of the local, state, and territorial associations, the NEA represented more than 1,700,000 teachers.

In 1966, the NEA merged with the 32,000 member American Teachers Association, a national organization of black educators, and also established an affiliate association composed of teachers in the schools operated by the U.S. Bureau of Indian Affairs [75:19]. However, race relations remain a problem in professional education as in many other fields, as witnessed by the expulsion of the Louisiana Teachers Association and the Mississippi Education Association by the NEA in 1970 for refusing to merge with the state's black teacher organizations [81:206].

A change in the membership qualifications provided that after August 31, 1964, eligibility for new members in the NEA would require an earned bachelor's, or higher, degree or a regular vocational or technical certificate [75:20]. If a person is not able to meet one of these qualifications, he may become an associate member without having the privilege of voting for delegates or of holding office in the organization.

The official purpose of the National Education Association is "To elevate the character and advance the interests of the profession of teaching and to promote the cause of education in the United States." At a July 6, 1970, Representative Assembly, the following goals were adopted for the Association: "an independent, united teaching profession; professional excellence; economic security for all educators; adequate financing for public education; human and civil rights for all educators and children; and leadership in solving social problems" [75:102–104].

The services performed by the NEA are of tremendous variety and scope, but in order to gain some understanding of the total program and activities these services can be listed under the following broad categories: professional growth, public relations, defense of the teaching

The many publications of professional organizations are of great benefit to educators in the improvement of educational practices. (*Photograph by Joe Di Dio, National Education Association.*)

profession, research, professional standards, teacher welfare, federal relations, curriculum and instructional development, international education, selective teacher recruitment, publications, and assistance in professional negotiations. The official journal of the NEA is *Today's Education*. The Association also provides various direct services to individual members including life and accidental death insurance, a mutual fund, a tax-sheltered annuity program, book purchase, and an auto-leasing program [75:21].

In its continuous efforts to elevate the standards of the teaching profession, the NEA provides services to local associations as well as to individual teachers. These services include various publications, consultative services, conferences, a clearing-house for ideas, and special materials to local committee chairmen. An example of one such service is that of the Research Division of the NEA. This division renders a real service to teachers, associations, and government officials by collecting and publishing nationwide data on such problems as teacher load, salaries, tenure, certification, retirement, finance, legislation, welfare, and status. These data have been of much help to teachers and teacher associations in appraising the status of local conditions in comparison with the status in the United States as a whole.

To encourage closer relationships and coordinated efforts on local, state, and national levels, the NEA has developed the unified membership plan in which teachers join all levels of associations at one time. By 1970, twenty-eight states had adopted the unified membership plan. A further attempt to strengthen local associations by bringing the services and resources of the state and national organizations closer to every teacher in Uniserv, in operation for the first time in 1970–1971. The goal is to have one staff man in the field giving direct and continuing service to every 1,200 teachers. The local, state, and national education associations pool their resources to finance each unit and to train and assist each Uniserv representative in providing service to teachers [75:22–23].

There has been much reorganization within the NEA during the past few years. For example, in 1966 there were thirty-three departments. However, in 1971, as may be noted in the organizational diagram, there were four departments, seventeen national affiliates, and twelve associated organizations. These changes represent, in most cases, a greater autonomy for the affiliates and associates. Within these various groups is an organization serving almost all levels or special interests and concerns in education.

As is indicated in the diagram, the NEA also has twenty-five commissions, committees, and councils. Illustrative of these groups, the National Commission on Teacher Education and Professional Standards has become increasingly more important since its creation in 1946. More familiarly known as the TEPS Commission, this group has evolved into a nationwide organization with parallel state commissions. As its name implies, the commission is concerned with the recruitment, selection,

ORGANIZATION CHART

FIGURE 6–5. Organizational chart of the National Education Association.

preparation, and certification of teachers, and with the standards of the schools which prepare teachers.

Perhaps the greatest prominence of any NEA commission was achieved by the Educational Policies Commission, in existence from 1935 to 1969. The commission considered issues facing the teaching profession, and proposed policy for the conduct of education in this country and in its international relationships. Among its most influential publications were *The Unique Functions of Education in American Democracy* (1937), *Education for All American Children* (1948), *Moral and Spiritual Values in the Public Schools* (1951), *Manpower and Education* (1956), *The Central Purpose of American Education* (1961),

Education and the Disadvantaged American (1962), and *American Education and the Search for Equal Opportunity* (1965).

Student Professional Associations

Many college students belong to the Student National Education Association, and many high school students belong to the Future Teachers of America. From 1937 to 1957 the name "Future Teachers of America" referred to both the high school and college groups. Since that time the high school organization has been known as the FTA and the college organization as the Student NEA. Student NEA is designed for college students preparing to teach, and FTA clubs are for high school students exploring teaching as a career.

In 1971 there were more than 250,000 high school students in 6,000 FTA clubs and more than 83,000 college students in 1,000 campus chapters of the Student NEA [75:118&131]. The Student NEA seeks to:

... develop in education students an understanding of the education profession to provide for a national student voice in matters affecting their education and their profession, to influence the conditions under which prospective teachers are prepared, and to stimulate the highest ideals of professional ethics, standards, attitudes, and training. The overall program strives to encourage its members to serve as change agents in the arena of teacher education, education more generally, society, and the profession.

Continuing SNEA programs include teacher education reform; minority education; political awareness (particularly in securing voter registration and political education); educational volunteer service, a student internship program at the NEA Center; local, state, and national programs to strengthen student governance, organizationally, in teacher education programs; and providing a national voice for education students about matters affecting them.

The FTA offers an opportunity to encourage the finest young men and women in high schools to enter the teaching profession. The official purposes of the FTA are as follows [75:130]:

To provide a means for secondary school students (a) to participate in making their education increasingly relevant to their present and future needs and (b) to engage in realistic education activities that are of assistance in making valid decisions about education careers. Among FTA's many activities are summer conferences (including the National FTA College and Career Seminar), and political and educational participation experiences.

Special attention is given to strengthening the relationship between local FTA chapters and local associations.

In 1969 the SNEA-FTA was made an NEA project with a special committee named to restudy the goals, structure, and administration of the organizations; to assess students' perceived needs; and to provide an organizational design which would provide for student self-determination. This pattern would identify mutually beneficial relationships between the student groups and the parent body [74:104]. Thus major changes in these organizations are occurring.

American Federation of Teachers

An increasingly important organization for all levels of classroom teachers in American education is the American Federation of Teachers (AFT), an affiliate of the American Federation of Labor-Congress of Industrial Organizations. The AFT originated in 1916 and, until the merger of the AFL and the CIO in 1955, it was affiliated with the AFL. *American Teacher* is the official monthly newspaper of the AFT, and *Changing Education* is the quarterly professional journal.

The AFT has experienced an appreciable increase in membership in the past 20 years, especially in some of our biggest cities, such as New York, Chicago, Detroit, Philadelphia, Cleveland, Baltimore, Pittsburgh, Boston, and Washington, D.C. Some of the reasons behind this increase include the success of the AFT in negotiating contracts for teachers, calling for substantial salary increases and improvements in working conditions. In 1971 the total membership was nearly 250,000 in 1,000 local organizations. The membership of the AFT is centered almost entirely in the large cities and in the suburban areas which surround these cities. AFT groups are rarely found in rural areas.

The long-range objectives of the American Federation of Teachers, as stated in its constitution, are [55:10]:

(1) to bring associations of teachers into relations of mutual assistance and cooperation; (2) to obtain for them all the rights to which they are entitled; (3) to raise the standards of the teaching profession by securing the conditions essential to the best professional service; (4) to promote such a democratization of the schools as will enable them to better equip their pupils to take their places in the industrial, social, and political life of the community; and (5) to promote the welfare of the childhood of the nation by providing progressively better educational opportunity for all.

More specifically, the AFT has promoted integration within the schools, supporting the idea of equal educational opportunities for all. It has instigated special programs, such as the More Effective Schools Program in New York City, geared to providing improved educational opportunities for inner-city youth. It has opposed any form of a merit-rating salary plan as educationally unsound. More recently it has launched a national campaign against what is called "educational gimmickry" such as performance contracting, voucher plans, and differentiated staffing [82:2].

The action program of the AFT lists the following goals [40:4–11]:

Collective bargaining goal: Recognition of the right of teachers and other non-supervisory educational employees to negotiate written agreements with their school boards through organizations of their own choice. Such agreements should cover salaries, fringe benefits, working conditions, and all other matters of interest to teachers. They should include strong grievance procedures for enforcement of the terms of the agreement and for the elimination of inequities suffered by individuals.

Collective action goal: To develop techniques of collective action which give teachers the power to make collective bargaining meaningful.

Salaries goal: To establish fully automatic salary schedules, free from "merit" rating requirements, which adequately reflect the professional status of teachers.

Tenure goal: State legislation protecting teachers from discharge except for proper cause, after a limited probationary period, and establishing impartial procedures guaranteeing a fair hearing and due process of law in the event charges are made against any teacher or other professional school employee.

Professional standards goal: To guarantee that any person employed as a teacher meet professional standards of education, practical training, and performance ability.

Fringe benefits goal: To establish sick leave, health insurance and other group benefits for teachers and other nonsupervisory employees equal to those enjoyed by employees in private industry and in public employment on the state and federal levels.

Retirement goal: To permit teachers to retire after 25 years of service on a retirement allowance which permits them to look forward to a life of dignity and comfort.

20/20 vision for teachers goal: Modern, properly equipped classrooms; limitation of maximum class sizes to no more than 20 pupils (and fewer in special and "difficult" classes); no more than 20 classroom periods a week; and complete relief from nonteaching chores such as keeping clerical records, supervising buses, lunchrooms, and playgrounds.

Handling student behavior problems goal: To establish an orderly, cooperative climate in the school so that student behavior problems are minimal, with a clearly understood policy of support for teachers by administrators, and proper procedures and facilities for handling students with chronic behavior problems.

Equal opportunity for all children goal: To give every child a good education in spite of any environmental or other handicaps which may inhibit his ability and desire to learn.

Vocational education goal: To develop a system of trade, technical, and business education which will provide young people with new skills, or enhance their present skills, to increase their productivity, economic status, and self-esteem.

Textbooks, teaching materials, and curriculum goal: Full teacher participation in selection of textbooks and materials as well as in curriculum planning and revision.

Teachers as citizens goal: To mobilize the civic power of teachers, in cooperation with organized labor and other liberal forces, in order to bring about the social reforms necessary to eliminate poverty and build a hopeful and progressive society.

Academic freedom goal: To protect the rights of teachers to use their professional judgment in selecting materials to be used in their teaching, in conducting discussions of controversial issues, and in presenting the basic facts about our nation and world.

Higher education goal: To establish a system of free college education for all students who wish to avail themselves of the opportunity, and to ensure rights and benefits for college teachers appropriate to their professional status.

The AFT is an organization for classroom teachers only. School superintendents, principals, and other administrators at or above the rank of principal are not admitted to membership in the AFT. Within the AFT the councils on educational problems include The National Council for Effective Schools, The National Council on Teacher-Supervisory Relationships, and The National Council on Professional Standards. As in the

NEA there may be Student Federations of Teachers chartered on college or university campuses, and a similar group may be chartered in a high school through application of the sponsoring local union of the AFT [55:14].

Although affiliated with the AFL-CIO, the AFT is a legal entity in its own right. It need not join the AFL-CIO in any specific action. The AFT sees itself "first and foremost a union seeking benefits and improved working conditions for its members. But it is also an educational organization, deeply committed to improving the quality of schools at all levels. Finally, the AFT is a social force, working with other unions to improve the quality of American life" [40:11].

International Educational Organizations

As the nations of the world grow closer together, educators find that they have many common interests. In the first place it is the desire of the free world to have peace and security. The best way to ensure this peace and security is through the development of international understanding, which is a crucial task confronting teachers throughout the world. In the second place, because of the increasing relatedness of nations today, the welfare of the teachers in any nation becomes the concern of teachers in all other nations. For these reasons efforts have been made to develop an organization for the educators of all nations.

The World Confederation of Organizations of the Teaching Profession was established in 1952 as a result of a merger of various international organizations, including the World Organization of the Teaching Profession which originally had been founded in 1946 at the invitation of the National Education Association. The organization consolidates teachers in ninety countries engaged in elementary, secondary, and higher education in order to "promote education for international understanding, material and moral rights and interests of the teaching profession, improvement of educational policy and practice, and representation of the profession in the international aspects of educational policy" [74:324].

UNESCO (United Nations Educational, Scientific, and Cultural Organization) was created in 1945 by the United Nations. According to the constitution of UNESCO, its purpose is "to contribute to peace and security by promoting collaboration among the nations through education, science, and culture in order to further universal respect for justice, for the rule of law and for the human rights and fundamental freedoms which are affirmed for the peoples of the world, without distinction of race, sex, language, or religion, by the charter of the United Nations."

Within the framework of these purposes, UNESCO has engaged in many different types of activities. Those most closely related to education have included the organizing of educational missions to assist under-developed countries, the dissemination of educational materials, the holding of international conferences and seminars, the planning of programs of fundamental education to combat illiteracy, the promotion of international understanding, and the carrying on of research in world educational problems.

Other Education Associations

The *Education Directory,* issued regularly each year by the U.S. Office of Education, lists many national, regional, and state educational associations in addition to the few that have already been discussed. A good share of these are designed to meet the needs of various specialized groups of educators. Some of them are departments of the NEA, but many others are not.

Elementary school teachers usually become members of an association such as the Association for Childhood Education International (ACEI), which is concerned with the education of children from 2 to 12 years of age. Most elementary teachers are interested in becoming members of the American Association of Elementary-Kindergarten-Nursery Educators, a national affiliate of the NEA. Each subject area in the high school has its own national association, such as the National Council for the Social Studies, and the National Council of the Teachers of Mathematics. The NEA *Handbook* contains essential information about each of the NEA departments, such as historical background, activities, names of national officers, and the amount of regular and student dues.

Curriculum supervisors and consultants usually become members of the national association in their subject area and the Association for Supervision and Curriculum Development (ASCD). Principals and superintendents usually become members of the National Association of Elementary School Principals (NAESP), the National Association of Secondary School Principals (NASSP), or the American Association of School Administrators (AASA). College and university professors in the field of education may join various specialized groups such as the National Society for the Study of Education, The John Dewey Society, The American Educational Research Association, and the American Association of University Professors.

The associations mentioned in this section are only a few of those in the field of education. The important point is that for every position and interest, there is a professional association composed of persons holding that position and sharing that interest. Furthermore, it is the journals and yearbooks of these associations that provide much of the professional literature in education.

Honorary Educational Associations

Professional and honorary groups in education include Pi Lambda Theta (for women) and Phi Delta Kappa (for men), or Kappa Delta Pi (for both men and women).

Pi Lambda Theta is open to undergraduate and graduate women students and women faculty members who meet the necessary qualifications. General qualifications include evidence of high professional standards, qualities of leadership, and ability to live and work with others. In addition, there are more specific requirements for both student and faculty eligibility for membership. The specific purposes are to:

recognize women of superior scholastic achievement and high potential for professional leadership; foster creativity and academic excellence at all educational levels; support, extend, and interpret the function of education in a democracy; demonstrate the power of competence in the body of knowledge unique to the profession; stimulate, conduct, and utilize research; accept responsibility for evaluation and improvement of the profession of teaching; contribute to the solution of educational, social, and cultural problems of national and international concern; and promote professional fellowship and cooperation as a means of positive action [99:i].

Membership in Phi Delta Kappa is by chapter invitation to male graduate or undergraduate students who have completed at least 90 semester hours toward the baccalaureate degree, who give promise of success in a professional career in education, and who will contribute to the purposes of Phi Delta Kappa. Additional requirements include 15 semester hours of courses in education, scholarship acceptable for admission to candidacy for a graduate degree, and commitment to a life career in educational service.

The chief purpose of Phi Delta Kappa shall be to promote free public education as an essential to the development and maintenance of a democracy, through the continuing interpretation of the ideals of research, service and leadership. It shall be the purpose of Phi Delta Kappa to translate these ideals into a program of action appropriate to the needs of public education [59:n.p.].

Membership dues in the organization includes a subscription to the *Phi Delta Kappan,* which is published monthly, October through June of each year. This journal carries many articles, reviews, and features of special interest to educators.

Kappa Delta Pi is open to both men and women and is composed of outstanding junior and senior undergraduates, graduate students, and faculty members. In addition to the functions commonly performed by honorary educational organizations, Kappa Delta Pi has contributed to the general cause of education by issuing several significant publications. These publications include *The Educational Forum, The Kappa Delta Pi Lecture Series,* and the *Kappa Delta Pi Research Publications.*

These honorary educational associations exert positive influences upon the profession. Membership is highly regarded and provides an opportunity for outstanding educators to join forces in worthy causes.

Parent-Teacher Association

An opportunity for parents and teachers to work together effectively on both local and national levels is provided through the Parent-Teacher Association. Teachers are usually expected to take an active part in this association in those communities where it is established. All official local PTA groups are members of their state congress and of the National Congress of Parents and Teachers. The objects of this group of nearly 12 million members are as follows [86:i]:

To promote the welfare of children and youth in home, school, church, and community.

To raise the standards of home life.

To secure adequate laws for the care and protection of children and youth.

To bring into closer relation the home and the school, that parents and teachers may cooperate intelligently in the training of the child.

To develop between educators and the general public such united efforts as will secure for every child the highest advantages in physical, mental, social, and spiritual education.

In most communities the PTA takes its work seriously, studies its problems realistically, and wields tremendous power in shaping trends toward better schooling. Unfortunately, some teachers feel that PTA work requires too much of their time. Some administrators feel that it provides another unnecessary opportunity for people to meddle in school affairs.

In most PTA groups, mothers far exceed fathers in number. Many PTAs fail to reach those parents in the community when response would be most advantageous to themselves, to their children, and to the improvement of the instructional program in school. These are typical problems which, through planning, hard work, and cooperation on the part of parents and school people, have been largely solved in individual communities.

As indicated in the organizational diagram, Figure 6-5, the National Education Association recognizes the value of the PTA through a joint committee of the NEA and National Congress of Parents and Teachers. *The PTA Magazine* has won the School Bell Award of the National School Public Relations Association for distinguished service in the interpretation of education.

Within the past decade or so, in some school districts where parents and teachers have preferred not to affiliate with a national organization but have wished to retain a cooperative group that would work for better schools and in the best interest of boys and girls, the Parent-Teacher Organization (PTO) or the Parent-Teacher-Student Organization (PTSO) has replaced the PTA.

Code of Ethics for the Teaching Profession

Besides joining and working earnestly to promote the purposes of various professional organizations, every teacher is expected to conduct himself and manage his work affairs in such ways as are approved by the profession at large. Should a teacher tutor his own students for pay? Should a teacher leave a position suddenly in the middle of a semester? Is it legitimate for a teacher to make speeches in his classroom favoring his political party?

The acceptable modes of behavior along these lines, and many others, are well established in a professional code of ethics. Medical doctors have such a code, lawyers have one, and teachers also have one. These codes are not legal enactments; nevertheless, they are definite and well understood by the great body of the profession. A prospective teacher should become well acquainted with the code of ethics of the teaching group.

The NEA has spent a great amount of time and effort in developing and revising the Code of Ethics of the Education Profession. It is designed to be acceptable to all workers in education in all parts of the nation. The first national code of ethics for teachers was adopted by the NEA in 1929 and revised in 1941, 1952, 1963, and 1968. The most recent revision is presented below [75:105–107]:

PREAMBLE

The educator believes in the worth and dignity of man. He recognizes the supreme importance of the pursuit of truth, devotion to excellence, and the nurture of democratic citizenship. He regards as essential to these goals the protection of freedom to learn and to teach and the guarantee of equal educational opportunity for all. The educator accepts his responsibility to practice his profession according to the highest ethical standards.

The educator recognizes the magnitude of the responsibility he has accepted in choosing a career in education, and engages himself, individually and collectively with other educators, to judge his colleagues, and to be judged by them, in accordance with the provisions of this code.

PRINCIPLE I

Commitment to the Student

The educator measures his success by the progress of each student toward realization of his potential as a worthy and effective citizen. The educator therefore works to stimulate the spirit of inquiry, the acquisition of knowledge and understanding, and the thoughtful formulation of worthy goals.

In fulfilling his obligation to the student, the educator—

1. Shall not without just cause restrain the student from independent action in his pursuit of learning, and shall not without just cause deny the student access to varying points of view.
2. Shall not deliberately suppress or distort subject matter for which he bears responsibility.
3. Shall make reasonable effort to protect the student from conditions harmful to learning or to health and safety.
4. Shall conduct professional business in such a way that he does not expose the student to unnecessary embarrassment or disparagement.
5. Shall not on the ground of race, color, creed, or national origin exclude any student from participation in or deny him benefits under any program, nor grant any discriminatory consideration or advantage.
6. Shall not use professional relationships with students for private advantage.
7. Shall keep in confidence information that has been obtained in the course of professional service, unless disclosure serves professional purposes or is required by law.
8. Shall not tutor for remuneration students assigned to his classes, unless no other qualified teacher is reasonably available.

PRINCIPLE II

Commitment to the Public

The educator believes that patriotism in its highest form requires dedication to the principles of our democratic heritage. He shares with all other citizens the responsibility for the development of sound public policy and assumes full political and citizenship responsibilities. The educator bears particular responsibility for the development of policy relating to the extension of educational opportunities for all and for interpreting educational programs and policies to the public.

In fulfilling his obligation to the public, the educator—

1. Shall not misrepresent an institution or oganization with which he is affiliated, and shall take adequate precautions to distinguish between his personal and institutional or organizational views.
2. Shall not knowingly distort or misrepresent the facts concerning educational matters in direct and indirect public expressions.
3. Shall not interfere with a colleague's exercise of political and citizenship rights and responsibilities.
4. Shall not use institutional privileges for private gain or to promote political candidates or partisan political activities.
5. Shall accept no gratuities, gifts, or favors that might impair or appear to impair professional judgment, nor offer any favor, service, or thing of value to obtain special advantage.

PRINCIPLE III

Commitment to the Profession

The educator believes that the quality of the services of the education profession directly influences the nation and its citizens. He therefore exerts every effort to raise professional standards, to improve his service, to promote a climate in which the exercise of professional judgment is encouraged, and to achieve conditions which attract persons worthy of the trust to careers in education. Aware of the value of united effort, he contributes actively to the support, planning, and programs of professional organizations.

In fulfilling his obligation to the profession, the educator—

1. Shall not discriminate on the ground of race, color, creed, or national origin for membership in professional organizations, nor interfere with the free participation of colleagues in the affairs of their association.
2. Shall accord just and equitable treatment to all members of the profession in the exercise of their professional rights and responsibilities.
3. Shall not use coercive means or promise special treatment in order to influence professional decisions of colleagues.
4. Shall withhold and safeguard information acquired about colleagues in the course of employment, unless disclosure serves professional purposes.
5. Shall not refuse to participate in a professional inquiry when requested by an appropriate professional association.
6. Shall provide upon the request of the aggrieved party a written statement of specific reason for recommendations that lead to denial of increments, significant changes in employment, or termination of employment.
7. Shall not misrepresent his professional qualifications.
8. Shall not knowingly distort evaluations of colleagues.

PRINCIPLE IV

Commitment to Professional Employment Practices

The educator regards the employment agreement as a pledge to be executed both in spirit and in fact in a manner consistent with the highest ideals of professional service. He believes that sound professional personnel relationships with governing boards are built upon personal integrity, dignity and mutual respect. The educator discourages the practice of his profession by unqualified persons.

In fulfilling his obligation to professional employment practices, the educator—

1. Shall apply for, accept, offer, or assign a position or responsibility on the basis of professional preparation and legal qualifications.
2. Shall apply for a specific position only when it is known to be vacant, and shall refrain from underbidding or commenting adversely about other candidates.
3. Shall not knowingly withhold information regarding a position from an applicant, or misrepresent an assignment or conditions of employment.
4. Shall give prompt notice to the employing agency of any change in availability of service, and the employing agent shall give prompt notice of change in availability or nature of a position.
5. Shall adhere to the terms of a contract or appointment, unless these terms have been legally terminated, falsely represented, or substantially altered by unilateral action of the employing agency.
6. Shall conduct professional business through channels, when available, that have been jointly approved by the professional organization and the employing agency.
7. Shall not delegate assigned tasks to unqualified personnel.
8. Shall permit no commercial exploitation of his professional position.
9. Shall use time granted for the purpose for which it is intended.

Enforcement of the Code of Ethics

Most states and local school systems have adopted the NEA code or, in some cases, have established their own codes of ethics. The Professional Ethics Committee of the NEA is responsible for the development and interpretation of the code and provides materials and assistance to the ethics committees of state and local associations in their activities and studies [24:4].

Enforcement of the code of ethics is the responsibility of the Commission on Professional Rights and Responsibilities of the NEA. It is also concerned with the defense of teachers and schools against unjust attack, development of professional personnel policies, tenure legislation, civil and human rights of the teaching profession, information regarding persons and groups criticizing and opposing education, and unethical conduct of members of the teaching profession [75:158–159]. However, serious questions have been raised about the willingness of the profession to enforce the code. Has the education profession done as good a job of policing itself as has the American Medical Association or the American Bar Association?

Future of the Profession

Teachers and the teaching profession have come far in achieving better salaries and salary schedules, better working conditions, greater professional recognition, greater prestige and status—both locally and nationally —and improved quality of service rendered to students and communities. These accomplishments have been achieved largely through the efforts of many, many dedicated teachers working through organized groups on the local, state, and national levels.

In recent years a spirit of greater militancy has been apparent in the efforts of teachers, including those representing the NEA as well as those representing the American Federation of Teachers of the AFL-CIO. In achieving professional goals, the terms "professional negotiations," "professional sanctions," and "withdrawal of services" have come into common use within the teaching profession, just as the terms "collective bargaining" and "strike" have been associated with labor for many years and are still associated with the AFT.

It is interesting to follow the dramatic change in opinion among teachers concerning the right to strike. In the period from 1965 to 1970, the percentage of teachers answering "yes" to an Opinion-Poll question, "Do you believe public school teachers should ever strike?" rose from 53 per cent to 73 per cent [134:27]. In 1960–1961 there were three strikes, and in 1969–1970 there were 180, with a total of 500 for the ten-year period [135:69]. Both the AFT and the NEA have official statements of policy concerning "withdrawal of services" and "work stoppages."

Within the past decade "professional negotiation" and "collective bargaining" have become a way of life for educators in many, many school districts. Points of view within the profession concerning the long-range accomplishments of these procedures range from the most optimistic to severely pessimistic. The optimistic view holds that it is only through these processes that the profession can realistically approach and solve its problems. The pessimistic view holds that short-range gains have been achieved at the expense of community understanding of, and sympathy for, school problems; that the processes establish an adversary relationship between teachers and administrators at a time when unity is tremendously important; and that long-range gains will not be any greater than they would have been without negotiations and bargaining. In view of the time-consuming element of the processes, for both school boards and teachers, it has been suggested that the next step may be negotiations at the state level [76:9].

In many communities, teachers have asked to decide by vote which group—the teachers association or the union—shall represent them before the school board. The AFT has had its greatest comparative success in the large cities where unionism has long been powerful, although there are many exceptions even here. The NEA has continued to show its great national strength in small cities, rural areas, and in entire states, for example, Utah, Oklahoma, and Washington. The first statewide professional negotiation law was passed in the state of Wisconsin in 1962.

A negotiation or bargaining agreement in a local school district may be quite simple and brief, or it may be quite complicated and detailed. The general trend is for agreements to become longer and more detailed as they are renegotiated. At any rate a typical agreement may contain sections on recognition and definitions, fair practices, integrated education, school calendar, class size, school day, discipline, report-card marks, parent-teacher conferences, personnel assignments, teacher competence, substitutes, leave policy, insurance, improvement of program, improvement of facilities, and grievance procedures [1:iv].

Principals, who are part of the management of schools but who in most cases continue to think of themselves as teachers, have sought to counsel both sides. For example, the National Association of Secondary School Principals [25:11–12]:

emphasizes that discussions and decisions on purely professional problems cannot be considered in an atmosphere characteristic of the bargaining table. It proposes instead that such considerations take place in an atmosphere of colleagues working together as a professional team. It welcomes the establishment of formal councils made up of representatives chosen by teachers, principals, and supervisors. . . . Such councils can evoke a partnership rather than an adversary relationship. They can encourage the search for solutions rather than victories.

The National Association of Elementary School Principals at its 1970 convention adopted much the same position. They did not wish to stand with either superintendents or teachers but to be "expert witnesses" who will advise both sides about the "educational and management consequences of decisions under consideration" [22:201].

The achievement of professional goals and the question concerning agencies and procedures through which to achieve those goals represent a complex problem. Although there are proponents of extreme points of view, there are also those who attempt to bring about agreement, even to the extent of a merger of the NEA and the AFT. It has become obvious that the major organizational issues which have historically divided the NEA and the AFT—membership of administrators and AFT affiliation with the AFL-CIO—are no longer so divisive [64:139–140]. In fact, the two organizations have merged on the local level in Flint, Michigan (1969), and in Los Angeles, California (1970). Although many problems still exist, it seems reasonable to anticipate a national merger between the two groups.

Another major problem, alluded to earlier in this chapter, which faces the education profession today is that of accountability. A number of educators feel that "self-governance" is essential before members of the profession are held accountable for educational outcomes—for what students learn. As Bain points out [4:413]:

. . . it is pure myth that classroom teachers can ever be held accountable, with justice, under existing conditions. The classroom teacher has either too little control or no control over the factors which might render accountability either feasible or fair.

As a beginning, the teaching profession must be afforded those legal rights necessary for it to assume responsibility and accountability for its own professional destiny. At a minimum, this includes transferring to the profession the following: (1) authority over issuing, suspending, revoking, or reinstating the legal licensure of educational personnel; (2) authority to establish and administer standards of professional practice and ethics for all educational personnel; (3) authority to accredit teacher preparation institutions; and (4) authority to govern in-service and continuing education for teachers.

One approach to accountability about which both NEA and AFT are justifiably concerned is performance contracting, in which a school district contracts with a private organization to perform instructional tasks. Teacher groups fear that widespread adoption of this concept may have an adverse effect on the overall quality of educational programs and turn professional teachers into mere teaching technicians, with little or no effective voice in policy and decision making.

SUMMARY

The advancement of teaching as a profession depends in great degree upon the vigorous work of professional organizations and their members. An individual teacher can contribute most to the profession by assuming an active role in one or more of the many organizations—striving to improve the status, conditions, and effectiveness of the profession.

Within the field of education there are professional organizations that are geographic in scope—local, state, regional, and national. There are organizations based on types of duties—teaching, counseling, supervision, and administration. There are organizations based on subject-matter specialties, and there are organizations that are comprehensive in nature and include all these types.

Teachers need to support one another and to work together cooperatively for the good of their schools and their pupils. Joining forces in professional organizations of various sorts, studying their purposes and procedures, and playing a responsible part in those groups is one way of accomplishing the necessary cooperation. To be effective, a teacher should take an active role in especially the local and state organizations, and at least maintain active membership in one or more national organizations that are most appropriate to his area of work.

One of the distinctive characteristics of a profession is a clearly formulated code of ethics to which its members adhere. Therefore, there is a moral obligation for a teacher to be familiar with, to respect, and to adhere to the Code of Ethics of the Teaching Profession, and to expect and insist that his colleagues do likewise. The status of the profession will grow as its membership becomes disciplined in terms of a code of ethics.

During the past several years, teachers have assumed a much more aggressive role in improving conditions within the profession. The complaints are many—inadequate salaries, few fringe benefits, heavy teaching loads, community pressures, lack of teaching materials and supplies, excessive nonteaching duties, lack of support in handling discipline problems, lack of decision-making participation in curriculum planning, arbitrary dismissals, lack of personal protection especially in inner-city situations, inadequate provision for minority groups—the list is long. This is one of the reasons why the NEA and the AFT urge teachers to become active within the profession and within the local community, state, and nation.

This is a time of critical decisions for teachers and the teaching profession. This is a time for teachers to work together in achieving greater autonomy for the profession, and in improving conditions within the profession so that the mission of our public school system may be more effectively realized. Decisions made in the next few years will determine the course of American education and the role of teaching as a profession for many years to come.

QUESTIONS TO CONSIDER

1. In your opinion, what should be the characteristics of a profession?
2. How does teaching as a profession differ from other professions such as medicine and law? How are they similar?
3. How do you account for teaching frequently not being accorded professional status? How might this condition be corrected?
4. What are the chief differences between the NEA and the AFT with respect to policies, services, and potential contributions to the improvement of education in the United States? In what ways are they similar? How would you justify joining one or the other?

5. Why should a teacher be expected to give some of his time to the profession itself?
6. Should teachers be required to join one or more professional organizations? Why?
7. There are many opportunities today for teaching abroad. What values usually come to the teacher who participates in such a program? What special responsibilities does he have?
8. Why do you suppose the Parent-Teacher Association has usually been more successful at the elementary level than at the secondary level?
9. What are the differences between professional negotiation and collective bargaining and between sanctions and strikes?
10. What procedures may the teaching profession ethically use in attempting to gain higher salaries and better working conditions?
11. What should be the role of teachers, principals, superintendents, and school boards in professional negotiation as well as in collective bargaining?
12. What are the values of a code of ethics for you as a teacher?
13. Consider the teachers whom you have had. To what extent did they seem to be aware of a code of ethics? To what extent did they seem to practice the provisions of this code?
14. Who should speak for the profession of teaching? Why?
15. How can you reconcile autonomy for the teaching profession and local control of schools?
16. What kind of provisions should the NEA and the AFT make to assure active involvement of racial and ethnic groups?
17. What are the pros and cons of teacher strikes?

PROBLEM SITUATION FOR INQUIRY

When the time came for salary negotiations, it became obvious that the school board was going to ask the teachers to "hold the line" for another year. But the teachers had already held the line for two straight years, and therefore it seemed that a work stoppage or strike was imminent. Phil Jones had strong reservations about the ethics of teacher strikes. He was aware of the need for salary increases because his personal budget was being taxed by inflation as much as anyone else's. He also was aware of his responsibility to the teaching profession, realizing that higher salaries might attract better teachers and encourage experienced teachers to decline lucrative offers outside teaching. Furthermore, he felt the need for supporting his fellow teachers. Still, Phil felt a deep responsibility to the pupils in his classes. Striking and closing the schools, he believed, would hinder the educational progress of the students. Since teacher strikes are illegal in the state in which Phil teaches, he also felt that breaking the law would set a poor example for his students.

If you were Phil, what would you do? Why?

ACTIVITIES TO PURSUE

1. Attend one or more local and state teachers' meetings. Make a careful study of the problems discussed and the values gained by teachers as a result of these meetings.
2. Learn about your campus chapter of the Student National Education Association. Secure information concerning its major purposes and its program.
3. Arrange a panel to discuss the meaning and value of a professional code of ethics. If possible include on the panel a clergyman, a medical doctor, a lawyer, an engineer, and a school superintendent.
4. Have a superintendent of schools or a principal discuss infractions of the Code of Ethics of the Teaching Profession which he has observed. Discuss with him how such infractions might be avoided in the future.

5. Watch the newspapers for a month for all NEA and AFT news releases. Try to classify the items as to types and purposes.
6. Invite representatives of various honorary groups in the teaching profession to explain the purposes and programs of their organizations.
7. Spend some time in the library examining the journals published by the various professional organizations. Make a list of those that may prove to be especially helpful to you when you begin teaching.
8. Discuss with a legislator how teachers might be more effective in improving conditions confronting teachers.
9. Formulate a plan of action on how you will proceed to enhance the teaching profession.

FIGURE CREDITS

FIGURE 6–1. (*Source: Milestones in Teacher Education and Professional Standards*, National Education Association, National Commission on Teacher Education and Professional Standards, Washington, 1970, p. 9, and data from "Highest Degrees Held by Teachers," *NEA Research Bulletin*, vol. 49, no. 2, National Education Association, Research Division, Washington, May, 1971, p. 56.)

FIGURE 6–2. (*Source:* "Profile of the American Public School Teacher, 1966," *NEA Journal*, vol. 56, no. 5, National Education Association, Washington, May, 1967, p. 15.)

FIGURE 6–3. (*Source:* "Profile of the American Public School Teacher, 1966," *NEA Journal*, vol. 56, no. 5, National Education Association, Washington, May, 1967, p. 12.)

FIGURE 6–4. (*Source:* Data from *Milestones in Teacher Education and Professional Standards*, National Education Association, National Commission on Teacher Education and Professional Standards, Washington, 1970, p. 27.)

FIGURE 6–5. (*Source: NEA Handbook for Local, State, and National Associations*, National Education Association, Washington, September, 1971, p. 18.)

7 | LEGAL LIABILITIES AND RESPONSIBILITIES OF TEACHERS

As we experience increases in population, in levels of educational attainment, in the complexity of society, and in concern for our health, education, and welfare, it is to be expected that lawyers and our courts will be busier than ever before. There is a tendency for the average citizen today to be more sensitive to legal affairs than he has been in the past. This tendency extends to students and their parents in their relationships with the schools.

We read frequently of lawsuits being filed against medical doctors and people in the other professions. Today teachers are sometimes the subjects of lawsuits brought by parents and other individuals. As is true in the other professions, it is highly probable that the frequency of lawsuits against teachers will increase in the future.

It is unfortunate that, as a general rule, teachers are woefully uninformed about their legal rights and responsibilities. Physicians, for example, normally receive courses in medical jurisprudence as a part of their professional education. Prospective teachers generally are not given a comparable type of instruction. It is also true that the work of a teacher, which normally does not involve the life-or-death responsibilities assumed so frequently by physicians, does not tend to stimulate an acute consciousness of the legal hazards involved in teaching. In planning a career in teaching, it is important to become familiar with the legal rights and responsibilities of teachers.

This chapter is much too brief to analyze all aspects of the law as it affects teachers. Problems of teacher contracts, tenure, strikes and collective bargaining, and retirement will be discussed in subsequent chapters. The reading list at the end of the chapter suggests numerous other resources which might be utilized for further study of these and other areas of legal concern.

An attempt is made here to provide an acquaintance with two major aspects of the law affecting teachers—*tort liability* and *pupil con-*

trol—since these are perhaps of more significance to teachers and prospective teachers generally than are any other legal topics.

In studying the materials concerning these two aspects, keep in mind that the courts are by no means antagonistic to teachers. Even though court decisions have gone against teachers in certain situations, they generally tend to uphold the actions of teachers so long as good judgment and common sense were used. It should be kept in mind, the cases referred to are drawn from a number of different states, and strictly speaking, precedent as established by the courts in one state may not necessarily be followed by the courts in another state. It is also important to understand that the law as it affects schools is in a period of change. The concept of tort liability is being questioned by the courts, and the area of pupil control is being affected by court extension of constitutional rights such as due process to students. The cases presented here represent the status of the law at the present time. Starting from this base, the teacher and the prospective teacher must be alert to changes which affect the legal liability and responsibility of the teacher.

THE SOURCES OF THE LAW

You may already be familiar with three great decisions of the United States Supreme Court which have vitally affected the public schools—the 1954 decision requiring desegregation of the public schools (*Brown v. Board of Education,* 347 U.S. 438, 74 Sup. Ct. 686); the 1962 decision banning a state-prescribed prayer in the public schools (*Engel v. Vitale,* 370 U.S. 421, 82 Sup. Ct. 1261); and the 1969 decision extending constitutional protections to students during their attendance in school (*Tinker v. Des Moines Independent Community School District,* 393 U.S. 503, 89 Sup. Ct. 733). These great decisions illustrate one of the major sources of American law—the judicial process whereby a court considers a problem and arrives at a decision, thereby establishing or creating "law."

If the man on the street is asked where the law comes from, the following answers might be received: "The United States Congress passes laws," or "The state legislatures enact laws," or "The United States Constitution is the basis of all American law." All these statements are basically accurate but are superficial at best. It is true that the Congress and the various state legislatures enact *statutes,* or laws, which cover a multiplicity of subjects. It is also true that the federal and state constitutions provide the basic framework of American government. The federal Constitution is the basis for congressional authority, and the state constitutions provide limitations beyond which the state legislatures may not go. A basic source of American law, however, is to be found in the federal or state system of courts.

The Judicial System and Precedent

One of the most important sources of law in the Anglo-American countries is the judicial, or court, system. The courts over a period of hundreds of years in England, and later in America, have been called upon to adjudicate disputes between parties arising from situations for which no legislature or constitution has made provision. In other cases the courts have been requested to interpret the meaning of portions of the various American constitutions as well as the statutes enacted by Congress or by the state legislatures.

Over the years, then, a body of court-made law has developed which has become known as *case law,* or in a broad sense, the *common law.* In developing the common law, the courts have tended to examine earlier similar court decisions and to follow *precedent,* which can be defined as an earlier court decision which furnishes an example or authority for a later decision on a similar point of law. A study of court decisions, then, can result in an understanding of how the courts are likely to rule on many questions involving teachers and the schools.

The law has been said to be an expression of public policy, whether the source is constitutional, statutory, or judicial. When the constitution and statutes are silent (as is the case in most states in the area of corporal punishment of school pupils, for example), a court is called upon actually to legislate, to formulate law, or to express public policy in deciding the dispute which is before it.

Types of Court Action

Court action may be either *criminal* or *civil* in nature. A criminal case is initiated normally by the prosecuting attorney acting for the state against an individual who has been accused of violating the criminal statutes of the state. If guilt is proved, the penalty assessed by the court is imprisonment and/or a fine payable to the state.

A civil case is normally brought by one individual or group of individuals, known as the *plaintiff,* against another, known as the *defendant.* In a civil case, the plantiff seeks some sort of *remedy,* which may be in the form of an *injunction* (prohibiting the defendant from doing something), *mandamus* (requiring the defendant to do something), or *monetary damages* (for an injury or loss). Most cases involving teachers and the school are civil in nature.

The Appellate Court System

Legal action is initiated in a *trial court,* or *lower court,* which may be known in the various states as "circuit courts," "superior courts," "county courts," or "district courts." Following the decision of the trial court, the loser may appeal the decision to a higher court, known as an *appellate court.* The highest appellate court in the state court system is the state supreme court. This court is known by various names. For example, the highest state court in Kentucky is known as the Court of Appeals, in Connecticut it is called the Supreme Court of Errors, and in Oregon it is termed the Supreme Court. Although the decisions of trial courts normally are not published in widely disseminated law journals and books and thus are not readily available to attorneys, the decisions of appellate courts are published and are available in any adequate law library. These published appellate court decisions form the basis for precedent and vividly portray the continuing development of the common law.

Many of the cases related to students and teachers involve the enforcement of rights found in the Constitution of the United States. Such cases usually start in a Federal District Court. Appeals go to the Court of Appeals in the circuit in which the case originated and may go ultimately to the United States Supreme Court for final decision. All the decisions of the federal courts are published and form the basis for precedent.

TORT LIABILITY OF TEACHERS

A *tort* is a private or civil wrong which does not flow from breach of contract and which results in loss or damage to an individual or to his property. Perhaps the most common torts are negligence causing personal injury, trespass upon property belonging to another, maintenance of a nuisance, and defamation of character.

In most states, the state itself is immune from tort liability. A school district, as a subdivision of the state, therefore enjoys immunity in these states. Although there are a number of legal reasons for this type of immunity, perhaps the most frequently cited reason is to be found in the ancient doctrine that "the king can do no wrong." Since the state in the United States has replaced the sovereign, this doctrine has been modified to "the state can do no wrong." Other reasons given in support of state immunity are that school funds can only be spent for the educational benefit of pupils and cannot be used to pay damages for claims; and that school district officers can only act to carry out the bona fide purposes of the school and that they are not acting for the school district when they act negligently.

State immunity from tort liability, however, is slowly changing. In recent years several states, including Arizona, California, Illinois, New York, Washington, and Wisconsin, have abolished, either by statute or by court decision, the immunity of school districts under certain circumstances. The trend toward the abolishment of sovereign, or governmental, immunity of school districts appears to be continuing.

To the teacher the question of state immunity is of little significance. Teachers are classified as employees of school districts and do not enjoy immunity even in states where the school district is immune. Teachers are liable for their torts. This is important because the teacher has an almost constant relation with and responsibility to students. Thus the teacher is in a position where the chance of being involved in litigation arising from tort liability is ever present.

The Standard of Negligence

The tort which results in by far the greatest number of lawsuits involving teachers is *negligence*. Negligence has been defined as conduct involving unreasonable danger to others which should be recognized by a reasonably prudent person. Since every factual situation in which an individual may be injured as the result of the actions or conduct of another is unique, the courts through the years have established the conduct of the "reasonably prudent man" as the hypothetical standard against which the actions of the person sued are measured.

A reasonably prudent man will behave differently under different circumstances. Although the courts do not expect an individual to be clairvoyant or psychic in making certain his actions do not result in injury to others, they do require the conduct of an individual in protecting others from harm to be that of the average person under similar circumstances.

The courts require teachers to exercise a greater degree of care to protect pupils from injury than they require of the ordinary person. Perhaps it would be more accurate to say that the standard of conduct demanded of a teacher is that of the "reasonably prudent teacher."

Injuries leading to litigation and sometimes to teacher liability often arise from common factual situations such as the following:

Immediately after lunch but prior to the start of afternoon classes, a senior high school student began "slap boxing" with a friend in the school gym area while waiting for classes to resume. The "slap boxing" continued for five to ten minutes while a group of thirty students gathered to watch. During the exchange of slaps, Michael was hit, fell backwards, and fractured his skull on the asphalt paving. He died later that night.

No supervision schedule had been set up for this area, and supervision had been "left to the person in the gymnasium office." While the "slap boxing" incident was in process, the teacher "in the gym office" was eating his lunch at a desk with a wall obscuring his view of the area where Michael was injured. There were no noises heard to indicate a disturbance in the gym area just before Michael fell.

Would a court be likely to find the teacher in this situation liable for negligence?

In order to answer this question, it is perhaps necessary to examine in greater detail the tort of negligence as it applies to teachers.

Criteria for Establishing Negligence

Liability for negligence rests upon three factors: (1) a duty to act so as to protect others from unnecessary risks, (2) the failure to so act, and (3) the injury of another causing loss or damage as the result of such failure to act. A teacher may be liable either for *an act* which a reasonably prudent teacher should have realized involved an unreasonable risk of injury to another or for *failure to do an act* which the teacher was under a duty to do for the protection of another.

The major criterion used by the courts in determining negligence is *foreseeability;* that is, should the defendant as a reasonably prudent teacher have foreseen the possible harmful consequences of his action or lack of action and did he disregard these consequences? If the answer of the court is in the affirmative, liability for negligence exists.

Liability for Pupil Injury: Classroom Activities

In order to illustrate the attitude of the courts with respect to teacher negligence resulting in injury to pupils in the classroom, court decisions from several different states are summarized in the following paragraphs.

The importance of proper instruction in dangerous activities was emphasized in a California case. A chemistry teacher during a laboratory period required pupils to perform an experiment as outlined in the textbook without giving additional instruction. A pupil used the wrong chemical and an explosion occurred, resulting in pupil injury. In finding the teacher negligent, the court in 1935 stated (*Mastrangelo v. West Side Union High School District,* 42 P.2d 634): "It is not unreasonable to assume that it is the duty of a teacher of chemistry, in the exercise of ordinary care, to *instruct* students regarding the selection, mingling, and use of ingredients with which dangerous experiments are to be accomplished, rather than to merely hand them a textbook with general instruction." Italics added.)

Normally a teacher is not responsible for injuries occurring to pupils off the school grounds or after school hours. Under certain circumstances, however, the teacher may be held liable, since teachers apparently have the responsibility of warning pupils about dangerous practices which arise out of classroom activities.

In another California case pupils in an industrial arts class had been constructing model cannons made of bronze with wooden gun carriages. The teacher had given no warning to the pupils about the danger of firing the cannons at home, although the evidence indicated that he was aware that the pupils were taking the cannons home and firing them, using powder from shotgun shells as an explosive and ball bearings as projectiles. A pupil was permanently injured as the result of an explosion which occurred when he attempted to fire one of the model cannons at home. Since, as indicated previously, California is one of the states in which suit may be brought against the school district, the district was sued for the alleged negligence of the teacher. In 1963 the court held the teacher negligent and pointed out that, even though the injury to the pupil was incurred off the school grounds and after school hours, the teacher had failed in his duty to warn the pupils of the potential dangers of firing the model cannons (*Calandri v. Ione Unified School District,* 33 Cal. App.2d 333).

A teacher has a responsibility to be present in his assigned classroom to supervise pupils or to notify his principal that it is necessary for him to be absent. In New York, a teacher was not present to supervise his pupils during the first period of the day and had failed to notify school authorities that he would be absent. In the teacher's absence, the pupils began to engage in "horseplay," and one boy openly began to brandish a knife. After a period of time another pupil was stabbed.

The court, in 1962, found that the teacher was negligent and stated that, had the teacher been present in the classroom, it would have been his duty to take action to relieve the pupil of the knife (*Christofides v. Hellenic Eastern Orthodox Christian Church,* 227 N.Y.S.2d 946). In other words, the teacher, if present, should have foreseen and prevented the injury.

Negligence may be assessed for injuries resulting from the mismatching of pupils engaged in physical education activities. During a physical education class held in a school in New York in 1963, groups of boys were placed on each side of the gymnasium and given numbers chosen at random. When a number was called by the teacher, two boys at opposite sides of the floor would run to a soccer ball in the center of the room and attempt to kick it. A boy suffered serious injury as the result of being kicked by a taller and heavier opponent, and suit was brought against the school district on grounds of negligent supervision by the teacher. The court held that the "mismatching" of the two boys constituted negligence (*Brooks v. Board of Education,* 189 N.E.2d 497).

The element of foreseeability, previously mentioned, is a major factor in determining negligence. In 1956, a California teacher of drafting took his class out on the school lawn, with each pupil carrying his own drawing board. On the way out of the building, a boy picked up a knife and, when the pupils were seated on the lawn, began repeatedly to flip the knife into the grass. The teacher noticed this game of mumblety-peg but did nothing to halt it. The knife eventually glanced off a drawing board and struck a pupil in the eye, which caused permanent injury. The court, in holding the teacher negligent, pointed out that, since the teacher had been aware of the dangerous activity and since the activity had gone on for a period of time, the teacher should have foreseen the possible dangerous consequences and should have halted the activity (*Lilienthal v. San Leandro Unified School District,* 293 P.2d 889).

A study of the negligence cases involving teachers reveals that teachers who have supervised potentially hazardous activities over a long period of time frequently may be lulled into a false sense of security concerning the dangers to pupils. What is perhaps the most flagrant case involving teacher liability for negligence occurred in South Dakota in 1941 and illustrates this point. For a number of years it had been the practice to initiate high school male athletes into a club known as the "H" club by subjecting the candidates to an electric shock produced by batteries and run through a transformer to reduce the current. The high school coach secured permission from the school superintendent to use the gymnasium for the initiation. The transformer and batteries were not available that year; so the boys prepared a rheostat consisting of a jar of salt water and obtained current from a 120-volt light socket. Each boy, blindfolded and clad in shorts, was made to lie down with a glass of water in his hand on a series of bare copper wires connected to the circuit. The electricity was then turned on, which caused electric shock and resulted in the spilling of the water. Five candidates were in the process of being initiated. After each of the first three received his shock, the coach mopped the floor and tested the current with his hands. The fourth candidate complained that the shock was too great, after which one-half of the solution of salt water was removed from the rheostat and replaced with city water, presumably to reduce the current. The fifth boy then took his turn. When the electricity was turned on, he partially arose, gasped "Oh, my God," and fell backward. All attempts to revive the boy failed—the electric shock had resulted in a fatality.

Suit was brought by the parents of the boy against both the coach and the school superintendent. The coach was found negligent. The court pointed out that he should have known electricity was dangerous and that he had failed to observe the high degree of care he owed his pupils. The superintendent, on the other hand, was absolved from responsibility. The court held that the superintendent had performed his full duty when he permitted use of the gymnasium with the knowledge that the coach would be present [*DeGooyer v. Harkness,* 13 N.W.2d 815 (1944)].

Liability for Pupil Injury: The Playground

Playground or outdoor athletic activities are probably inherently more physically dangerous than most classroom activities. Teachers who are charged with the responsibility for such outdoor activities should therefore make certain that pupils are warned against unreasonable hazards and should supervise these activities very carefully.

A teacher who is given playground duty, however, is not expected by the courts to protect every pupil against every possibility of injury, since the courts will use the reasonably prudent teacher as the standard measure of conduct. For example, while a Colorado teacher was supervising a playground, a pupil threw a rock which struck another pupil in the eye. The court refused to impose liability on the teacher and stated: "There is no requirement that the teacher have under constant and unremitting scrutiny the precise spots wherein every phase of play activity is being pursued; nor is there compulsion that the general supervision be continuous and direct" [*Carroll v. Fitzsimmons,* 384 P.2d 81 (1963)].

A teacher who is given responsibility for playground supervision should be on the playground rather than be "supervising" the pupils by watching through the classroom window. In New York, for example, a six-year-old pupil climbed up and fell from a fire escape which the "supervising" teacher could not see from the classroom window, since it was located around the corner of the building. The court held that the teacher was negligent [*Miller v. Board of Education,* 50 N.E.2d 529 (1943)].

The importance of adequate safety rules for playground activity was illustrated in a California case. The school principal had been aware for some time that boys on the playground were playing a game known as

What teacher liability might be involved in this situation? *(Photograph from the National Education Association.)*

"blackout." The game consisted of one boy taking a deep breath while another squeezed him tightly from behind with the object of rendering the subject unconscious. Upon being rendered unconscious, one of the boys fell, struck his head on a concrete pavement, and was fatally injured. Suit was brought against the principal, and the court found him negligent, primarily because he had known of the practice for some time and had done nothing to stop it [*Tymkowicz v. San Jose Unified School District,* 312 P.2d 388 (1957)].

Liability for Pupil Injury: The School Patrol

Teachers are frequently required to assume general supervision of school patrol activities. When school-age pupils are called upon to shepherd other pupils across streets and highways it might be thought that the teacher selecting or supervising such patrolmen could be held liable in case of pupil injury.

Surprisingly, perhaps, there appears to be no case in courts of record dealing with teacher liability for actions of school patrolmen. Legal authorities, however, have pointed out that a teacher with the responsibility for selecting school patrolmen should make certain that the pupils selected are competent, are reliable, and are properly instructed and that the patrol activity is voluntary and engaged in with the permission of the parent (see, e.g., *Opinions of the Attorney General of Indiana,* 1929, p. 257; 1954, p. 143).

A Maryland case involving a school bus driver apparently supports the principle that the use of a school patrolman to help pupils across the street is not unreasonable. In this case the school bus driver was not found negligent when a child was injured while being escorted across a highway by a responsible older pupil who was a member of the school safety patrol. The use of a safety patrol, stated the court, was "generally regarded as a reasonable and adequate provision for the safety of school bus riders" [*Ragonese v. Hilferty,* 191 A.2d 426 (1963)].

Liability for Pupil Injury: Errands and Field Trips

A teacher should avoid sending pupils on errands off the school grounds except in cases of real emergency. Two areas of possible liability exist: (1) injury to the pupil himself, in which case a court might be called upon to determine whether a reasonably prudent teacher would send a child on such an errand, and (2) injury or damage done by the pupil to a third party or to his property, in which case a court might hold that the pupil was acting as the agent of the teacher and that the teacher was liable.

Most educational authorities agree that field trips are desirable and should be a recognized part of the curriculum. A teacher should not

Upon being confronted with this type of situation, what should a teacher do? *(Photograph by Joe Di Dio, National Education Association.)*

hesitate to take pupils on field trips because of the possibility of liability. The teacher should, however, make certain that pupils are properly protected and that dangers are minimized. The following steps are recommended:

1. Plan the trip carefully in advance.
2. If the trip is to be a visit to an industrial plant or to some other potentially dangerous place, visit the plant in advance and discuss possible hazards with the plant manager or his representative.
3. Discuss the potential hazards with the pupils who are to make the trip. Establish safety rules for the trip and inform pupils of these.
4. Obtain the permission of the school administrator who is the immediate superior.
5. Send parental permission slips home with the pupils to be signed by the parents, and returned.
6. Provide extra supervision if this seems necessary. Parents can be utilized in this role.
7. If automobiles must be used, be certain that the drivers are properly licensed and that such drivers carry adequate liability insurance in case of an accident occurring in transit.

Keep in mind that a signed parental permission slip does not relieve the teacher of liability, since one individual (even a parent) may not sign away the right of another to sue. However, parental permission slips at least inform parents about the proposed field trip, and might be used as evidence of reasonable prudence on the part of the teacher.

Strangely, perhaps, most of the lawsuits arising out of injury to pupils on school field trips have been brought against the industrial plants in which the injuries occurred. Whether the pupil was legally a licensee or an invitee has been significant in these cases. A *licensee* can be defined as one who visits the premises of another for his own benefit; an *invitee* visits the premises of another for the benefit of the owner or for the benefit of both himself and the owner. Although a plant owner owes only a normal degree of care to protect a licensee from harm, he owes a much higher degree of care to an invitee.

In a Maryland case, a class visited the plant of a traction company. The pupils were warned of the dangerous apparatus and then told to "look around" for themselves. (The teacher in charge should have ended the visit at this point.) A pupil fell into an open vat of boiling water flush with the floor in an inadequately lighted portion of the plant, and suit was brought against the traction company. The court held that since the pupils were licensees, the plant owed them only an ordinary degree of care. The pupils had entered the plant at their own risk, and therefore the injured pupil could not recover from the traction company. The court further pointed out that if any negligence existed, "it consisted in bringing thirty-odd boys at one time to a building filled with dangerous machinery." The court obviously felt that the teacher, rather than the traction company, should have been the defendant in the lawsuit [*Benson v. Baltimore Traction Company,* 26 Atl. 973 (1893)].

In a Missouri case, the court held that a pupil injured while visiting a bakery and creamery company was an invitee. The company had advertised widely and had encouraged inspection of the plant by the public. Each year, five or six classes from the local high school visited the plant. On one such visit, a girl was seriously injured when her arm became caught in an ice crusher, which later resulted in the amputation of the arm. The court held the industrial plant liable, since the invitation to the public to visit the plant was used as a part of its advertising. As an invitee, the girl was owed a much higher degree of care than ordinarily would be required, and the plant officials had failed to properly warn her of the dangerous machinery [*Gilliland v. Bondurant,* 59 S.W.2d 679 (1933)].

Liability Arising out of Cocurricular Activities

Teachers who supervise pupil activities of a cocurricular nature or activities which take place after school hours are held to the same standard of conduct as that required during school hours in the classroom. A teacher should exercise the same high degree of care in supervising such activities as is exercised during any other school activity.

Athletics is a particularly likely area for litigation. The problem is illustrated by a Louisiana case in which a football player died after being "denied" treatment for two hours after symptoms of heat stroke and shock had appeared. The high school football coaches were found negligent in this case. Administrators in the school were found not to be negligent, because they were not present at the practice and had no duty to be there [*Mogabgab v. Orleans Parish School Board,* 239 So.2d 456 (1970)]. Coaches need to be especially alert to their responsibility to provide for the safety and protection of student athletes.

The following statements summarize other problems and aspects of teacher liability with which teachers should be familiar:

1. A teacher probably has a responsibility to report to the proper authorities unsafe or deficient instructional or playground equipment.
2. Should a pupil be injured, the teacher probably has the responsibility to administer emergency first aid. One good rule to follow is that seriously injured pupils should not be moved until competent medical personnel arrive and take charge. In any case, the principal or appropriate supervisor should be notified immediately whenever a pupil is injured.
3. A teacher would not be expected by the courts to be able to diagnose every type of contagious disease with which pupils might become infected. Teachers therefore are unlikely to be held liable by a court in case a pupil contracts a disease in the classroom. However, teachers would be expected to utilize reasonable care in recommending the exclusion of pupils from the classroom if they are suspected of carrying an infectious disease.
4. Teachers are sometimes in the habit of dispensing medication, such as aspirin, to pupils who have a headache or who appear ill. A teacher should avoid giving medication to pupils. Ill pupils should be sent to the school nurse or to the school sickroom until parents can be notified. Good judgment should be used in such cases. If a pupil brings medication from home as prescribed by his family doctor, it is probably reasonable to permit the pupil to take such medication at prescribed times.

Defenses against Negligence

A number of legal defenses against negligence which relieve the teacher of liability have been rather clearly defined by the courts. The first and most common defense is, of course, a denial that any negligence exists. The person bringing suit (plaintiff) must prove negligence by proving that the conduct of the defendant fell below the standard of reasonable prudence.

A Minnesota case illustrates this defense. Suit was brought against a teacher for injuries sustained by an elementary pupil during a rope-jumping activity in a physical education class. The pupil stepped on the rope as it was being rotated, and the wooden handle affixed to one end was pulled from the grasp of the teacher. The wooden handle struck the front teeth of the pupil and caused injuries for which recovery was sought. The plaintiff maintained that the teacher should have foreseen the injury and could have prevented it by furnishing a longer rope or by providing a rope without wooden handles. The court absolved the teacher from any negligence and pointed out that the jumping rope was of the kind normally used by children for "many years" and that the teacher could not have reasonably anticipated the injury [*Wire v. Williams,* 133 N.W.2d 840 (1965)].

Contributory Negligence

In most states an individual is relieved of liability if the actions of the injured person had the effect of contributing to his own injury, and proof by the plaintiff that he had done so is known as *contributory negligence.* In recent years in such states as Arkansas, Georgia, Mississippi, Nebraska, South Dakota, and Wisconsin, the doctrine of *comparative negligence* has been gaining acceptance. In states where comparative negligence is recognized, the court seeks to "apportion the blame" between the two parties and may assess some degree of liability to the defendant even though the plaintiff contributed to his own injury.

An example of contributory negligence occurred in a North Carolina case. A chemistry teacher granted a high school boy and several classmates permission to go to the chemistry laboratory to set up a specific experiment in the absence of the instructor. Instead of performing the experiment agreed upon, the boys made gunpowder. An explosion of the gunpowder resulted in serious injury to one of the boys. As a result, a suit was brought against the teacher. The court, in relieving the teacher of liability, held that the injured boy had contributed to his own injury, and was therefore guilty of contributory negligence. "Even an eight-year-old would have known better," stated the court [*Moore v. Order of Minor Conventuals,* 267 F.2d 296 (1959)].

The giving of proper instructions can be an important factor in determining contributory negligence. In a recent case in Oregon the court held that a student who had sustained an injury while mixing potassium chlorate and powdered sugar could not recover from the teacher because the student had had full knowledge of the risk (proper instructions) and had contributed to his own injury [*Hutchinson v. Toews,* 476 P.2d 811 (1970)].

There appears to be an age below which the courts are unlikely to assess contributory negligence. In determining whether a child is guilty of contributing to his own injury, the court normally asks itself whether a child of similar years and similar mental and physical ability would reasonably be expected to protect himself from the dangers inherent in the particular situation. As may be expected, the defense of contributory negligence is less often successfully used in situations involving injuries to elementary school pupils than it is in situations involving injuries to high school pupils.

The defense of contributory negligence will be weighed carefully by the courts. In the "slap boxing" case, presented previously, it might be assumed that the courts would have been influenced by the age of the students. However, despite the fact that the students were high school seniors, the court still found the teacher negligent. The court said: "Recognizing that a principal task of supervision is to anticipate and curb rash student behavior, our courts have often held that a failure to prevent injuries caused by the intentional or reckless conduct of the victim or a fellow student may constitute negligence" [*Dailey v. Los Angeles Unified School District,* 2 C.3rd 741 (1970)].

Proximate Cause

Causal connection is a major factor considered by the courts in assessing whether negligence exists; there must be an unbroken "chain of causation" between the negligence of the teacher and the resultant pupil injury. In other words, the negligence of the defendant must be the *proximate cause* of the injury. A "break" in the chain of causation which results from the *intervening act* of a third party, for example, may mean that the court will conclude that the proximate cause of the injury was not the negligent conduct of the defendant and thus relieve the defendant of liability.

A sudden action by a pupil which causes injury to another pupil that could not have been foreseen by the teacher usually results in the court's absolving the teacher from liability. For example, a New Jersey teacher was standing outside the classroom door as two pupils came down the hall together. One of the pupils hit the other lightly on the arm. The teacher, believing that nothing more was likely to happen from this incident, entered the classroom. The second pupil then pushed the first through the classroom door, causing him to strike his foot against a metal desk, which resulted in an injury that eventually necessitated the amputation of the foot. Suit was brought against the teacher for negligence on the ground that he should have foreseen the action on the part of the second pupil. The court held that the first incident in the hall was not of a nature to reasonably attract the attention of the teacher, and therefore the injury to the first pupil was not *proximately caused* by the negligence of the teacher. Rather, the injury to the first pupil was the result of the *intervening act* of the second pupil [*Doktor v. Greenberg,* 155 A.2d 793 (1959)].

Although a teacher should not leave his classroom unsupervised, the courts have sometimes been lenient to teachers in this regard. For example, a Maryland teacher left her classroom for a few minutes while the class was engaged in calisthenics. The teacher had given proper instructions to the students for performing the exercise. An injury resulted when a nine-year-old boy failed to follow the instructions. His feet struck a nine-year-old girl, badly chipping two of her front teeth. The court held that the teacher was not liable because her absence from the classroom was not the proximate cause of the injury [*Segerman v. Jones,* 259 A.2d 794 (1969)].

Comparing the case just described with the earlier case in which one pupil stabbed another with a knife after brandishing it for a period of time may give further understanding of the reasoning of the courts in cases where the teacher is absent from the classroom. In the latter case, the court held that the teacher, if present, would have seen the knife and could have taken it from the pupil. In other words the teacher could have "foreseen" the possible injury. The court in the "chipped teeth" case evidently felt that the failure to follow instructions and the resulting injury could have occurred even if the teacher had been present. While the court did relieve the teacher of liability in the "chipped teeth" case, it should be remembered that a teacher runs a serious risk of liability if he leaves the classroom unsupervised.

Assumption of Risk

An adult who knowingly engages in a dangerous occupation or activity normally is considered by the courts to have assumed the risk of the occupation. Except in the case of gross negligence of his employer or any other person, he may not recover any compensation if he should be injured. This is known as the doctrine of the *assumption of risk.* Except in cases of athletic injuries, in which the pupil and his parents know that the activity may be physically hazardous, this doctrine is seldom used as a successful defense in cases involving the schools.

Other Reasons Assigned by Courts for Nonliability

As indicated earlier in this chapter, a court will use the reasonably prudent teacher as the standard against which the allegedly negligent conduct of a teacher is measured in a particular situation. *Proper instruction* and *due care* are terms frequently used by the courts in determining whether the teacher against whom suit is brought behaved with reasonable prudence. In New Jersey, a 14-year-old boy was injured in a physical education class while jumping over a piece of apparatus known as a "horse." The instructor had demonstrated the proper method of performing the exercise and had warned the pupils that they should not try if they felt they could not accomplish the exercise safely. The court found that the teacher had not been negligent, since he had exercised due care in warning the pupils and had properly instructed the pupils by demonstrating the exercise [*Sayers v. Ranger,* 83 A.2d 775 (1951)].

In California, an industrial arts teacher had promulgated safety rules for the automobile shop and had frequently repeated the rules to the pupils during the school year. A pupil was assigned the job of adjusting the valve tappets on an automobile. In violation of the safety rules, another pupil started the car. The vehicle, which was in gear, pinned a third pupil against the wall of the shop and caused serious injury. The evidence showed that the teacher had personally inspected the car immediately prior to the accident. The court exonerated the teacher, primarily because he had established and repeated the safety rules. Since he had used due care, he could not have foreseen the accident [*Perumean v. Wills,* 67 P.2d 96 (1937)].

Teachers should keep in mind that it is important to establish adequate *safety rules* for potentially dangerous activities.

Defamation of Character

Another tort for which teachers occasionally are sued is *defamation of character,* which may be defined as damage to a person's reputation through communication involving ridicule, disgrace, contempt, or hatred. Written defamation is known as *libel,* and spoken defamation is known as *slander.*

Teachers are involved in possible liability for defamation of character in such activities as (1) writing letters of recommendation to or talking to prospective employers or college representatives about pupils, (2) entering comments on pupil records, (3) making comments to parents or to other teachers about pupils, or (4) making public or newspaper statements concerning pupils.

Truth as a Defense

In many states truth is a defense against defamation-of-character lawsuits. Should the person against whom a suit is brought be able to prove the truth of his statements, no liability exists in these states.

In other states (and the number appears to be growing), truth is not a full defense unless it can be shown that spoken or written publication of the defamatory material is made without malice or with good intentions and justifiable ends.

Privilege as a Defense

In many instances the law excuses the publication of defamatory material under the doctrines of *absolute privilege* or *qualified privilege.* Absolute privilege is based upon the proposition that in some cases a person must be completely free to speak his mind without fear of reprisals in the form of lawsuits for libel or slander. Absolute privilege is extended to comments by judges in court proceedings, statements by legislators during legislative sessions, and comments by certain executive officers of government in the exercise of their duties. Absolute privilege is not usually extended to school personnel as a defense against defamation.

Qualified (or conditional) privilege, on the other hand, is frequently used as a defense by school personnel against whom suit is brought for defamation. Qualified privilege rests upon the assumption by the courts that certain information should be given to certain individuals or agencies in the protection of the interests of the individuals, of the agencies, or of society as a whole. The existence of qualified privilege depends upon the *reason* which exists to communicate the information. If the person to whom defamatory information is communicated has a valid reason to receive such information, the communicator may be protected by qualified privilege. Recognizing the problem that school personnel have in this area, the Indiana General Assembly, in a 1965 statute, extended to counselors immunity from disclosing "privileged or confidential communication" from pupils.

Defamation of Character: Case Examples

In California, an instructor in a teacher education institution made statements to a local newspaper that a female student was "tricky and unreliable" and "destitute of those womanly characteristics that should be the first requisite of a teacher." The court held the instructor liable for defamation of character [*Dixon v. Allen,* 11 Pac. 179 (1886)]. It is quite possible that no liability would have existed had the instructor communicated the same information to a person with *reason* to have the information, such as a prospective employer, since the teacher probably would have been protected by qualified privilege.

Teachers who report grades on school registers are normally protected so long as they report facts (or perhaps even opinions) reasonably related to the pupils' school activities. However, the limits of qualified privilege were exceeded in an Oklahoma case, where a teacher added the comment "ruined by tobacco and whisky" on the school register after the name of a pupil. The court held the teacher liable [*Dawkins v. Billingsley,* 172 Pac. 69 (1918)].

In brief, teachers have little to fear insofar as defamation of character is concerned, so long as information—even rumor or suspicion—is communicated in good faith to those having reason to possess the information. The doctrine of qualified privilege protects the teacher in such situations.

Gossip about pupils, however, is another matter. Teachers who communicate defamatory information about pupils to persons outside the school system or to other teachers who have no reason to have such information (e.g., who do not now have or who are not likely in the future to have the pupil in class) are acting imprudently, since it is possible that a successful lawsuit for defamation of character may be initiated.

Liability Insurance and Other Protection

One means of protection against judgments resulting from tort suits is liability insurance. For a relatively modest sum a teacher may obtain a personal liability insurance policy insuring him against judgments for negligence and other torts.

As is the case with most insurance policies, tort liability insurance may be secured at a lesser cost on a group basis than on an individual basis. Many state teachers' organizations are now including liability insurance as a part of their services to members. In addition, school boards in some states are empowered by law to carry liability insurance on school employees.

There is also an increasing trend whereby state legislatures have authorized or mandated school districts to provide for the legal defense and/or pay damages for employees in claims resulting from tort liability. Such provision is known as "save harmless" legislation.

PUPIL CONTROL

Large numbers of legal cases have been concerned with the extent to which a school board, a school administrator, or a teacher may establish rules setting limits on pupil conduct. In determining whether such rules are legally valid, the courts invariably attempt to determine the reasonableness of the rules, or whether the rules are reasonably related to the discipline, morale, or good order of the school. Regardless of the specific punishment incurred for violation of a school rule, a basic common-law principle established by the courts is that the rule itself must be reasonable.

Not only must a rule governing pupil conduct be reasonable; the punishment itself must also be reasonable. Punishment may not be excessive; excessive punishment is usually defined as punishment which results in permanent injury, is performed with immoderate severity, or is administered with malice or wicked motives.

Reasonable Rules

Most of the general rules governing pupil conduct, such as rules dealing with pupil dress, marriage, pregnancy, leaving of school premises, pupil driving, and membership of pupils in secret societies, are established by school boards or by school administrators pursuant to authority granted by the boards rather than by the teachers. An analysis of court decisions dealing with general rules of pupil conduct will perhaps reveal the criteria used by the courts in determining reasonableness of conduct.

The reasonableness of a rule governing pupil conduct depends upon circumstances and does not exist in the abstract. This was graphically illustrated by two cases which reached the Court of Appeals of the Fifth Federal Circuit on the same day in 1966. Both involved rules forbidding students in all-black high schools in Mississippi from wearing buttons which expressed political positions. In the one case the Court of Appeals invalidated the rule [*Burnside v. Byars,* 363 F.2d 744 (1966)]. In the other case the Court of Appeals upheld the rule [*Blackwell v. Issaquena County Board of Education,* 363 F.2d 749 (1966)]. The only significant difference in the two cases was that in the latter case the rule forbidding the wearing of buttons had been made following disturbances caused by students talking in corridors, absenting themselves from classes, and attempting to pin the buttons on other students. These differences in the two situations evidently caused the Court of Appeals to reach exactly opposite judgments regarding the reasonableness of rules which were almost identical.

Student Expression

In 1969 the Supreme Court of the United States handed down a decision of far-reaching significance regarding the free-speech rights of students. The Court invalidated a school rule forbidding the wearing of black armbands as an objection to the hostilities in Vietnam and in support of a truce. The Court ruled that the wearing of symbols such as armbands is "speech" and that students retain their rights to freedom of speech or expression while in school. Regarding the authority of schools to restrict free speech, the Court said: "undifferentiated fear or apprehension of disturbance is not enough to overcome the right to freedom of expression . . . The State must be able to show that its action was caused by something more than the desire to avoid the discomfort and unpleasantness that always accompanies an unpopular viewpoint" [*Tinker v. Des Moines Independent Community School District,* 393 U.S. 503, (1969)].

The immediacy of the free-speech issue has been demonstrated in a number of court decisions relative to the publication and distribution of student newspapers. The Court of Appeals of the Seventh Federal Circuit ruled in an Illinois case that a school could not forbid the distribution of a "literary journal" which criticized school administrators and urged other students to disregard school rules [*Scoville v. Board of Education of Joliet,* 425 F.2d 10 (1968)]. Federal courts have also held that students can distribute an underground newspaper on school grounds even though the paper is extremely critical of the school principal, so long as the distribution does not interfere with proper school activities [*Sullivan v. Houston Independent School District*, 307 F.Supp. 1328 (1969)]; that students cannot be suspended for refusing to comply with regulations that a privately printed newspaper be submitted to school administrators for approval [*Eisner v. Stamford*, 39 U.S.L.W. 2037 (1970)]; and that a school newspaper which had discussed the war in Vietnam on its editorial pages had to accept an anti-war advertisement. In the latter case the court said: "Here the school paper appears to have been open to free expression of ideas in the news and editorial columns as well as in letters to the editor. It is patently unfair in light of the free speech doctrine to close to the students the forum which they deem effective to present their ideas" [*Zucker v. Panitz*, 229 F.Supp. 102 (1969)].

The court did, in the Eisner case, recognize that students could be required to conform to reasonable regulations as to "time, exact place in school, and manner of distribution of the newspaper." That the courts are not in agreement regarding free speech and student newspapers was demonstrated by a California case in which the federal court upheld ten-day suspensions of students for distributing an off-campus newspaper containing "profanity and vulgarity" [*Baker v. Downey City Board of Education*, 307 F.Supp. 517 (1969)].

Pupil Dress and Appearance

Most of the recent court decisions regarding the dress and appearance of pupils have dealt with rules regulating the length of student hair. The federal courts are not in agreement regarding the reasonableness of such rules. Recent cases in which the federal courts have invalidated haircut regulations include: [*Griffin v. Tatum*, 425 F.2d 201 (1970)]: [*Richards v. Thurston* 424 F.2d 1281 (1970)]: [*Danhom v. Palsifer*, 312 F.Supp. 411 (1970)]: [*Sims v. Colfax Community School District*, 307 F.Supp. 485 (1970)]. Cases in which haircut regulations have been upheld include: [*Jackson v. Dorrier*, 424 F.2d 213 (1970)]: [*Brownlee v. Bradley County, Tennessee Board of Education*, 311 F.Supp. 1360 (1970)]: [*Corley v. Daunhauer*, 312 F.Supp. 811 (1970)]: [*Stevenson v. Wheeler County Board of Education*, 426 F.2d 1154 (1970)]. These cases are representative of the numerous equally conflicting decisions handed down relative to haircut regulations.

Recent decisions have also dealt with the clothing and apparel of students. In one case the student, with the parent's permission and in violation of a school rule, was suspended from school for wearing dungarees which had been neatly cleaned and pressed. The court invalidated the rule [*Bannister v. Paradis*, 316 F.Supp. 185 (1970)]. A New York court nullified a school regulation prohibiting girls from wearing slacks. The court said school regulations were "valid only to the extent they protect the safety of the wearer or prevent disturbances that interfere with school operations" [*Scott v. Board of Education*, 305 N.Y.S. 2d 701 (1969)]. In another interesting case, a court was called upon to decide when a student could wear a hat. The court ruled that a regulation forbidding the wearing of hats in the classroom was reasonable [*Hernandez v. School District No. 1. Denver*, 315 F.Supp. 289 (1970)].

The conflicting nature of court decisions regarding the dress and appearance of students is indicative of the fact that court attitudes in this area are in a period of change and transition. It is not over-generalizing to say that courts are showing an increasing concern for student rights and are demanding that school rules and regulations be limited to those directly related to the effective operation of the school. Given this trend, it would be advisable for school personnel to reexamine rules regarding the dress and appearance of students to make certain that they are based on something other than personal preference.

Payment for Destruction of School Property

Rules requiring pupils to make financial restitution for damage to or destruction of school property generally have not been upheld by the courts, especially if the damage is accidental or due to simple carelessness. An Indiana court held that a rule requiring such financial restitution was unreasonable, since "carelessness on the part of children is one of the most common, and yet one of the least blameworthy of their faults." The court went on to state that "in simple carelessness there is no purpose to do wrong" [*State v. Vanderbilt*, 18 N.E. 266 (1888)]. Courts in other states have held similar positions. [See, e.g., *Holman v. Trustees*, 43 N.W. 996 (Mich. 1889); *Perkins v. Independent School District*, 9 N.W. 356 (Iowa 1880).] The reasoning of these courts seems to be as follows: (1) Accidental damage to school property is not a breach of morals or discipline; (2) children from families of limited financial means may be denied an education illegally if required to make restitution; and (3) pupils are usually financially unable to make restitution, and if parents refuse to do so, pupils should not be punished for the failure or unwillingness of parents to make such a payment.

The courts do not look with favor upon willful or malicious destruction of school property. Although it is doubtful whether pupils may be required even in such case to pay for the damage, other kinds of punishment have been upheld by the courts, so long as such punishment is considered to be reasonable [*Palmyra Board of Education v. Hansen*, 153 A.2d 393 (N.J. 1959)].

Prohibitions concerning Leaving of School Premises

School board regulations prohibiting pupils from leaving the school grounds during the noon lunch period have generally been upheld by the courts. In Virginia, a school board rule forbade pupils to leave the school campus between 9:00 A.M. and 3:35 P.M. A parent contested the rule on the ground that he wished his child to eat a hot meal at home. The court, in upholding the school board regulation, commented that it could discover no detriment to the health of pupils resulting from the eating of a cold meal at noon [*Flory v. Smith,* 134 S.E. 360 (1926)]. Similar rules have been upheld in Michigan [*Jones v. Cody,* 92 N.W. 495 (1902)], in Kentucky—where the court felt that the regulation was for the "common good" of all the children [*Casey County Board of Education v. Luster,* 282 S.W.2d 333 (1955)], and in Texas, where the board rule prohibited pupils from "taking lunch during the noon recess except from the school cafeteria or that . . . brought from home" [*Bishop v. Houston Independent School District,* 29 S.W.2d 312 (1930)].

Pupil Driving

The increasing number of student drivers has resulted in rules by school boards prohibiting automobile driving during the noon hour. Surprisingly, perhaps, only one lawsuit bearing upon the reasonableness of such regulations has reached an appellate court in the United States.

A school board in Texas required students driving to school to park automobiles in the school parking lot in the morning and not to move the automobiles until school was dismissed in the afternoon. A girl was suspended from school for violation of the rule. The parents brought suit against the school board, contending that the board had no authority to adopt rules controlling streets and highways. The board countered with the argument that the rule had been adopted for the safety of all the pupils in the school, since there had been safety hazards created by student joyriding during the noon hour. The court upheld the school board, commenting that the rule was obviously not enacted to control traffic on streets and highways, but rather to control pupil conduct to the end that other pupils would be safe. This, according to the court, was a legitimate exercise of the power of the school board [*McLean Independent School District v. Andrews,* 33 S.W.2d 886 (1960)].

Pupil Marriages

Numerous school boards have attempted to discourage pupil marriages either by providing for the expulsion or suspension of married pupils or by prohibiting married pupils from participating in cocurricular activities. The weight of authority seems to be that pupils may not be excluded from school solely because they are married. [See, e.g., *McLeod v. State,* 122 So. 737 (Miss. 1929); *Nutt v. Board of Education,* 278 Pac. 1065 (Kans. 1929).] A Texas court even struck down a rule which provided that upon marriage a student would be suspended for three weeks following which application for readmission could be made to the principal. The court ordered two married students readmitted for "scholastic purposes" only [*Carrollton-Farmers Branch Independent School District v. Knight,* 418 S.W.2d 535 (1967)]. The reasoning of the courts in these cases can be summarized as follows: (1) Marriage is a domestic relation highly favored by the law; therefore, pupils associating with married pupils would be benefited rather than harmed; (2) the fact that married pupils might desire to further their education is evidence in itself of character warranting favorable consideration; and (3) exclusion of married pupils denies the guarantee of free public education provided in most of the state constitutions.

Although unwilling to permit the suspension of students solely because they are married, courts did, until recently, almost uniformly hold that married pupils could be excluded from cocurricular activities. [See, e.g., *Kissick v. Garland Independent School District,* 330 S.W.2d 708 (Tex. 1959); *Cochrane v. Board of Education,* 103 N.W.2d (Mich. 1960); *State ex rel. Baker v. Stephenson,* 189 N.E.2d 181 (Ohio, 1962); *Board of Directors of Independent School District of Waterloo v. Green,* 147 N.W.2d 854 (1967).] The reasoning of these courts may be summarized as follows: (1) Pupils have no "right" to participate in cocurricular activities in the same sense that they have a right to attend school; (2) cocurricular activities are not a regular part of the school program; and (3) it is reasonable to limit the activities of married pupils to the end that they will be better able to assume the responsibilities of married life.

However, recent cases indicate a developing unwillingness by the courts to accept any restrictions placed on participation of married students in school activities. In one state, Indiana, the high school athletic association suspended enforcement of a rule excluding married students from participation in interscholastic athletics. This action was taken following several lower court decisions in which the rule was held to violate the constitutional rights of married students. It may be that the time is approaching when courts will insist that married students be permitted to attend school with the same rights and privileges as their unmarried peers.

Pupil Pregnancy

The courts have seldom been called upon to rule on the question of the legality of the exclusion of pregnant pupils. However, there are at least two such cases on record. In a 1961 Ohio case, a board rule required pregnant pupils to withdraw from school "immediately upon knowledge of pregnancy." The purpose of the rule was clearly indicated by the board, i.e., to protect the physical well-being of the pregnant pupil. In addition, home instruction was provided to enable the pupil to maintain her school standing. The Ohio court upheld the rule of the school board under these circumstances [*State ex rel. Idle v. Chamberlain*, 175 N.E.2d 539 (1961)].

In a 1969 case in Mississippi, a federal court ruled that unwed mothers could not be excluded from high school solely on the basis that they were unwed. The court stated they could be excluded only if they "were so lacking in moral character they would taint the education of others" [*Perry v. Grenada Municipal Separate School District*, 300 F.Supp. 748 (1969)].

Prohibition of Pupil Membership in Secret Societies

Some states have enacted statutes prohibiting membership of elementary or secondary school pupils in secret societies and permitting expulsion of pupils holding such membership in violation of school board rules. (See, e.g., *Acts 1907 Indiana*, ch. 278.) Most state legislatures, however, have remained silent on this question, and in several of these states, court cases have arisen challenging the authority of the school board to prohibit participation in cocurricular activities by pupils who hold membership in Greek letter fraternities or other similar secret societies. Courts in Arkansas [*Isgrig v. Srygley*, 197 S.W.2d 39 (1946)], Washington [*Wayland v. Board of School Directors*, 86 Pac. 642 (1906)], Oregon [*Burkitt v. School District*, 246 P.2d 566 (1952)], Ohio [*Holroyd v. Eibling*, 188 N.E.2d 797 (1962)], Illinois [*Wilson v. Board of Education*, 84 N.E. 697 (1908)], and California [*Robinson v. Sacramento City Unified School District*, 245 Cal. App.2d 278 (1966)] have upheld such rules of school boards. Missouri is one of the few states holding that a board may not take such action against pupils for membership in such organizations [*Wright v. Board of Education*, 246 S.W. 43 (1922)].

The Teacher *in Loco Parentis*

In the eyes of the court, the school board and school administration have the right to make rules governing pupils, and the teacher may establish reasonable rules relating to the good order and discipline of pupils in his classroom, so long as such rules are not inconsistent with higher authority. [See, e.g., *Patterson v. Nutter*, 78 Me. 609 (Maine 1866); *Sheehan v. Sturges*, 53 Conn. 481 (Conn. 1885); *Russell v. Lynnfield*, 116 Mass. 365 (Mass. 1874); *Fertich v. Michener, supra.*]

A public school teacher stands in a unique legal relationship with his pupils. This relationship is known as *in loco parentis,* meaning "in the place of the parent." Under the *in loco parentis* doctrine, the teacher's authority over pupils under his supervision is substantially the same as that of a parent, but it is restricted to the limits of his jurisdiction and responsibility as a teacher.

Even parents are limited to some degree with respect to the punishment of children. Every state has enacted statutes, for example, which prohibit cruelty to children.

Although the *in loco parentis* doctrine gives teachers substantial authority in dealing with pupils, teachers should be careful not to exceed this authority. In Pennsylvania, two teachers attempted to treat the infected finger of a 10-year-old pupil by holding the finger under boiling water, even though no situation existed requiring first aid or emergency treatment. In holding the teachers liable for the resulting injury, the court made clear that the doctrine of *in loco parentis* was limited and stated:

Under the delegated parental authority implied from the relationship of teacher and pupil there is no implied delegation of authority to exercise her lay judgment, as a parent may, in the matter of treatment of injury or disease suffered by a pupil. . . . [The teachers] were not acting in an emergency. . . . Whether treatment of the infected finger was necessary was a question for the boy's parents to decide [*Guerreri v. Tyson,* 24 A.2d 468 (1942)].

Reasonable Punishments

As indicated previously, the rules governing pupil conduct must be reasonable under the existing circumstances. In the last analysis, the courts are the determiners of the reasonableness of school rules. Not only must a rule be reasonable; the enforcement of the rule or the punishment meted for violation of the rule must also be reasonable.

There seems to be little doubt that withholding of privileges, removal from the classroom, and reasonable detention after school (where, of course, a child is not subjected to unreasonable hazards such as being required to walk home where pupil transportation is normally provided) are punishments with which it is unlikely a court would find fault. Most litigation in the area of specific punishments falls into three other categories: academic punishments for disciplinary infractions, suspension and expulsion, and corporal punishment.

Academic Punishments for Disciplinary Infractions

In a recent case a federal court was asked to consider academic penalties which had been assessed against students as a result of absences from class resulting from suspensions related to the violation of a "dress code." The court ruled that such penalties were "unrelated to academic performance" and were "illegal and unconstitutional" (a decision in the case of *Christopher v. Smith,* United States District Court for the Northern District of Indiana filed March 10, 1971).

Denial of diplomas for violations of school rules has been declared illegal by at least two courts [*Valentine v. Independent School District,* 183 N.W. 434 (Iowa, 1921)]; [*Ryan v. Board of Education,* 257 Pac, 945 (Kans. 1927)]. From these cases, it is obvious that the courts regard academic accomplishment and school discipline to be separate and distinct, and have held that the use of such academic punishments as grade reductions or the withholding of diplomas for disciplinary infractions is unreasonable.

Suspension and Expulsion

Suspension can be defined as exclusion of a pupil from school for a specified brief period of time, such as a few days. Expulsion differs from suspension only in length of time. Expulsion usually involves a relatively long period of time, such as a semester or a school year.

Most authorities appear to agree that expulsion, being a more severe punishment than suspension, should involve school board rather than teacher action [see, e.g., 97]. Moreover, there is doubt as to whether even a school board may expel a pupil *permanently* [see, e.g., *Board of Education v. Helston,* 32, Ill. App. 300 (Ill. 1889)] from the public schools for disciplinary offense, since this gives the pupil no opportunity to make amends or to rehabilitate himself and would be contrary to the entire philosophy of Anglo-American law. The courts have specifically held that expulsion is not "forever" [see e.g., *Alvin Independent School District v. Cooper,* 404 S.W.2d 76 (Tex. 1966)].

In the absence of school board rules to the contrary, a principal or teacher probably has inherent authority to suspend pupils for disciplinary infractions. The following case examples illustrate the reasoning of the courts in this regard.

In Wisconsin, a school principal suspended a pupil for misconduct and refused to readmit him until he gave "sincere promise of future good conduct." The pupil declined to do so, and his parents brought suit against the principal, contending that only the school board had authority to suspend the pupil from school. The court did not agree, pointing out that a principal or teacher does not derive all of his power with respect to pupil control from the school board. Teachers, according to the court, stand *in loco parentis* to pupils and therefore are entitled to exercise authority over pupils in many "things concerning which the board may have remained silent." In upholding the principal, the court commented that, even though the law gives him the power to punish pupils corporally, this is often an inadequate punishment. If the presence of a pupil is detrimental to the school, it is "essential" that the principal or teacher have the authority to suspend the pupil from school [*State v. Burton,* 45 Wis. 150 (Wis. 1878)].

In South Carolina, pupils refused to drink milk which was in containers bearing a certain label. No cause for refusing to drink the milk was advanced. The principal called an assembly and indicated he would suspend pupils who refused to drink milk. Certain pupils were subsequently suspended. The court held that a principal has the inherent authority to suspend pupils unless deprived of that authority by board regulation [*Stanley v. Gary,* 116 S.E.2d 843 (1960)].

It should be noted that it is not a common practice on the part of teachers in the public schools to suspend pupils from school. Many school systems have established policies which limit such action to principals or other administrative officials. It is likely that such action should only be taken by an administrator in compliance with established school policy.

Due Process

One of the most significant legal developments of the 1960s was the frequency with which due process questions involving students were brought to the courts. Very often the issue centered around the procedures used in expulsion from school. The question of due process is in an evolutionary stage, and it is difficult to identify clear legal guidelines. For example, some courts have held that a student is entitled to a hearing before expulsion [see *Dixon v. Alabama State Board of Education,* 294 F.2d 150 (1961)]. Other courts have held that no hearing is required [see *Banks v. Board of Public Instruction of Dade County,* 314 F.Supp. 285 (1970)].

An especially instructive case regarding due process occurred in Michigan. A student who had been given repeated warnings for absences was apprehended smoking in the building in violation of a school rule. Following a conference with the parents, the student was given the opportunity to appear before the school board at which time he was accompanied by his mother and counsel. He was then suspended indefinitely. The court rejected a subsequent request for a full-scale judicial hearing. The court ruled that: "The standard is whether he has been treated with fundamental fairness in the light of the total circumstances. . . . The student has been fully informed as to the offenses charged; he has been heard with respect thereto; and he has had due process in ample measure" [*Davis v. Ann Arbor Public Schools,* 313 F.Supp. 1217 (1970)].

It is possible to conclude that courts will continue to consider the due process rights of students. It may not be overly venturesome to predict that minimum due process in cases of severe student discipline eventually will lead to the following procedures: (1) a notice of the charges against the student and the nature of the evidence to support these charges; (2) a hearing; and (3) a decision based on the evidence presented in the hearing. Other issues such as the right to be represented by counsel and to cross-examine witnesses will also be litigated. While it is impossible to predict where the courts will draw the line relative to student due process, the cases already decided are indicative of a more aggressive court attitude in the protection of student rights. Teachers should understand this trend and should make every effort to comply with the standard of "fundamental fairness" in dealing with students.

Corporal Punishment

Since 1833, there have been more than sixty cases decided in American appellate courts dealing with corporal or physical punishment of school pupils by teachers. Most of these cases were decided prior to 1900, which leads to a belief that the common law in this area is now fairly well settled.

New Jersey is the only state in which corporal punishment of public school pupils by teachers is forbidden by statute. In several states (e.g., Florida, Hawaii, Montana, New York, Vermont, Virginia, Georgia, Ohio, Michigan), corporal punishment is expressly permitted by statute. The California Education Code clearly provides that "The governing board of any school district shall adopt rules and regulations authorizing teachers, principals, and other certificated personnel to administer reasonable corporal punishment when such action is deemed an appropriate corrective measure" (California Education Code, Section 10854). It may safely be assumed that in most of the other states the right of a teacher to administer reasonable corporal punishment is protected by the common law.

Rules of School Boards Forbidding Corporal Punishment

In some school districts, however, school board rules forbid corporal punishment of pupils. It is possible that a teacher who violates school board rules prohibiting corporal punishment might be guilty of insubordination and thus might be considered to have breached his teaching contract. However, a concurring opinion in a 1963 Indiana case may indicate a growing attitude on the part of the courts to the effect that a school board has no right to prohibit the use of corporal punishment by teachers:

. . . I have serious doubts that a teacher confronted with . . . responsibility under the law for maintaining order and a respect for authority before a classroom of pupils, can be deprived by a "rule" of the right to use physical force to eliminate . . . a disturbance. As long as teachers or parents are obligated under the law to educate, teach and train children, they may not be denied the necessary means of carrying out their responsibility as such teachers and parents [*Indiana State Personnel Board v. Jackson,* 192 N.E.2d 740 (1963)].

It should be kept in mind that the opinion stated by this judge did not represent the majority opinion of the court. Teachers who are employed in districts where corporal punishment is forbidden by school board rules should abide by such rules.

In any case, most school districts have established policies relating to procedures to be followed by teachers in administering corporal punishment, including a provision requiring witnesses. A teacher would be wise to follow closely the established corporal punishment policy of the district in which he is employed.

Assault and Battery

Assault and battery consists of striking or threatening to strike or harm another person. Consequently, a pupil may be guilty of such a charge. An action for assault and battery may be a *criminal action,* brought by the prosecuting attorney on behalf of the state, for which conviction would result in a fine and/or imprisonment. On the other hand, it may be a *civil action* in tort, brought by the injured party, for which the penalty would be monetary damages to the injured party.

Reasonableness of Corporal Punishment

The reasonableness of the corporal punishment administered is usually a major factor in determining the liability of the teacher. The courts normally will assume that corporal punishment which results in permanent injury is excessive or unreasonable. Corporal punishment administered with malice, which usually means with wicked motives or in anger, is also likely to be considered unreasonable. An Alabama court has listed certain guidelines which the courts tend to follow in determining whether corporal punishment is reasonable: "In determining the reasonableness of the punishment or the extent of malice, proper matters of consideration are the instrument used and the nature of the offense committed by the child, the age and physical condition of the child, and other attendant circumstances" [*Suits v. Glover,* 71 So.2d 49 (1954)].

The legality of corporal punishment of school pupils, perhaps more than any other aspect of pupil punishment, depends upon circumstances. What might be considered reasonable corporal punishment for a child of a certain age or sex might be considered unreasonable for another child of a different age or sex. Community attitudes also may affect the decision of courts. An examination of several court decisions in which action was brought against teachers for assault and battery may reveal the factors which determine reasonableness.

Corporal Punishment: Case Examples

In Ohio, a teacher corporally punished a boy who had thrown a stone at another pupil on the way home from school and who, when questioned, had "fibbed" about it. The teacher struck the pupil six to fifteen times with a paddle of "normal" proportions, which caused vivid discoloration of the buttocks. A complicating factor in the case was the fact that the pupil was an epileptic and had suffered three seizures following the spanking. Action was brought against the teacher for criminal assault and battery. The court listed the following as "fundamental propositions of law" which should be followed when a teacher is charged criminally for assault and battery arising from the corporal punishment of a school pupil: (1) A teacher stands *in loco parentis* and is not liable for an error in judgment; (2) a teacher's authority attaches from home to home; (3) there is a presumption of correctness in the actions of the teacher; (4) there is a presumption that the teacher acts in good faith; and (5) mere excessive or severe punishment is not a crime unless it produces permanent injury or unless it is administered with malice. The court found that no permanent injury had resulted to the child and that no malice was involved. The teacher, therefore, was found to be not guilty [*State v. Lutz,* 113 N.E.2d 757 (1953)].

In Alabama, a teacher corporally punished an eight-year-old boy who was "well developed, fat and in good health" for insubordination and for "scuffling" in the hall contrary to school rules. Civil action was brought against the teacher for assault and battery. The court indicated that, according to the evidence, the boy had been struck only five times on the buttocks. The evidence conflicted as to whether the instrument used was a Ping-Pong paddle or a slat from an apple crate. In any case, no permanent injury resulted. In relieving the teacher from liability, the court stated: "To be guilty of an assault and battery, the teacher must not only inflict upon the child immoderate chastisement, but he must do so with legal malice or wicked motives or he must inflict some permanent injury" *(Suits v. Glover, supra)*.

It can be inferred from the foregoing cases that teachers may be found liable for immoderate corporal punishment (1) if the punishment results in permanent injury or (2) if the punishment is administered with malice. Three cases in which teachers were held liable for excessive corporal punishment serve to further illustrate the importance of these factors.

In Pennsylvania, a teacher's corporal punishment of a child involved a blow on the pupil's right ear, which injured the eardrum and permanently impaired the hearing of the pupil. Since permanent injury had resulted, the court held the teacher liable and pointed out that, if corporal punishment were necessary, nature had "provided a part of the anatomy for chastisement" and tradition held "that chastisement should be there applied" [*Rupp v. Zintner*, 29 Pa. D. & C. 629 (1937)].

In Connecticut, a principal ordered a ten-year-old third-grade pupil to go to his office following an altercation between the pupil and a teacher. The boy refused, and the principal grabbed his wrists and tried to drag him. The boy was struggling to escape and became hysterical. The principal, who weighed 190 pounds, pushed the boy, who weighed 89 pounds, to the floor and sat on him. The boy was injured, and the court found that the principal had used "unreasonable force" [*Calmay v. Williamson*, 36 A.2d 377 (1944)].

In Louisiana, a boy who had not followed instructions in a physical education class was ordered to the sidelines. Three times he tried to return to the floor against the instructions of the teacher. As a result of the teacher using force to enforce his instructions, the student struck the floor and broke his arm. The court noted that the teacher was a foot taller and weighed twice as much as the boy and found that the teacher's actions were clearly in excess of the physical force necessary either to discipline the pupil or to protect himself [*Frank v. Orleans Parish School Board*, 195 So.2d 451 (1967)].

SUMMARY

The most common tort involving teachers is negligence resulting in pupil injury. A teacher's actions which fall below the standard of the reasonably prudent teacher and which result in injury to pupils may make the teacher liable for negligence.

Defenses against negligence include contributory negligence, proximate cause, and assumption of risk. In spite of the existence of these legal defenses, a teacher should make every effort to foresee and to prevent pupil injury.

The importance of adequate instruction in potentially hazardous activities and the establishment of safety rules cannot be over-emphasized. These two factors, in addition to the exercise of sound common sense, are vital to teachers in protecting themselves against successful negligence suits.

In addition to cases involving negligence teachers occasionally are sued for defamation of character. Written defamation is known as libel, and spoken defamation as slander. Teachers who communicate information about pupils should be certain the person to whom such information is given has a reason for having it. Teachers who follow this rule probably have little to fear from defamation-of-character lawsuits, since such communication is privileged.

School boards, administrators, and teachers have wide authority to establish rules of pupil conduct. So long as the rules are reasonable and bear reasonable relation to the welfare of the school (even though they may to some extent govern pupil conduct off the school grounds and after school hours), they are likely to be upheld by the courts. It should be remembered, however, that the courts are the final determiners of the reasonableness of a particular school rule.

Methods of enforcing school rules must also be reasonable. Such enforcement procedures as academic punishments for disciplinary infractions or the requirement that children pay for school property accidentally damaged or destroyed are likely to be struck down by the courts. Suspension and expulsion, withholding of privileges, removal from the classroom, and reasonable corporal punishment probably would be upheld.

Probably the most important trends for teachers to note are the willingness of the courts to consider legal challenges involving the reasonableness of school rules and the extent to which courts are providing protection for the constitutional freedoms of students. Courts have not removed the authority of schools to regulate the conduct of students; however, they are demanding that rules and regulations be directly related to the effective operation of the schools. There is no longer any tendency for the courts to regard the authority of the school over the student to be absolute.

QUESTIONS TO CONSIDER

1. How would you define the term "common law"?
2. Why do you think the courts have established the concept of the "reasonably prudent man" as the standard for determining negligence?
3. Why do you think the courts have established "foreseeability" as the first test of negligence?
4. If you, as a teacher, were given the responsibility for supervising the school safety patrol, what precautions would you take?
5. What policy do you feel a teacher should follow regarding elementary pupils who forget to bring books from home and request permission to go home after them?
6. As a teacher, what should you do about a pupil who complains of a severe headache?
7. What seems to be the determining factor as to the liability of a teacher for pupil injury in the classroom while the teacher is out of the room?
8. What is the reason the courts have established "privilege" as a defense against defamation of character?
9. What disadvantages result from a teachers' association carrying a $50,000 liability insurance policy on all members of the association?
10. What seems to be the controlling factor as to whether teachers may punish pupils for acts off the school grounds or after school hours?
11. Under what circumstances might a teacher be liable for injuries to pupils off the school grounds or after school hours?
12. As a teacher, what action should you take against a pupil who hits a baseball through a classroom window during playground activities at a school where a rule is in effect that baseball is not to be played close to the school building?

13. Are there any circumstances under which a teacher ever suspends a pupil from school? Cite specific cases.
14. What do you think the attitude of the courts would be toward a school rule providing for a 3 per cent grade reduction for each "unexcused" absence?
15. Why do you think the courts have established the *in loco parentis* doctrine?
16. Do you think it is desirable or undesirable that a school board establish a rule forbidding corporal punishment by teachers? Justify your position.
17. In what ways will the further implementation of the "due process" concept affect the teacher's role in relationship with pupils?

PROBLEM SITUATION FOR INQUIRY

Mr. Sennett is an instructor in biology at Russellville Junior High School. His second period class, composed of twenty-eight freshmen, was in the process of learning to dissect the clam. Because of the toughness of the muscle fibers that hold the two clam-shell halves together, the separation of these two halves can be a hazardous undertaking unless performed properly. For this reason Mr. Sennett took more time than usual to explain the dissection procedure. He placed special emphasis on the proper way to hold the clam and make the incision. He also restated the importance of reporting any injury, no matter how minor, immediately after it occurs. Having finished these instructions, he told the class to proceed with their work, while he slowly moved throughout the room to give any help he could.

Bill, one of the less conscientious students in the class, did not give his full attention to any of Mr. Sennett's opening comments. Consequently, he set to work without any significant knowledge of the possible danger involved in the task. While trying to open the shell in one swift slash, his scalpel slipped and cut a gash in the side of his left hand. The bleeding was not severe, however, and in an attempt to save himself the embarrassment of facing Mr. Sennett, he quickly wrapped a paper towel around the wound and concealed it for the remainder of the period.

That night, Bill noticed pronounced swelling around the cut area. He showed it to his parents, who, in turn, notified the family doctor. The infection resulted in a sizable medical bill. Bill's parents asked Mr. Sennett to pay this medical bill, or they would bring suit against him for negligence. If you were Mr. Sennett, what would you do? Why?

ACTIVITIES TO PURSUE

1. Outline the points which might have been made by the attorney for the plaintiff in the case involving the "slap-boxing" incident.
2. Set up a mock court, including the attorney for the plaintiff, the attorney for the defendant, a judge, a bailiff, a plaintiff, a defendant, and a jury to "try" the "slap-boxing" case outlined in this chapter.
3. Go to a courthouse law library and look up the United States Supreme Court prayer and Bible-reading cases cited in the chapter. Analyze these cases, including the facts, the issues, the decisions, and the reasons given by the Court in reaching the decisions.
4. Analyze the 1954 desegregation decision of the Supreme Court cited in the chapter. Try to find out why the Court held that separate public school facilities for black and white pupils were "inherently" unequal.
5. Assume that you are a school principal. Establish a set of guidelines which you might suggest that your teachers follow in order to avoid tort liability for negligence.
6. Develop a parental permission form which might be used for pupil field trips.
7. Develop a set of pupil safety rules for the classroom, assuming that you are an

elementary teacher (or a high school teacher of physical education, chemistry, industrial arts, or homemaking).

8. Assume that you are a school principal. Develop a set of rules for teachers who wish to administer corporal punishment.

9. From the references cited in the chapter and/or from your state school code, see what you can learn about the following: (*a*) Must a pupil's cumulative-record folder be shown to the parents of the pupil upon their request? (*b*) May a pupil-composed prayer be said at the noon meal in a public school cafeteria? (*c*) Do teachers have the legal right to strike? (*d*) May the King James Version of the Bible be used as a textbook in the public schools? (*e*) Under what circumstances may teachers be dismissed for unbecoming conduct after school hours? (*f*) May a person in college who will receive a teaching license in August legally contract with a school district the previous spring? (*g*) Would a school counselor likely be held liable for the suicide of a student because the counselor failed to recommend psychiatric care for the student? (*h*) What authority does the state legislature have over the public schools?

10. Discuss with a lawyer the probable effects of the further implementation of the "due process" concept upon the teacher's role in the governance of pupils.

8 | RECURRING CONTROVERSIAL ISSUES AND PROBLEMS IN EDUCATION

No major improvement takes place in society without attendant problems. Difficulties are certain to be present whenever changes in the thinking and behavior of people are involved. This is true in the field of education as well as in any other major field of endeavor.

This chapter is concerned primarily with some of the educational issues and problems that have confronted educators for many years. For example, schools have been criticized as long as they have existed, and will continue to be criticized. There is abundant evidence of a communication gap between the general public and the school system. The relationship between the public schools and our religious institutions has been a basic issue since not long after this country was founded. Freedom to teach has been a long-time goal of teachers. The 1954 desegregation decision made the schools the continuing battleground for efforts to eliminate the vestiges of segregation in our society. Meanwhile the issue of what the schools should teach and the importance of academic versus vocational training continue to be debated.

In the following pages these recurring issues are examined in some detail.

Why Do Schools Continue to Be Criticized?

There probably has never been a time when the public schools were so besieged by criticism from so many diverse and varied sources.

What are the reasons for the attacks? Are they due in part to the increased amount of education which each succeeding generation has gained? As people become more educated, they tend to place a higher value upon schooling and to become increasingly critical of educational practices. Have the two major opposing ideologies in the world today contributed to an outburst of concern for the education of the young? Are these attacks due to an increasing awareness upon the part of the general public of the importance of education as a means of preserving and promoting democratic living? Are these attacks sincere efforts designed to improve the education of the young, or are they motivated by desires to weaken our schools, curtail educational costs, or spread seeds of suspicion? To what extent do these attacks represent differences in opinion or confusion in regard to the school's function in a democratic society? To what extent are the attackers misinformed or unaware of valid research findings in terms of which modifications have been made in educational practices? These are only a few of the questions to keep in mind in appraising criticisms of the public schools.

The public has a right, in fact an obligation, to prescribe policies by which the public schools shall abide and to appraise the extent to which these policies have been fulfilled. Furthermore, the public for many years has exercised the right to criticize educational endeavors. Aristotle in 384 B.C. wrote the following: "There are doubts concerning the business of education, since all people do not agree in those things they would have a child taught." Some of the people at that time, and even earlier, complained that the children preferred sitting around chatting to participating in athletic activities, had bad manners, were disrespectful of their elders, and ruled the household. Confucius, approximately 2,500 years ago, noted: "The teachers of today just go on repeating things in a rigmarole fashion, annoy the students with constant questions, and repeat the same things over and over again. They do not try to find out what the students' natural inclinations are so that the students are forced to pretend to like their studies, nor do they try to bring out the best in their talents" [89:1].

Horace Mann, in his report of 1838, stated:

I have devoted special pains to learn, with some degree of numerical accuracy, how far the reading, in our schools, is an exercise of the mind in thinking and feeling, and how far it is a barren action of the organs of speech upon the atmosphere. . . . The result is, that more than eleven-twelfths of all the children in the reading classes, in our schools, do not understand the meaning of the words they read; that they do not master the sense of the reading lessons, and that the ideas and feelings intended by the author to be conveyed to, and excited in, the reader's mind, still rest in the author's intention, never having yet reached the place of their destination.

In 1845 the Grammar School Committee of Boston, after having administered various tests to the pupils, reported that:

They [tests administered] show beyond all doubt that a large proportion of the scholars in our first classes, boys and girls of 14 and 15 years of age, when called on to write simple sentences, to express their thoughts on common subjects, without the aid of a dictionary or a master, cannot write, without such errors in grammar, in spelling, and in punctuation, as we should blush to see in a letter from a son or daughter of their age.

John Erskine, in *My Life as a Teacher,* said, regarding his teaching at

Amherst in 1903, "A large proportion of my first Amherst freshmen were unable to spell."

Do these statements have a familiar ring, even though some of them were made over 2,000 years ago?

Older people often appraise present conditions and practices in terms of "the good old days." There seems to be a human tendency to glamorize and "haloize" days past. Furthermore, there is a tendency to resist change and to impose an element of rightness to our own past experience. These tendencies may operate as older people appraise the products of today's schools.

How do children in present-day schools compare with the products of an earlier system? It is difficult to find meaningful comparisons except in quantitative measures. However, data that are available would indicate that schools have performed and continue to perform a tremendous job with reasonable competency. In 1900, 11.3 per cent of the population 15-years-old and older was illiterate. By 1930 the percentage had dropped to 4.8 per cent of the population 14 years and older, and by 1960 the percentage was down to 2.4. Tentative 1970 census data indicate that the percentage has dropped below 1.0.

The median number of years of school completed by adults 25-years of age or older has increased continuously. The data are as follows [27:39]:

Year	Median Years of School
1940	8.6
1950	9.3
1960	10.5
1969	12.1

These statistics are reinforced by the fact that the number of public high school graduates in 1970 was estimated at 2,640,338, which was an increase of 61.7 per cent over 1960 [27:37].

These data indicate the increasingly important role the school is playing in the lives of Americans—which may have resulted in more attention being given to the effectiveness of schools. The expanded use of the public schools has contributed to increased costs, which, in turn, have tended to produce increasingly negative public reactions. During the ten-year period of the sixties, for example, the cost of public elementary and secondary schools more than doubled—going from $15.6 billion in 1959–1960 to $39.5 billion in 1969–1970 [27:40].

In the "Third Annual Survey of the Public's Attitude Toward the Public Schools, 1971" [36], an effort was made to determine what the public believes is right about public schools. To the question: "In your own opinion, in what ways are your local public schools particularly good?" The significant factors identified by respondents were: Teachers—21 per cent; Curriculum—15 per cent; Facilities—9 per cent; and

Up-to-date teaching methods—5 per cent. The only other response which exceeded 5 per cent was from the 7 per cent who indicated they could find nothing good to list [36:37].

The same poll gave the respondents the opportunity to list the biggest problems relative to the public schools in their communities. The five major problems cited and the percentage of respondents identifying each problem were [36:37]:

Problem	Percentage
Finances	23
Integration/Segregation	21
Discipline	14
Facilities	13
Dope/Drugs	12

A survey finding of equal significance may be the fact that 68 per cent of those surveyed indicated the high schools place too much emphasis on "preparing students for college" and not enough emphasis on "preparing students for occupations that do not require a college degree" [36:42].

Regardless of the strengths or weaknesses of American public education, criticism is present today in many quarters and probably will continue. There is no reason to assume that the schools will ever be free of criticism, public discussion, and controversy. Few would argue that such criticism and discussion are undesirable. Constructive criticism is at the heart of the democratic process, and improvements in American public education undoubtedly can continue to be made.

Unfortunately not all the criticism seems to be constructive by intent. Finn points out that [30:31]:

Books that have good things to say about our society do not sell very well; very few orders for pamphlets and reprints are received when the pamphlets and reprints have something worthwhile to say in favor of a person or institution. It's small consolation, but the last best seller that sang praises was probably the Book of Psalms.

At the moment, there's money, prestige and almost sure publication without much chance of getting slapped back awaiting anyone willing to kick an educationist in the stomach. Aggressions are also relieved. By creating a new minority group (the education-ists) to push around, most of the critics . . . (but not all critics) have discovered a form of therapy that brings wonderful release . . . and money.

As teachers are confronted in the future with criticisms of the schools, they will need to examine the apparent motives behind the author, as well as the accuracy, objectivity, logic, and depth of understanding with which he writes or speaks. Teachers need to be prepared to react positively to criticism which is well intentioned and based on fact, willing to defend education against that which is not, and enlightened enough to distinguish between the two.

How Can the Communication Between the General Public and the Schools Be Improved?

Many of the attacks upon public schools, mentioned previously, are caused by a lack of understanding and facts. The results of a Gallup Poll illustrate the problem faced by the American schools relative to public information. To the direct question, "How much do you know about the local schools?" 18 per cent responded that they knew "Quite a lot," 40 per cent felt that they knew "Some," and 42 per cent indicated that they knew "Very little" [34:27, 36, 37]. Additional questions and responses were as follows:

Question	Percentages	
	Yes	No
Do you happen to know the name of the superintendent of schools?	56	44
During the last year, have you received any newsletter, pamphlet, or other material telling what the local schools are doing?	35	61
During the last month, have you read any articles in the newspapers about local schools?	60	34
Have you heard anything about local schools on radio during this period?	36	58
Have you heard anything about local schools on television during this period?	35	59

While these responses are not particularly encouraging, a heartening fact was the indication that two-thirds of those surveyed wanted and would appreciate more information about the public schools [34:39].

The necessity for developing an informed public is indicated by the response to a question asked in a 1971 Gallup Survey: "Suppose the local public schools said they needed much more money. As you feel at this time, would you vote to raise taxes for this purpose, or would you vote against raising taxes for this purpose?" [36:33]. A total of 40 per cent responded affirmatively to this question, but a majority of 52 per cent indicated they would not vote to raise taxes to provide money for schools. Since a public school system is dependent upon tax dollars, the survey responses clearly indicate the need for increased attention to programs of public information [36:33].

In general, it is difficult to convey to the public the economic value of education to the individual and to society. It is not possible to translate into dollars and cents the exact capital gains that accrue from having studied American literature for one year or music in the third grade.

When asked to pay more taxes for schools, however, the American public tends to ask such questions as "Will we get our money's worth?" or "Can we afford better schools?"

You have heard of the staggering costs of education with which the public will be confronted if future generations are to be at least as well educated as children are today. Actually, the quality of education must be improved if future generations are to be prepared to deal adequately with the increasing complex social, economic, and technological problems. Somehow the general public must remember an old saying that may be paraphrased as follows: "We cannot use yesterday's tools for educating youth to do the job today and expect to be in business tomorrow."

There are a number of activities at the community level that are being used, and perhaps could be used even more effectively, to acquaint the general public with the activities, purposes, and outcomes of schools. These include such activities as participation in parent-teacher groups and various educational associations; the observance of special days and weeks devoted to education; wide use of television, radio, and newspapers; the formation of study groups, local conferences, board-appointed lay advisory committees, counsel groups, and scheduled individual parent-teacher conferences; work on school newspapers; community use of school buildings; cocurricular activities; preparation of illustrated annual reports by school boards; class reunions; student participation in community activities; teacher participation in community affairs.

One aspect of public relations has generally been neglected in most of America's school systems. Although we teach pupils about local, state, and national government in "government," "civics," or other social studies classes, very few school systems have ever made any attempt to

FIGURE 8–1 The percentage of teachers who use various public relations techniques who consider these techniques to be effective. Are there other techniques that should be used?

Per cent   0   20   40   60   80   100

☐ Percentage of teachers considering them effective
■ Percentage of teachers using them

educate pupils with respect to local school government or to help them understand and appreciate the American educational system as an expression of our society. Yet teachers and school administrators apparently expect pupils in later life to become effective school board members and informed school patrons and to financially support the public schools through tax levies and bond issues, even though they have little knowledge of the public school as a legal and social institution. Some thought should be given to the advantages which might accrue on a long-range basis to any school district which attempts to provide instruction to pupils in such areas of local school government as school purposes, school board authority, local taxation for schools, and state authority.

Many of the suggestions already given require action by the school board, administration, or the organizations which represent teachers. This should not be taken to minimize the role which the individual teacher can and should play in improving the public image of the schools. That which the teacher does behind the closed classroom door remains the most effective means the school has for communicating with the community it serves. The major impact of the school comes in the intrapersonal relationships which parents, students, and concerned community residents have with school personnel. An effective and formal school information program can help to build a base of community approval and support. However, it cannot replace or overcome weaknesses in the best communication device—effective teaching.

What Should Be the Relationship Between Religion and the Public Schools?

Any discussion of the relationship between religion and public education must, at least initially, be approached from a historical base. From your study of history you will recall many of America's early colonists came to the New World to escape religious persecution in Europe. These early settlers had lived in European countries where a certain church or churches were given sanction or approval by the government and where religious freedom as we know it today did not exist.

When many of these early colonists arrived in America, they made provision for an established church sanctioned by the colonial government and began to persecute religious dissenters at least as vigorously as they themselves had been persecuted in Europe. In fact, in many of the American Colonies dissenters such as Baptists, Roman Catholics, Quakers, and Jews were denied the right to assemble and to worship publicly, and punishments for violation of these early religious laws ranged from a fine or imprisonment to, in some cases, death.

During the years prior to the American Revolution, opposition to the practice of persecution of religious minorities grew, and by the time the federal Constitution was drafted, colonial leaders such as Jefferson and Madison were firm in their determination that never again would government in America sanction or support a particular religion or prohibit any religious faith from public worship or from expressing publicly its beliefs.

Out of the reaction against governmental involvement in religion grew the First Amendment to the federal Constitution. This amendment provides, in part, that "Congress shall make no law respecting an establishment of religion, or prohibiting the free exercise thereof."

The First Amendment originally applied only to Congress or the federal government. Following the Civil War, however, the Fourteenth Amendment was enacted, which guaranteed to citizens of all states the basic rights protected by the federal Constitution. In recent years, the United States Supreme Court has interpreted the Fourteenth Amendment to mean that the First Amendment applies not only to Congress but also to the states. The First Amendment, as interpreted today, means, then, that neither Congress nor a state may establish a religion or prohibit the free exercise of a religion.

The public schools are a part of state government. In fact, a local school district is a legal subdivision of the state, and the members of local boards of education are state officers. Since a state may not establish a religion, neither may a local school district, because such a district is a state entity. This legal concept has been the basis for many of the most significant and critical court decisions involving the schools which have been decided by American courts in recent years.

The McCollum case, decided by the United States Supreme Court in 1948, was one of the first wherein this concept was tested. It involved a situation common to many schools of the day—that of *released time,* which was a practice whereby public school pupils were released from their normal classes to attend religious classes held in the same public school building and taught by church school teachers who came from outside the school. Suit was brought to prevent the continuation of such a program of religious instruction in the public schools of Champaign, Illinois, primarily on the grounds that such a program violated the "establishment of religion" clause of the First Amendment.

The Supreme Court declared that the Champaign religious education program violated the First Amendment and ordered the program discontinued. The practice of permitting outside religious teachers to conduct religious classes on public school property during the school day constituted "too great" a cooperation between government and religion and thus amounted to an establishment of religion by government, according to the Court (*McCollum v. Board of Education,* 333 U.S. 203, 68 Sup. Ct. 461).

For some four years, religious educators in America were in a quandary. Did the McCollum decision mean that released time programs were prohibited entirely? Could such programs be conducted off school grounds rather than within public school facilities? Did the decision mean that the Supreme Court was antagonistic toward any religious teaching of public school youngsters?

In 1952, another case reached the Court, which at least in part answered these questions. This case, known as the Zorach case, involved a challenge brought by parents in New York City against a public school practice which permitted pupils to be released from classes to attend religious instruction off the school grounds. This practice differed from the McCollum case in that the religious instruction was not given in the public school buildings.

In upholding the release of pupils to attend religious classes held away from the public school buildings, the Supreme Court made it clear that, although the government was compelled to remain "neutral" in religious matters, this by no means meant that the government was "hostile" to religion. According to the Court, cooperation between government and religion, such as releasing pupils for off-school religious classes, was permissible under the First Amendment (*Zorach v. Clauson,* 343 U.S. 306, 72 Sup. Ct. 670).

Many questions involving the public schools and religion remained, however. In nineteenth-century American public schools, teachers were expected to impart to pupils religious and "moral" training, including use of the Holy Bible as a text, as a moral guide, and as a basis for classroom "devotions." Pupils were also expected to participate in prayer in many public school classrooms. Vestiges of these religious practices remained in American public schools as late as 1962.

In 1962, challenge of a prayer adopted by the New York Board of Regents (the state board of education) reached the Supreme Court (*Engel v. Vitale,* 370 U.S. 421, 82 Sup. Ct. 1261). The prayer, developed by representatives of several religious faiths and designed to be interdenominational, had been recommended by the Board of Regents for use in the public schools of New York.

After lengthy consideration, the Supreme Court held that the use of a governmentally composed prayer in the public schools violated the establishment clause of the First Amendment—in other words, the government of New York was establishing a state-approved religion. Even the fact that children might be excused from the classroom during the saying of the prayer made no difference. According to the Court, the mere existence and use of a state-approved prayer constituted an establishment of religion by the state. Mr. Justice Black, speaking for the majority of the Court, stated (370 U.S. 424, 82 Sup. Ct. 1263):

We think that by using its public school system to encourage recitation of the Regents' prayer, the State of New York has adopted a practice wholly inconsistent with the Establishment Clause. There can, of course, be no doubt that New York's program of daily classroom invocation of God's blessings as prescribed in the Regent's prayer is a religious activity. It is a solemn avowal of divine faith and supplication for the blessings of the Almighty. The nature of such a prayer has always been religious.

Justice Black went on to say (370 U.S.429, 82 Sup. Ct. 1266):

The First Amendment was added to the Constitution to stand as a guarantee that neither the power nor the prestige of the Federal Government would be used to control, support or influence the kinds of prayer the American people can say, that the people's religions must not be subjected to the pressures of government for change each time a new political administration is elected to office. Under that Amendment's prohibition against governmental establishment of religion, as reinforced by the provisions of the Fourteenth Amendment, government in this country, be it state or federal, is without power to prescribe by law any particular form of prayer which is to be used as an official prayer in carrying on any program of governmentally sponsored religious activity.

In 1963, the Court was faced with another decision of far-reaching importance to American public education. At this time, two cases, known as the Schempp and Murray cases, which dealt primarily with the legality of devotional use of the Holy Bible in the public schools, reached the Court (*School District of Abington Township v. Schempp; Murray v. Curlett,* 374 U.S. 203, 83 Sup. Ct. 1560).

In the Schempp case, suit was brought to prevent enforcement of a Pennsylvania law which required that at least ten verses from the Holy Bible be read without comment at the opening of each school day in the public schools of that state. In the Murray case, a rule of the Baltimore school board provided that opening exercises in the public schools of that city consist of the reading, without comment, of a chapter from the Holy Bible and/or the use of the Lord's Prayer.

The Supreme Court handed down a single opinion dealing with both cases, holding that both the Pennsylvania law and the Baltimore school board rule were unconstitutional. In reaching this decision, the Court pointed out that the religious exercises were a "prescribed part of the curriculum" and were "held in the school buildings under the supervision and with the participation of teachers" and therefore constituted a state sanction or establishment of religion. The Court made clear, however, that although devotional use of the Bible was prohibited, use of the Bible as a literary or historical document was permissible.

Mr. Justice Brennan, speaking for the Court, stated (374 U.S. 283, 83 Sup. Ct. 1603):

There are persons in every community—often deeply devout—to whom any version of the Judaeo-Christian Bible is offensive. There are others whose reverence for the Holy Scriptures demands private study or reflection and to whom public reading or recitation is sacrilegious. . . . To such persons it is not the fact of using the Bible in the public schools, nor the content of any particular version that is offensive, but only the manner in which it is used.

Justice Brennan went on to outline the position of the Court on the relationship between religion and government (374 U.S. 294, 83 Sup. Ct. 1609):

I believe that the line we must draw between the permissible and the impermissible is one which accords with history and faithfully reflects the understanding of the Founding Fathers. It is a line which the Court has consistently sought to mark in its decisions expounding the religious guarantees of the First Amendment. What the Framers meant to foreclose, and what our decisions under the Establishment Clause have forbidden, are those involvements of religious with secular institutions which (*a*) serve the essentially religious activities of religious institutions; (*b*) employ the organs of government for essentially religious purposes; or (*c*) use essentially religious means to serve governmental ends, where secular means would suffice. When the secular and religious institutions become involved in such a manner, there inhere in the relationship precisely those dangers—as much to church as to state—which the Framers feared would subvert religious liberty and the strength of a system of secular government.

A recent ruling, added to the earlier decisions, appears to have settled the question of prayer. A teacher in a classroom in Illinois had her students repeat the following verse before going to the cafeteria:

> Thank you for the world so sweet,
> Thank you for the food we eat,
> Thank you for the birds that sing,
> Thank you for everything.

How do recent decisions of the Supreme Court affect the use of prayer in public schools? What guidelines should a teacher follow in regard to this matter? *(Photograph from the National Education Association.)*

The court ruled that even this kind of nondenominational prayer violated the First Amendment to the Constitution [*DeSpain v. DeKalb County Community School District,* 384 F 2d 836 (1967)].

In considering court rulings on the prayer issue, teachers should remember that what the Supreme Court has barred is religious exercises. It has not barred, but rather has encouraged, teaching about religion. While teachers and schools cannot and should not promote any single religion or creed, the historical aspect of religion can and should be communicated to students.

How Can Freedom to Teach and to Learn Be Assured?

Freedom to think, speak, and write as reason and conscience dictate is basic to the survival of a democratic society. Our forefathers recognized this fact as they formulated the First Amendment to the Constitution of the United States. It would seem, therefore, that the development of skill in thinking and expression constitutes one of the very important tasks to which the school should give attention. The development of this skill takes place most effectively in an environment where individuals feel free and are encouraged to think and express themselves, one which offers opportunities for young people to come to grips with problems of real concern to them. Many such problems will be of a controversial nature.

Academic freedom refers to the freedom of teachers to seek and to present the truth on problems and issues without fear of interference from school boards, governmental authorities, or pressure groups. From a learner's standpoint it refers to the opportunity to study all points of view in regard to a problem or an issue and to arrive at reasoned conclusions. The teacher does not have a right to tell pupils what to think, nor does he have the right to advocate one theory only. The teacher's concern is the development of skill in thinking, expression, and problem solving on the part of his pupils. Unless both teachers and pupils feel free to examine, discuss, think, and arrive at reasoned conclusions on issues affecting their daily lives, the school is handicapped greatly in fulfilling its function in a democratic society.

Do teachers and pupils today feel free to teach and to learn? Teachers in some communities feel that they would run considerable risk of losing their jobs if they permitted students to examine all sides of issues concerning trade unions. In some sections of the country it would be extremely hazardous to encourage free inquiry and discussion of the racial problem. The discussion of sex education is questionable in some school systems. Certain textbooks in some communities have been censored. A number of teachers have been accused of being Communists if they permit pupils to learn *about* communism. These and many other instances which could be cited indicate that teachers and pupils are not entirely free to teach and to learn.

Yet the picture seems to be changing. Materials prepared by the U.S. Office of Education and other agencies pertaining to teaching *about* communism and other controversial subjects are becoming plentiful. Surveys of school administrators have indicated that these leaders increasingly favor teaching about controversial issues, and the teaching of such issues appears to be more accepted today than ever before. The National Education Association believes that academic and professional freedom is essential to the teaching profession.

Controversial issues should be a part of instructional programs when judgment of the professional staff deems the issues appropriate to the curriculum and to the maturity level of the student. Academic freedom is the right of the learner and his teachers to explore, present, and discuss divergent points of view in the quest for knowledge and truth.

Professional freedom includes the teacher's right to evaluate, to criticize, and to advocate his personal point of view concerning the policies and programs of the schools. The teacher also has the right to assist colleagues when their academic or professional freedom is violated [75:79].

Recent Supreme Court decisions have expanded teachers' constitutional rights of self-expression. In 1969 the Court observed that neither "teachers or students shed their constitutional freedoms at the schoolhouse gate" [*Tinker v. Des Moines Independent Community School District,* 89 S. Ct. 733 (1969)]. In an earlier decision the Court had protected a teacher's right to comment upon his conditions of employment and to speak critically of his school board [*Pickering v. Board of Education of Township High School District,* 88 S. Ct. 1731 (1968)]. These decisions are sufficiently extensive to justify the conclusion that courts will provide protection to teachers in the reasonable exercise of academic freedom.

The exercise of academic freedom also places a substantial responsibility upon the teacher. It is important for teachers to remember that academic freedom should never be used as a protective device in terms of which society suffers. Teachers in our democratic society have a basic responsibility to their pupils and to their communities to promote freedom of thought, freedom of expression, and the pursuit of truth. Society, in turn, has an obligation to provide and to promote these conditions.

How Can Problems of Discrimination and Segregation Be Resolved?

In addition to the financial inequalities that have existed within the American school system, educators also have been confronted with problems arising from racial discrimination and segregation. These problems are precipitated when attempts are made to provide equal educational opportunities for boys and girls regardless of race, color, and religion. Although much progress has been made since 1954 in lessening the amount of discrimination and segregation, problems still remain. Teachers are confronted with the task of helping resolve these very complex problems.

From the study of social problems, it is obvious that there are varying degrees of prejudice and discrimination existing throughout the United States wherever minority groups are involved. Race, color, and religion affect to some degree job opportunities, housing, churches, labor unions, clubs, and political groups. In various parts of the country definite discriminatory practices still exist with respect to such minority groups as Jews, Orientals, Latin Americans, and blacks. As an example, the large influx of Puerto Ricans in New York City presents a major problem of integration.

As Thayer indicates [140:479–480], court decisions affecting the education of blacks, oddly enough, date back to a decision of a Massachusetts court in 1849 [*Roberts v. the City of Boston,* 5 Cush. 198, 206]. In this particular case a black child claimed the right to attend the school nearest her home rather than the one to which she had been assigned, since the Massachusetts constitution stated that all persons are equal before the law without distinction of age or sex, birth or color, origin or condition. In denying this right, the court maintained that,

when the great principle (of equality) comes to be applied to the actual and various conditions of persons in society, it will not warrant the assertion, that men are legally clothed with the same civil and political powers, and that children and adults are legally to have the same functions and be subject to the same treatment; but only that the rights of all, as they are settled and regulated by law, are equally entitled to the paternal consideration and protection of the law, and their maintenance.

Following the termination of the Civil War, Congress took steps to ensure the equality of blacks and whites. As a result, the Thirteenth, Fourteenth, and Fifteenth Amendments were added to the Constitution. Furthermore, states applying for statehood were required to include in their constitutions provisions for the establishment and maintenance of free public schools [140:479].

In meeting their educational obligations, the Southern states segregated blacks upon grounds that they would be provided with equal facilities. This action was upheld in various courts, using as a precedent the "separate but equal" decision that had been pronounced by the Massachusetts court in 1849. In 1896 the United States Supreme Court, in the famous case *Plessy v. Ferguson* [163 U.S. 537, 16 Sup. Ct. 1138], validated the "separate but equal" practice of dealing with blacks. Although the actual case involved segregation on a railroad engaged in interstate commerce, in a number of states the policy was subsequently applied to public facilities, such as parks, beaches, and golf courses, and eventually to public schools.

After the turn of the century, a number of decisions rendered by federal courts began to weaken the rigid tradition and state laws regarding segregation. In 1915 the Court declared that the grandfather clause was a violation of the Fifteenth Amendment [*Guinn v. United States,* 238 U.S. 347, 35 Sup. Ct. 926]. Subsequent cases, involving such matters as housing and seating on buses, further weakened the legality of segregation practices. In 1950, a black student sought admission to the Law School at the University of Texas. The Court [*Sweatt v. Painter,* 339 v. 629, 70 Sup. Ct. 859] ruled that he must be admitted. In May, 1954, the Supreme Court [*Brown v. Board of Education of Topeka,* 347 U.S. 483, 74 Sup. Ct. 686], interpreted the Constitution to mean that compulsory segregation is unconstitutional. In the words of Chief Justice Warren, the decision was as follows:

Today, education is perhaps the most important function of state and local governments. Compulsory attendance laws and the great expenditures for education both demonstrate our recognition of the importance of education to our democratic society. It is required in the performance of our most basic public responsibilities, even service in the armed forces. It is the very foundation of good citizenship. Today it is a principal instrument in awakening the child to cultural values, in preparing him for later professional training, and in helping him to adjust normally to his environment. In these days, it is doubtful that any child may reasonably be expected to succeed in life if he is denied the opportunity of an education. Such an opportunity, where the state has undertaken to provide it, is a right which must be made available to all on equal terms.

   We come then to the question presented: Does segregation of children in public schools solely on basis of race, even though the physical facilities and other "tangible" factors may be equal, deprive the children of the minority group of equal education opportunities? We believe that it does. . . .

   We conclude that in the field of public education the doctrine of "separate but equal" has no place. Separate educational facilities are inherently unequal. Therefore, we hold that the plaintiffs and others similarly situated for whom the actions have been brought are, by reason of the segregation complained of, deprived of the equal protection of the laws guaranteed by the Fourteenth Amendment.

Teachers are generally familiar with some of the problems encountered in the implementation of this decision. In a great many cases, the integration of the races in the public schools has been without difficulty. In some cases, however, efforts to implement the ruling have met with defiance and subterfuge. Obviously, it takes time to implement such a ruling, since in a number of cases it strikes deep into the heart of tradition, feelings, and emotions. Legislation does not quickly change such factors.

   In 1964, however, a significant attempt to reduce segregation legislatively occurred when the federal Congress enacted the Civil Rights Act. Title IV of this act provides for a cutoff of federal funds to any school district which maintains a segregated system. It is anticipated that this type of federal legislation may hasten the day when all school districts are fully integrated.

   There also is evidence that the Supreme Court will insist upon compliance with its 1954 decision. In a 1969 case, the Court emphasized the responsibility of local school boards and the immediacy of the problem by stating that: "The burden on a school board today is to come forward with a plan that promises realistically to work now . . . until it is clear that state-imposed segregation has been completely removed" [*Green v. County School Board,* 88 S. Ct. 1689 (1969)]. In a 1971 decision the Court further stated that [*Swann v. Charlotte-Mecklenberg Board of Education,* 91 S. Ct. 1267 (1971)]: "Today's objective is to eliminate from the public schools all vestiges of state-imposed segregation that was held violative of equal protection guarantees by *Brown v. Board of Education.*" In this decision, the Court referred to the "broad powers" which lower federal courts have "to fashion a remedy" to end segregation. The Court also recognized that court ordered bussing could be "one tool of desegregation" and was within the power of the courts to order.

The involvement of the individual teacher also extends beyond the responsibility of providing equal and nondiscriminatory treatment for students. In the years immediately following the Brown decision of 1954, the courts were occupied with students and gave little attention to faculty desegregation. However, beginning in 1965, the courts began to require simultaneous staff and student desegregation. In the Swann case of 1967 the Supreme Court referred to faculty desegregation and specifically pointed to its approval of a lower court plan which required the ratio of black and white teachers in each school in a given school corporation to approximate the ratio of black and white teachers in the total corporation.

The courts are distinguishing between *de facto* and *de jure* segregation in relation to the integration of schools. Intentional maintenance of segregation, as prohibited by the 1954 decision of the Supreme Court, is known as *de jure* segregation. Any school board which consciously maintains segregated schools, through gerrymandering of school attendance zones so as to promote segregation, for example, is guilty of furthering *de jure* segregation and may be required by a court to end such segregation. Since the 1954 Supreme Court decision clearly prohibits *de jure* segregation, it is reasonable to suppose that it will finally be eliminated in American schools.

As *de jure* segregation recedes, another problem relating to segregation has taken its place—*de facto* segregation. *De facto* segregation can be defined as segregation of school pupils which results primarily from the housing patterns in many of America's large cities. Blacks and other racial minority groups tend to congregate in certain areas of such cities, owing perhaps in part to discrimination in matters of housing, and thus the neighborhood schools which serve such areas tend to become almost entirely populated by members of the minority race.

From an educational standpoint, teachers are responsible for understanding the problems of discrimination and segregation in evidence in all aspects of life and for relating these problems to the basic tenets of a democratic society. A teacher has the opportunity to help pupils as well as adults to identify these inconsistencies in our society and to formulate ways for effectively resolving them.

Without doubt, teachers have played a very significant role in the progress that has been made over the years. Teachers work primarily with younger people, who tend to be more tolerant than their elders. Furthermore, research indicates that people tend to become more tolerant as they become better educated.

A careful examination of countries throughout the world will reveal that problems of segregation and discrimination are not unique to the United States. They exist in every society. In many countries they are of much greater magnitude than they are here. Furthermore, in some countries the problems are becoming decidedly more acute. Teachers have a responsibility for understanding these problems as they exist on a worldwide basis and for aiding in the resolution of them. Most of all, teachers should do everything possible to foster progress in the solution of these problems in the United States, so that our country may be increasingly effective in demonstrating to the world a better way of life.

To What Extent Should the Public School Provide Vocational Education?

As indicated in Chapter 1, the modern world is changing so rapidly that many of today's pupils will be working in jobs that do not exist at present. M. J. Rathbone, chairman of the board and chief executive officer of Standard Oil Company of New Jersey, points out that approximately 70 per cent of the skilled trades in American manufacturing in the year 1900 do not exist today and that "a large proportion of today's skills will become obsolete in the shorter period between now and the year 2000, which is a period shorter than the average man's working lifetime" [103:8].

This era of rapid change poses a dilemma for the public schools. Can or should the public schools attempt to specifically prepare pupils for the world of work? The problem is made more acute by the fact that of every ten pupils presently in elementary school, two will not finish high school and only five will continue their education beyond high school.

The report of the Project on Instruction of the National Education Association states that competence in basic understandings and skills is still the best contribution of the elementary schools to future workers, but that the schools should also help pupils to learn more about the world of work. The report suggests that high schools offer some direct vocational education to pupils who do not plan to continue their formal schooling beyond the secondary school, with special programs being provided for the physically handicapped and the culturally deprived [111:112]. The importance of adequate vocational guidance programs in high schools, including testing programs and the providing of information to pupils about opportunities in the various occupations, has been cited as a special need for American high schools by many authorities.

All too often when a need is discovered in American education, a crash program is quickly developed to meet the need. There are those today who feel that such a program is needed in vocational education. Harris [48:365], however, points out that the essential purpose of American education is to train citizens rather than workers and that such crash programs are not defensible. Harris also feels that separating pupils into two different kinds of high schools, one academic and the other vocational, is not the answer to the need for vocational education. Rather than have this type of separation, Harris suggests post-high school education of at least one or two years' duration for the majority of American youth and cites the community junior college as the best answer to the problem.

The American Association of School Administrators [54:24] points out another aspect of the problem of vocational education. The more specific the vocational training of an individual becomes, the more vulnerable he is to changes in employment opportunities over which he

The objective of economic efficiency highlights the need for secondary schools to be concerned with the vocational interests and needs of students. In what forms should this concern be expressed? *(Photograph by Joe Di Dio, National Education Association.)*

has little or no control. The association suggests that the vocational education program be directed toward "general vocational excellence" in "broad occupational areas," leaving to the specific industry or craft the training of workers for particular assignments.

In 1969 the National Advisory Council on Vocational Education reported to the Secretary of Health, Education, and Welfare that 25 per cent of the young men and women who turn 18 each year are not educated to "a level of employability." The Council cited this condition as an important cause of the unrest and violence prevalent in the country. The Council maintained that: "At the very heart of the problem is a national attitude that says vocational education is designed for somebody else's children." The Council deplored this attitude as "snobbish, undemocratic, and a revelation of why schools fail so many students." The Council further charged that local school districts concentrate on college preparatory students in "reckless disregard of the fact that for 60 per cent of our young people high school is still the only transition to the world of work" [90:11].

While the Council saw the provision of additional federal financial support as a solution to the problem, it is clear that the charges, if true, impose a significant responsibility upon teachers. Teachers are in a position to diagnose the ability and potential of students; to help them understand their potential; and to assist them in coming to realistic decisions relative to career choices. Not all students are suited for college training, and the economy does offer many opportunities for noncollege-bound students who develop employable skills. The preparation of students for diverse kinds of employment is a responsibility of schools and teachers.

SUMMARY

This chapter has been concerned with some of the problems and issues with which educators have been confronted for many years. Teachers moving into the profession will encounter these problems and can play a vital role in determining how successful the schools may move toward their solution.

Prospective teachers should be aware of the kinds of criticisms directed at the school, and understand their underlying causes and assess the validity of the criticisms. Undoubtedly much of it springs from a lack of understanding of what the schools are doing. Teachers can do much to develop this understanding. They are in direct contact with students and parents, and much of the community reaction to the schools is based upon the interactions they have. It is also likely that some of the criticisms directed at the schools are valid and require positive responses.

Some of the criticism of the schools also can be attributed to problems concerning discrimination and segregation. Courts are now demanding that desegregation plans give promise of immediate results and that faculty and student desegregation occur simultaneously.

Freedom to think, to speak, and to write as reason and conscience dictate is basic to the survival of a democratic society. The development of skill in this regard constitutes one of the very important tasks to which teachers and schools must give attention. The restraints placed on teachers in determining what the instructional program will be have been eased as the courts have shown an increasing tendency to protect teachers in the exercise of academic freedom. Having this freedom also places a grave responsibility upon teachers to be certain that the experiences they provide for boys and girls contribute to the development of skills necessary for effective living in a democratic society.

Continuing attention must also be given to what the schools should teach. Prospective teachers should study the function of the school in promoting moral growth and character without providing instruction in particular religious faiths and doctrines.

The extent to which the public schools should provide vocational education will continue to be a major issue, especially in view of the changes in occupational requirements resulting from the rapid advance of technology. Undoubtedly problems resulting from unemployment, the quest for relevance in education, the demands of industry, the increasing concern of government for education, and a host of other factors will thrust educators into major roles of leadership in determining the public school's function in meeting the vocational needs of youth.

QUESTIONS TO CONSIDER

1. What, in your opinion, are the reasons for so much criticism being made of public schools today? How do you plan to handle these criticisms when you become a teacher?
2. When you begin teaching, how will you attempt to lessen the communication gap between the general public and the schools?
3. What responsibilities do you feel a teacher has for promoting a high level of support for schools in any given community and in what ways should this be accomplished?
4. In what ways will you attempt to promote moral and spiritual values in your pupils?
5. A number of people feel that an amendment should be written into the Constitution proclaiming the United States to be a "Christian nation and giving full legal sanction to religious expressions in public schools and other governmental activities." What would be your reaction to such a proposal? Why?
6. Do you feel the Bible can be used effectively in public schools as a historical document? As literature? If so, how would you determine which version of the Bible to use? What are some of the problems a teacher would face in attempting to use the Bible as history or literature?
7. How might teachers misuse academic freedom?
8. Are there any controversial issues that should not be discussed in public schools? Explain.
9. Do you feel a teacher should be able to take a public stand on any issue without fear of reprisal? How would you justify your position?

10. What suggestions do you have for resolving the problem of discrimination and segregation in schools?
11. What should be the function of the public schools with respect to vocational education?

PROBLEM SITUATION FOR INQUIRY

Mr. Ward had taught social sciences for three years in a large city high school before he and his wife moved to Milford Center, a small conservative community, over a year ago. He was very popular with students because of his robust physical appearance, his liberal, relaxed class presentations, and his vibrant out-of-class personality. The students came to look to him as an authority on things beyond their rural community and state. He was unanimously chosen as the faculty advisor to the senior class.

Mr. Ward's teaching was above average, and his students scored high on achievement tests in the subject areas for which he was responsible. In essence, he performed all his school-oriented duties in a highly satisfactory manner.

Mr. Ward had strong feelings about war and did not hesitate to make his feelings known in his classes. Upon learning that the local American Legion would have a military parade on Veteran's Day, for which school was to be dismissed, Mr. Ward suggested and organized a student march protesting a recent decision of Congress to extend military assistance to a foreign country at war. The student march caused some disruption of the parade of the American Legion. A large segment of the citizens of Milford Center were angered, and demanded that, unless Mr. Ward were fired, they would withdraw their sons and daughters from his "unsavory and subversive influence."

If you were Mr. Ward's principal, what would you do? Why?

ACTIVITIES TO PURSUE

1. Construct a list of key questions that would reflect an individual's feelings toward schools and teachers. Use these questions in conducting a representative community survey. To what extent are their criticisms typical of those reported in educational literature? How do you account for the criticisms they express?
2. Have a group of your colleagues visit one or more of the modern schools and one or more of the very traditional schools. Compare and contrast the learnings gained by the pupils. Which type of school is helping pupils the most in terms of effective democratic living?
3. Discuss with your college or university admissions officer the question of whether college freshmen are better prepared for college today than they were a decade ago. You might ask him to speak to your class on this subject.
4. Question some teachers and school administrators on how they attempt to bridge the communication gap between the general public and the schools. When you begin teaching how will you attempt to communicate effectively with the general public?
5. Arrange for a public school official, such as a superintendent of schools, to discuss with your class the ways in which schools develop moral and spiritual values in boys and girls. You may wish to discuss this matter with several teachers.
6. Conduct some research on how many different versions of the Holy Bible are in existence, some of the differences between the versions, and the faiths which subscribe to each version.
7. Have a group of students talk with their former public school teachers regarding the extent to which the latter feel they have academic freedom. Compile a list of any restrictions which they note.

8. Spend some time in one or more ghetto schools talking with teachers, administrators, and students regarding problems of discrimination and segregation. Upon the basis of your findings, what suggestions would you make for resolving this problem?
9. Investigate the area of vocational education through reading, research, and conferences with educators and laymen. Upon the basis of your findings, prepare a philosophical statement which indicates the role of public schools in meeting the occupational needs of students.

FIGURE CREDITS

FIGURE 8–1. (*Source:* "Teachers View Public Relations," *NEA Research Bulletin*, vol. 37, no. 2, National Education Association, Research Division, Washington, April, 1969, p. 39.)

9 | CURRENT CONTROVERSIAL ISSUES AND PROBLEMS IN EDUCATION

The traditional problems and issues which schools and teachers have faced are joined today by a series of relatively new problems, many of which are rooted to a very considerable extent in the rapid social, economic, and technological changes that are taking place. Students, especially in the secondary schools and in colleges, are demanding changes in educational practices and in conduct. The public is seeking evidences of quality education in our schools and of practices for assuring this quality. Increased pressure is being placed upon schools and teachers to deal more adequately with various disadvantaged groups of students and with the problem of racism. These problems are explored in the remaining sections of this chapter.

STUDENT DEMANDS FOR RELEVANCE, RECOGNITION, AND CHANGE

As students become increasingly aware of the complex problems of society which they will face in the future, they frequently feel frustrated. They may experience difficulty in finding channels open to discuss their problems, concerns, fears, and frustrations. These feelings may lead to the desire to protest various conditions with which they are confronted. Hence, it was not alarming to find that 18 per cent of all the nation's high schools had faced a serious student protest in the 1968–1969 school year. The major issues of protest were "disciplinary rules, dress codes, school services and facilities, and curriculum policy" [112:145]. The most popular forms of protest were sit-ins in smaller schools and the use of underground newspapers in the larger schools.

In the years to come, it is reasonable to assume that students will continue to seek change through the use of organized protests, although the issues and the forms of protest may differ. Teachers and school administrators are confronted with the task of trying to understand the sources of student concerns and frustrations. They should listen to students, talk with them as human beings who have individual and unique problems and concerns, and encourage them to get together intellectually for open discussion on controversial issues [148:407]. By recognizing and dealing with students on these bases, teachers may be able to lessen the undesirable causes of student protests, and at the same time, provide more positive learning experiences.

How Can Schools Become More Relevant?

One of the most common areas of concern to students involves the relevance of the school curriculum. In discussing the relationship of "relevance" to student protest groups, Shaffer maintains that the crusade toward a more relevant education involves the provision of courses and the reform of instructional programs to bring them more closely into line with student interests [115:647].

The striving for relevance has taken many forms, one aspect of which has been the request for educational experiences which are of immediate value and significance. Use of school time for protest against governmental activities, the demand for a "black studies" program, and sugges-

Youth today want to have the opportunity to discuss their problems, concerns, fears, and frustrations. They want to participate increasingly and more meaningfully in shaping their school experiences. *(Photograph by Joe Di Dio, National Education Association.)*

tions that grading be eliminated are representative of proposed changes advanced as part of the thrust for relevant education.

Van Til believes that much of the content taught in schools is unrelated to the lives of the learners. He identifies the problem faced by the teacher in the following manner [147:14, 16]:

Classes do exist in your community and mine in which an uninterrupted academic content bores young people. Classes do exist where subject matter is quite unrelated to the dilemmas and struggles and aspirations of many prospective learners.

The teacher who realizes that his content of instruction isn't meaningful has two viable alternatives. He can change his content from irrelevant to the relevant. Or, if he cannot change the required content, he can teach it in such a way as to give it relevance.

Yes, a third possibility does exist. One can continue with the meaningless content, break his heart trying to teach, and achieve very little.

The alternatives listed by Van Til may oversimplify the problem. Obviously teachers cannot give to elementary and secondary school students the responsibility for deciding what education is relevant and should be retained. This is a professional responsibility for which the mature, adult teacher is specifically prepared. Yet, the students' reactions should not be ignored. As the one most affected, the student can be a valuable source in aiding teachers in determining the relevance of curricular offerings.

The phenomenal expansion of technological knowledge and skills creates new demands in the education of youth. Relevance today includes familiarity with, and at least minimal skill in the use of, computers. *(Photograph by Joe Di Dio, National Education Association.)*

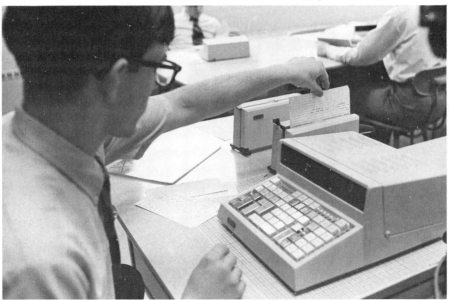

In all likelihood most school programs are more relevant than critics of the schools would have us believe and less relevant than school personnel would like them to be. Teachers are in the best position to assess course offerings, to gauge student reaction, and to continuously "tune" the curricular offerings so that they will be designed to meet changing student needs.

What Is the Role of Students in School Government?

Student protests, the demand for relevance in education, and a general awareness of the problems and concerns of young people have helped to produce demands for a greater role for students in the governance of the schools they attend. The reduction of the voting age in federal and in most state elections, as well as military service for 18 year olds, has added incentive and logic to this trend. High school graduates go into the world as adults with the responsibility and authority to become practicing members of a democratic society. If they are to be ready for this role, the preparation must come in the experiences students have as they move through school. The need for graduate students who are ready to participate in government is a powerful argument for student participation in school governance.

Surprisingly the school board members who have the authority for directing the schools appear to agree with the need for greater participation by students. When asked to give their views on student participation, a group of school board members made the following comments [7:27–28]:

Anybody enlightened enough to take a seat on a school board ought to recognize readily "that our youth, for numerous reasons, are capable of responsible thinking and should be given the opportunity to express the logic of their opinions." Students should and do have excellent ideas for improving policies that govern their education. I think they should be encouraged to develop these ideas systematically; to research them as to legality, possibility of accomplishing anticipated results, and effect on the school system. They should take part in discussions prior to the vote of the school board and be willing to assume some of the responsibilities of implementing policies.

Santa Barbara, California, for example, has a student board of education that assists the "senior" school board in making policy. The student board, which meets on the day preceding the "senior" board meeting, considers the agenda to be taken up by the "senior" board and reports its actions to the "senior" board during its regular meeting [72:29].

The attitude of students toward their own role in school government was indicated in a survey in Ohio in which 90 per cent of the students interviewed expressed a desire to be involved in the decisions that affected them, specifically "curriculum planning, dress codes, and rules

Student councils should provide excellent opportunities for students to assume meaningful roles in the governance of schools. *(Photograph by Carolyn Salisbury, National Education Association.)*

of conduct." The students in the survey expressed the opinion that a major problem in schools was the lack of communication between "themselves and school administrators and teachers" [88:85].

As in other areas relating to students, the teacher's role is extremely significant. While much of the discussion and writing relative to student participation in school government is concerned with the school board and administrative structure, the fact remains that students spend most of their school hours in direct contact with teachers. This relationship offers much of the opportunity for effective student involvement in school government. Teachers should recognize that students have ideas, and that they want to be involved. The primary responsibility for directing the schools should remain with administrators and teachers. However, carrying out this responsibility will be easier if the views of students are actively sought and considered.

Can the School Curriculum Be Adapted to Changing Needs?

The traditional school curriculum has undergone many changes in recent years. In addition to changes being made in the usual subject areas, the schools have attempted to adjust the curricula to meet the new and changing problems of society. Two of the most significant areas of curriculum expansion have been in sex education and drug education.

The growth in the number of family life and sex education programs in the schools has, according to one authority, been a reaction to the increasing number of premarital pregnancies, forced marriages, early divorces, abortions, and an increased venereal disease rate [114:3]. These problems have demonstrated the need for students to have factual knowledge of and an orientation to sexuality. That students have not received the necessary information from nonschool sources was shown in a Purdue University poll in which 53 per cent of the boys and 43 per cent of the girls stated that they "got the word" from their friends. Another 15 per cent "pieced things together" from a variety of sources. Only 15 per cent of the boys and 35 per cent of the girls received sex information from their parents [114:3].

While the public has generally favored school efforts to fill the need for responsible sex education programs, there are those who believe that schools should not be involved in such programs. Organizations have been formed to fight the spread of sex education programs in schools, and individual parents have become actively concerned. There is a tendency on the part of some school people to feel that these reactions come from right-wing radicals. However, even the proponents of sex education agree that this is not necessarily the case. As one writer indicates ". . . there are nevertheless many astute parents who recoil from something as psychologically important as sex being taught by teachers who may have few or no qualifications for such a job and may have sexual hang-ups of their own" [56:2].

The effort to provide drug education also has been a response to current problems. In 1970 the Drug Abuse Education Act was passed by Congress providing money for state departments of education to use in planning and carrying out drug abuse education programs [77:77]. Enactment of this program followed a report that drug use by students was extensive in half of the nation's urban schools and in 30 per cent of the rural schools. The report indicated that there were 100,000 heroin addicts in New York City's high schools alone [146:7].

The challenge involved in providing drug education may be summarized as follows [19:9]:

The urgent need for drug education in our schools goes beyond the task of conveying the facts of drug use and abuse—at best a difficult and sensitive job. It challenges the very meaning and methods of education.

The challenge comes in answers to the fundamental question: Why do students use drugs? Ignorance, curiosity, peer pressure, the desire to rebel are all considered factors in stimulating drug use by high school students—and increasingly by elementary school pupils. Students also use drugs because they enjoy them. But equally significant motives for student drug use are described as loneliness, unhappiness with one's self or one's family, and lack of fulfillment.

This challenge to the schools has produced many kinds of reactions including the development of courses of study in the problems of drug addiction, insertion of units on drugs in teacher preparation courses, and the distribution of pamphlets and materials designed to acquaint students with the dangers of drug abuse. Hope that the problems of drug abuse can be dealt with is heightened by a Purdue University poll indicating that high school students are "cautious" in their outlook on drugs. Only 11 per cent of those surveyed favored legalizing the sale of marihuana, and a majority indicated they would not try drugs even if the threats of addiction or arrest were absent [80:26].

The efforts of schools to react to drug and sex problems are probably a forerunner of more active school involvement in the problems of our society. This trend places a heavier responsibility upon teachers and administrators. It means they will often be at the center of controversy, since the issues involved and the solutions are seldom uniformly clear. School involvement in current issues also reemphasizes the importance of continuing education for teachers and other adults. Remaining up-to-date on the drug problem alone is a challenging responsibility. Adding to the school's curriculum also creates the problem of finding room in an already crowded program.

CONCERNS FOR THE QUALITY OF THE EDUCATIONAL PRODUCT

A second set of current problems and issues centers upon the quality of the educational product. The public has become more "results-oriented," and they are talking in terms of benefits derived from dollars spent, or cost-benefits analysis. Taxpayers are increasingly demanding that schools and school personnel be held "accountable" for educational results. One of the more controversial responses to this demand has been the use of "performance contracting" in an attempt to guarantee a specified level of pupil achievement. Educational results vary widely throughout the country, and many parents rightfully contend that their children are the victims of unequal educational opportunity. All this activity, the criticisms and the reactions, has been focused in demands for the institution of a program of national assessment.

Can the Process of Education Be Made Accountable?

A growing number of individuals concerned with education have become convinced that it is possible to hold schools responsible for the results of their activity. The emphasis on accountability is not upon the teacher or the teaching process. Rather it is upon results as reflected by the degree to which students actually develop the knowledge and skills which are the objectives of instruction.

The search for accountability has taken many forms. Descriptive terms, such as educational engineering, management by objectives, systems analysis, and performance contracting, have become a part of the vocabulary of education. Regardless of the terms used, it is apparent that the idea of holding schools responsible for achievement is popular with those outside the field of education.

A survey taken by a professional polling firm in the early 1970s asked the adult public to respond to the question: "Would you like to see students in the local schools be given national tests so that their educational achievement could be compared with students in other communities?" A total of 70 per cent responded favorably to this question [36:33]. In one Gallup Survey, the following question, dealing directly with the concept of accountability, was asked: "Would you favor or oppose a system that would hold teachers and administrators more accountable for the progress of students?" In response to this question, 67 per cent responded in favor, 21 per cent were opposed, and the remaining 12 per cent had no opinion [35:101]. In response to the question "Should each teacher be paid on the basis of the quality of work or should all teachers be paid on a standard scale basis?" 58 per cent favored a "quality of work" base as compared to 36 per cent favoring "a standard scale basis" [35:101].

While enthusiasm within the field of education relative to "accountability" has not matched that of the general public, a number of school systems are moving in this direction. For example, the New York City Schools have employed the Educational Testing Service at a cost of "not more than $100,000" to develop a systemwide plan for accountability [84:134]. Given this kind of impetus and the favorable public reaction, it is probable that the search for accountability will be of long duration.

Can Performance Contracting Guarantee Pupil Achievement?

One of the chief devices used in attempts to provide accountability has been that of performance contracting. A major thrust in this direction occurred in 1969 when the Texarkana school district entered into a contract by which a private business firm took over the operation of a part of the instructional program. The firm guaranteed to produce specific instructional results in the areas of reading and mathematics with payment under the contract conditioned on the success the company realized in raising student achievement to the guaranteed levels.

Other school systems have ventured into the field of performance contracting with encouragement and financial assistance being provided by the U.S. Office of Education. For example, in 1970 the Gary, Indiana School Board received a four-year federal grant in excess of $2,000,000 to experiment with performance contracting in an attempt to overcome the "gross underachievement" of Gary's children [96:39]. A private firm was given the management and instructional responsibility for an all-black elementary school. The company agreed to refund the approximately $800 it received for teaching a pupil if, at the end of the instructional period, the pupil's achievement was not up to national norms on tests administered by an independent evaluator.

Whether performance contracting will develop into a basic part of the instructional program of the public schools is uncertain and will depend, in part, upon the degree to which early efforts are successful.

Certainly the development of performance contracting has its share of critics and skeptics. The National Education Association has taken an attitude of extreme caution in advising affiliates "not to become parties to a performance contract without careful prior planning and consultation" [83:86]. Among the conditions which the NEA believes should be present are: involvement of teachers in every phase of planning from contracting to evaluation; use of professionally trained and certificated personnel; and compliance which the negotiated agreements already in effect between school boards and teacher groups [83:86]. There are also legal problems to be considered. Many of the early performance contracts have required temporary suspension of statutory regulations and administrative rules in areas such as class size and teacher certification. Almost certainly some of these contracts have involved the delegation of school board authority in ways which can be considered extra-legal. If performance contracting is to flourish, a firm legal basis will have to be provided.

Despite the problems already encountered, performance contracting is not likely to go away. Education is big business, and many private firms are looking toward the instruction of public school pupils as a promising source of productive investment. Also, the public is receptive to the idea of "guaranteed results." These conditions present a challenge to teachers to attempt to provide within the public schools the type of innovation and experimentation that would have even greater appeal to the public than performance contracting. At the same time, teachers need to be alert to the techniques used by private firms so that those which prove successful can be integrated into the public school program.

How Can Educational Opportunity Be Equalized?

The emphasis on accountability in education has given new significance to a fundamental ideal in the American school system: equal educational opportunity for all children. Since early colonial days, considerable progress has been made, but much yet remains to be done. One factor in limiting the progress which has been made has been the seeming inability to provide a sound financial base for all schools. Inequalities in financial support of public schools among the various states and communities are a basic fact of educational life.

In recent years those working to guarantee equal educational opportunity have turned to the courts in an attempt to gain improved state programs of school financing. Early efforts were unsuccessful. In a typical Illinois case the court held that the "equal opportunity" controversy could not be adjudicated because there were "no discoverable and manageable standards by which the court can determine when the Constitution is satisfied and when it is violated" [*McInnis v. Shapiro,* 293 F. Supp. 327 (1968)]. However, more recent efforts have met with a success which many believe could lead to alteration of state finance programs throughout the country. The California and the Minnesota court cases of 1971 found the public school state financing systems, and in particular the local property tax, to be in violation of the "equal protection clause" of the 14th Amendment because they produced inequalities in the financial ability of individual school districts. While these decisions were concerned with state plans, those who argue in favor of federal aid to education believe the reasoning used by the courts supports their contention that only the federal government is in a position to equalize educational opportunity throughout the United States through provision of funds to needy states and school districts.

Another type of education inequality involves the educationally deprived. In considering the objective of equal educational opportunity, Kirp maintains that [61:635]:

While educators have long spoken of equality of educational opportunity, it has been tacitly understood for at least as long that the quality of education that a school child received depended in large part on the community in which he happened to grow up. Suburban towns have had sufficient financial resources to afford the finest facilities and the best qualified teachers; their students have come almost exclusively from upper middle-class backgrounds. In contrast, at least since World War II, the big cities have been poor cities, poor both in money available to spend for facilities and teachers, and in vitally important human resources.

The educationally deprived youngster is often poverty-stricken and frequently lives either in a depressed rural area, on an Indian reservation, or in one of the ghettos of large cities. He comes from a family which typically exists on a low economic and educational level and which is likely to place little value on formal education. His family tends to be mobile, moving in an attempt to find a better life. But this mobility seldom solves the family's problem. Unable to achieve success in one location, the family frequently is also unable to establish a better living standard elsewhere, primarily because of the inadequacy of its cultural and educational background. It is easy to see that the problems of educating a child from such a family are tremendous.

In 1965, the Congress moved to provide better educational opportunities for the educationally deprived through passage of two of the most significant legislative acts dealing with public education that have ever been passed. The first of these, the Economic Opportunity Act, established Project Head Start, providing for preschool experiences for educationally deprived children. The second act, the Elementary and Secondary Education Act, bases much of its financial support to school districts upon the economic level of families living within each district and requires that those school districts which seek to take advantage of the act make provision for special programs for disadvantaged children.

The explosion of technology has resulted in a demand for workers and technicians possessing more training than ever before. This situation is likely to become even more critical in the years ahead. The educationally deprived child is therefore less and less likely to become a productive member of society when he reaches adulthood. Not only must we find ways to finance a more adequate educational program for this child, but educators must be willing to make whatever changes in our traditional school programs are necessary to meet his unique needs.

Teachers need to study the background of efforts to provide equal educational opportunities and see the relevance of current attempts to remedy inequities. To do this it will be necessary to study carefully and critically the current legislation and the agencies and forces which are at work to promote or defeat this imperative need in our time.

In the face of the great differences that exist in educational opportunities, it is difficult to help young and old alike maintain their faith in democracy despite its limitations in American life. Teachers have to teach youngsters and adults the actual state of affairs today, at the same time fostering a belief in the American ideal of equality for all and a democratic respect for the uniqueness of the individual. This is a task of a political nature, a task of statesmanship, and one of the most important aspects of the role of the teacher today.

Will National Assessment Answer the Critics?

In 1969 a program of "national assessment" was initiated. The program resulted from many years of discussion and six years of planning and preparation, dating from 1963 when the Carnegie Foundation asked a group of educators to explore the feasibility of making a "national assessment" of education.

From the very beginning the concept of assessment on a national basis has been surrounded by controversy. Proponents believe that:

1. The program will give the nation as a whole a better understanding of the strengths and weaknesses of the educational system.
2. Information secured from a national testing program will be invaluable to educational leaders in planning for innovation and change in educational practices.
3. It is unrealistic to expect Congress and the state legislatures to continue to increase educational expenditures without having some tangible measurement of results.

Those opposing a national assessment program contend that:

1. A national testing program is the first step in what could develop as a federal system of education and could be the basis for federal coercion of local school systems.
2. No test or series of tests can measure all the varied outcomes of education or take into account different state and local educational aspirations and objectives.
3. A national testing program will result in teaching for the "tests" and will stifle curriculum development, innovation, and change.

While the controversy continues, the program of national assessment is underway. It started in 1969 under the direction of the Education Commission of the States, with the testing of 9- 13- and 17-year olds and young adults in the 26–35 age group in the areas of citizenship, science, and writing. Testing followed the next year in the areas of reading and literature, and the following year in music and social studies. Additional testing areas are mathematics, art, and vocational education. Tests are to be repeated on a cyclical basis so that progressive comparisons can be made. The testing is being carried out by private contractors. Results are reported using the following subdivisions: male and female; four geographic regions (Northeast, Southeast, Central, and West); different types of communities (large city, urban, fringe, middle-sized city, and rural-small town); race (black, white, and other) and two socioeconomic levels [52:13].

The early results are so tentative and a basis for comparison so lacking that they cannot be used to judge the assessment process itself. Sample conclusions based on the first round of testing include the following [11:72]:

1. Large percentages of the nation's school-age youngsters and young adults don't understand or value some basic Constitutional rights.
2. The least understood or valued right is the freedom to express controversial or unpopular opinions.
3. Fifty-four per cent of the 17-year-olds and 61 per cent of the young adults believe they can personally influence government.
4. A total of 50 per cent of the 17-year-olds, compared with only 38 per cent of the young adults, can write an acceptable description of an automobile accident after studying a conventional accident diagram.
5. Only 28 per cent of the 9-year-olds can include all the information needed to address an envelope correctly.

As testing continues, information of the kind illustrated by the above conclusions and findings will be voluminous, and proponents hope that it will become highly significant as future testing enables comparisons and measurement of progress.

Almost certainly national assessment will continue. Prior to 1970, the federal government has spent $3.9 million on the program, and additional expenditures of $4.5 million were scheduled for 1971 [31:234]. The Education Commission of the States also has volunteered to aid states in setting up their own assessment programs, and Florida has become the first to accept the opportunity. A statewide assessment program costing the State of Florida as much as $12 million per year is underway [173:229].

The evidence of potential controversy continues to surround the assessment concept. The National Education Association included the following among its 1971 resolutions [75:89]:

The National Education Association notes that the first report of the National Assessment of Educational Progress on writing, citizenship and science has been issued.

The Association will continue to resist any attempt to transform national assessment results into a national testing program that would seek to measure all students or school districts by a single standard, and thereby impose upon them a single program rather than providing opportunities for multiple programs and objectives.

The cautious attitude expressed in the second paragraph of the resolution is representative of the views of those who continue to view national assessment with concern. Whether such fears will prove groundless may be determined as annual testing continues, data accumulate, and results are interpreted.

CONCERNS OVER DEPRIVATION AND RACISM[1]

American society is a mixture of national origins and social classes. In some schools as many as fifty nationalities are represented in the pupil body. Because of local conditions and pressures to integrate the schools, children of the poor and the wealthy, the illiterate and the educated, are sometimes found in the same school. But in the inner city the Negroes and the Puerto Ricans are forced by circumstance to live off by themselves, and thus their children attend schools in which there is less variation of cultural background and wealth. The same observation can be made about the children who live in rural poverty, or in Mexican communities, or on Indian reservations. Such variety among communities and pupils demands that all educational personnel be prepared to cope with problems arising from all kinds of social circumstances.

Even where the children come from apparently similar social and racial situations, as in suburbia or the black ghettos, a teacher ought to have a broad background, not only better to understand a child's situation but to direct him in his search for broader experiences. For example, a teacher who knows that use of a dialect is in itself no indication of shallowness of thought or feeling may be able to relate to the child by showing an understanding of the depth and vigor of that dialect. From

[1]This section has been reproduced from *Teachers for the Real World,* pp. 11–20, 1969, written by B. Othanel Smith and others, with permission granted by the American Association of Colleges for Teacher Education, Washington.

this the teacher may expand the ability of the child to use language in a way that helps him maintain respect for both his old and new manners of speech. To extend his language habits is to expand the child's possibilities of human associations. . . .

Should teachers for culturally deprived children be given some special type of training as are the teachers of the blind or mentally handicapped? One answer to this question is that the special motivations, attitudes, language system, and conduct of disadvantaged children require that their teachers be trained in methods different from teachers of middle-class children. Another answer is that under-privileged children learn in the same way as other children and that their teachers need no special training. This latter is the view taken here. The problem of preparing teachers adequately for the disadvantaged is the same as the problem of preparing teachers adequately for all children. We do not need special teachers for the children of different ethnic and social groups. Rather, we need teachers who are able to work effectively with children regardless of race or social situation, but mindful of what that is in each case.

The special circumstances from which children come cannot, indeed, be ignored in the preparation of teachers. On the contrary, teachers should be trained to work with the cultural and racial background of each child. A child's cultural heritage should be considered by his teacher to be the basis for his education, not a stumbling block. A child should learn because of what he already knows, not in spite of it. "Culturally deprived" is not an accurate term. No one is lacking in culture whether he be from the vast ranks of the poor, or the middle or upper class, or from differing areas of the country. The poor are not lacking in culture; theirs is as different from that of the middle class as the Southern culture is different from the New England culture. For example, one of the authors of *The Disadvantaged: Challenge to Education* speaks of interesting an eighth grade class in poetry. The teacher presented them a poem by Langston Hughes written in a dialect close to their own and known in Hughes' time as "jive." The class came alive and participated as any good teacher dreams of his class doing, illustrating "an approach to nonstandard dialect in such a way that the pupils feel that learning standard English dialect doesn't mean that they must discard their own" [29:382].

The teaching of poor children does not require unique skills, as does teaching the blind, for the handicap comes not from the children themselves but is placed upon them by the situations in which they live and the schools to which they go. But it does require broad life experiences which few middle-class teachers have had. Unless we stress this view of teacher education, we can unintentionally aggravate a potentially explosive division between the social classes and ethnic groups in our society.

False Ideas about the Disadvantaged

So much has been written and said about the extreme want and educational starvation of these children that a false image has been created. It is easy to imagine that they are somehow emotionally and intellectually inferior. These children are basically the same as all other children. Though their experience may be different, they too are interested in their world, attached to their families, and have important hopes and aspirations. If these characteristics are not visible to their teachers, it is because the teachers see only with the narrow vision of the middle class.

Another false image of deprived children is that they are all alike. In truth they are as different from one another as the children of other elements of the population. The poor are different in life styles: the Appalachian white child, the Mexican child, the [black] child and the Indian child have distinct outlooks and modes of behavior, although the differences within these groups are as large as the differences among them. The black youth of the ghetto is greatly influenced, often controlled, by the norms and power of his peer group. The Appalachian youth is influenced more by his family and the adult community. Like the youth of the ghetto, he also is inclined to be resourceful and independent. The Mexican-American so closely identifies with his family and its cultural milieu that he is often more at variance with the norms of the school than either the Appalachian white or the [black] of the ghetto. The Indian child lives in a culture almost entirely apart from the culture of the white man or Appalachian, Mexican, or [black] variations.

If one considers affluent children, he will find differences among them as striking as those among the poor. There will be physical as well as cultural differences attributable to social origins, occupations of their parents, and family income. Many children of the very affluent have had a great deal of experience at sophisticated levels. To them school is apt to be dull and lack the sensational experiences to which they are accustomed. The children of the families from skilled occupations and proprietary groups are apt to be ambitious, although they do not always pursue the knowledge that could fulfill their ambitions. These are rather gross distinctions and in some cases they will not hold. But they will suggest the differences that often seem unexpectedly great to teachers moving from a "comfortable" school to a different one.

If we look again at disadvantaged children, we see that some of them come from families which are chronically poor. These people live on the barest necessities of life and are for the most part demoralized and hopeless. Many live in filth and degradation and would perish without some form of public aid. At this level of cultural existence children see little in the future except the kind of life their parents have had. The schools appear to offer them neither hope nor learning. For this hard core, poverty is a way of life.

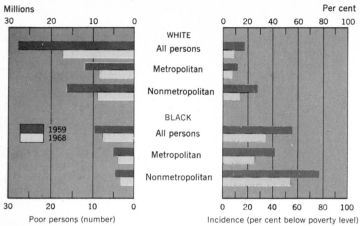

FIGURE 9–1   Number and percentage of persons in the United States in 1959 and 1968 classified as impoverished.

Economically, socially, and educationally disadvantaged children are ot new to American society. Throughout American. history since colonial days, disadvantaged youths and their families have made heroic efforts to avail themselves of schools.The existence of the free public school system itself can be attributed largely to the struggle of the laboring man to provide an education for his children. Even though the public school system is now well fixed in the American institutional structure, the struggle for an adequate program of education for the children of low-income groups continues.

Disadvantages and Deprivations

It is futile to look at the disadvantaged as a homogeneous group. What is emerging from the mass of literature on the deprived is that it is more profitable, certainly for pedagogical purposes, to look at the social and economic factors which cause problems for children in relation to the school.

One of the central conditions which affects many disadvantaged school children is simply lack of money. Many studies indicate that the cost of schooling (dues, trips, out-of-pocket expense, collections for various causes, loss of family income, etc.) places an undue hardship on the child whose family is poor. If school is expensive, the child who cannot afford the cost of schooling must either avoid the cost and not participate in the school's program or accept the charity of the school. Either route is unacceptable. If the child does not participate, his experience is limited and his self-esteem may be damaged. If he accepts the charity of the school, the injury to his self-concept is apt to be even greater. For, as the Webbs pointed out long ago, charity degrades both the giver and the receiver.

The children of poverty suffer chronically from malnutrition. Depression, apathy, limited amounts of energy, and lethargy are but some of the effects of poor nutrition. The impact of malnutrition on the functioning of the child in school indicates the close interrelation between the school and community life of the child. The hunger which a child carries to school lessens his performance and affects his attitudes.

The disadvantaged child is often affected adversely by the instability of his family and the unemployment of his parents. There is considerable evidence showing the close connection between the degree of family stability and the child's ability to profit from schooling. It is very difficult in school for a child who comes from a home that is broken but has economic security, but it is almost devastating for one who comes from a home where there is neither family nor economic stability.

One of the conditions which induces a sense of futility among the disadvantaged is the failure of the helping professions to perform their tasks adequately among the poor whites, the black, the Indian, and the migrant. Legal services for these people are almost nonexistent. The record of police discrimination is one of the salient features of the Kerner Report. Medical services are often unavailable to the poor, causing some groups to forfeit, on the average, as much as a quarter of a century of their lives. The failure of the medical profession to respond to the needs of the poor stems partly from a desire to be compensated for services rendered, but it is also a commentary on the nature of our social priorities: profit is placed above service where people are concerned. The lack of response of psychiatrists and psychologists to the needs of the poor is notorious. Similar examples document the failure of human services to meet social responsibilities and show the classic bias that is built into our social system.

The massive evidence which has been assembled to document the plight of the [black] shows only too well the prejudices of the white man and the effects of racial discrimination upon black children. The recent Racial Isolation Report, the Coleman Report, and the Kerner Report add weight to years of scholarly findings and indicate the immense impact of segregation on the black children of society. Segregation has created in many [black] children a sense of inferiority, a negative self-image, and a feeling that blackness is a stigma.

When one takes all of these facts into account, the failure of deprived children to respond to traditional programs of schooling is understandable. Yet some conclude that the children's serious environmental deficits make adjusting to the work of the school impossible. Others believe that the curriculum, teachers, and school organization simply cannot be adapted to the uniquenesses of disadvantaged children. The blame can be placed on the child or on the school. But the fact of the school's

How may the attitudes, beliefs, and behavior of these children be affected as a result of their home environment? How can the school effectively meet their educational needs? *(Photograph by Carl Purcell, National Education Association.)*

ineffectiveness remains. The disadvantaged child seems to get progressively further behind in his achievement, in his adjustment to the demands of schooling, and in his relationships to teachers.

The school system itself is one of the conditions that accentuates the problems of the deprived child. Recent evidence from the disadvantaged themselves, in the Kerner Report, indicates that the school is not as high on the list of complaints as other social agencies. Still, the teaching profession would be foolish to ignore evidence in dropout rates, comparative scores on tests, turnover of teachers in poor and ghetto areas, and other measurements indicating a pattern of discrimination to which the schools wittingly or unwittingly contribute.

If the education of the teacher is looked at in the context of the great variation among the children of the American people, the enormous dimensions of the teacher's task become only too clear. The educational system, no less than the American people, is devoted to the idea of a common school. It is the only institution through which all the children of all the people share in the wide range of experience that is both the richness and the poverty of American life. The teacher who can work with the children of only one social stratum or minority group is inadequately prepared to teach in the common school. The idea that the backgrounds and interests of the child must be understood if he is to be properly taught must now be put into practice. Furthermore, skills and techniques of effective interaction with children and adults at all points on the social spectrum must be built into the competency of every teacher.

The Disadvantaged and Racism

The problem of educating disadvantaged children can too easily become confused with the problems caused by the white man's prejudice and discriminations against the black man. The disadvantaged child is a product of his social class, and his deficiencies are attributable to the race of his parents only to the extent that white prejudice creates their poverty and other environmental limitations. The problem of educating the deprived child would exist if the total population of the country were either entirely white or entirely black. To be disadvantaged is to be a member of the lower social class, regardless of race or minority group.

Educational and economic deprivation is drastically increased by the existence of racism. Racism would deny any individual, because of color, the privilege of living in any part of the community he prefers, of being buried in any spot of earth he can afford, of holding a job for which he is fully competent, of getting an adequate education, and of associating freely with his friends regardless of their race.

Human beings have always set themselves apart from others on the dogma that some are by nature superior. This dogma was used as the justification of all forms of slavery, and, while a great proportion of the peoples of the earth have discarded it legally, there are still many who hold to it tenaciously. This dogma is the ultimate rationalization of the militant white when he is forced to justify his discriminations and crimes against the [black man]. He may not say it in so many words, but what he means is that, by nature, the blood of the white is superior to that of the black.

In racism, not only is the total group discriminated against, but the individual must carry the injustices which the white man's prejudices place upon the group. No matter how well the [black] may be educated or how wealthy he may be, the racist considers him to be inferior and enforces this belief in a thousand ways frequently too subtle to be perceived. In a democracy it is by the principle of achievement that the social position of an individual should be determined, not by his blood or his wealth. In actual practice, however, achievement has been combined with wealth. Racism has denied even the nation's most famous [blacks] the respect to which they were entitled by achievement.

The condemnation of the total group because of blood is the dogma of racial superiority that underlay Nazism. The basic idea of Nazism was not that the state is superior to the individual, but that the state is the instrument of the superior race in its efforts to reconstruct the world in its own image. In this sense, white prejudice in this country is much like the doctrine of racial superiority of the Nazi movement.

The [black] is not in the ghettos by his own choice. He is not in the work camps and the rural slums of the South because he wants to be there. He is in these places because that is where racist discriminations have placed him. The Irish once populated the ghettos [blacks] occupy today. The Italians and Jews also lived there. These people had their own schools, policemen, commercial enterprises, and small shops. In time they accumulated enough wealth and education to move out of the inner city to places more comfortable to live and rear children.

In these earlier ghettos there were jobs, industries, strong traditions, and morale to nourish and sustain the individual. But there are no jobs, no enterprises, and few traditions in the black ghettos, only hopelessness and loss of identity. The [black] has not been able to better himself while in the ghetto and to enjoy social mobility because American society is closed to him in countless ways. A great deal is said about our "open" society, but what we overlook is that it is open differentially to people according to their economic status and color. No one wishes to condemn the ideology of an open society just because American society at this point in its history is not completely open. It is the ideal by which men live and struggle to improve their social institutions and practices. The ideology must not be used to gloss over the hard fact that the ideal has yet to be realized.

As long as the political bureaucracies of the cities discriminate against the [black] in the appointment of police and teachers and in providing social services, and just as long as the financial system discriminates against the [black] by not giving him loans for business and housing, as long as real estate interests are able to build boundaries around the [black] by zoning and other means of exclusion, just that long will the ghettos continue to exist. The white man's hostility is deplorable enough, but even worse than hostility is his insidious patronage and discrimination in education, employment, and business, and countless other ways.

Social Integration and the Schools

In recent years a great deal has been written about apartheid in South Africa. Actually it is only the word that is new in American culture. Segregation and political and economic discrimination against the black people have existed here for over 350 years, and until recently they were reinforced by legal enactments and court decisions. The legal and judicial barriers to racial integration are being reduced. Eventually white prejudice may begin to erode, and the time may not be too distant when many of the worst features of racial discrimination will be wiped out.

But at the very time when the nation is moving toward the elimination of its legal and judicial impediments to an open society, some black militants are moving to close ranks and to insist upon separation. Social change always lags far behind the promises and hopes of men. The suffering in the ghettos and in rural slums of the South is intolerable to a self-respecting people who constantly find their hopes and efforts to improve their lot thwarted by the prejudices and discriminations of the whites. But democracy cannot continue to survive in a society that follows a policy of segregation and isolation of its races. The very essence of democracy is that men are equal one to another and that this equality can be honored only in unfettered human association. Were the white militants who favor a doctrine of apartheid and the black militant who follow a separatist doctrine to succeed, the ideal of democracy in this country would perish. There would then be no guides left for those who criticize society and work for its improvement.

Social integration is a means and a goal. As a means, it is a partial solution to problems created by white prejudice. As a goal, effectively achieved, it is a true sign that massive prejudice has been eliminated. So it is with school integration. But a token integration of the schools is hardly more than a gesture.

School integration is more fundamental than the mere mingling of different races in a school building. Integration is the incorporation of individuals of different races as equals into a social group. Furthermore, school integration involves the hierarchical system by which the schools are administered and education carried on.

Malcolm X pointed out several years ago that school segregation meant not only the separation of the races into different buildings but also the control of the black schools by the white power group [65]. He went on to point out that integration simply brought the black and white children together and left the white power structure in control. At that time, he was arguing for black schools under black control. There is nothing undemocratic about a community predominantly [black] which exercises control over its schools in the same sense that a community predominantly white or upper middle class exercises control over its schools. As long as social and economic integration is denied the [black] there is no reason to deny him the privilege of managing the affairs which affect his life. No group can run the affairs of another without debilitating it. Human development depends upon the involvement of the individual in the affairs that concern him. The right of the [black] to participate in his own affairs cannot on any moral principle be denied. If integration of the schools is to occur, it must involve the participation of the [black] in the control and management of the schools as well as the classrooms.

Because of discrimination in business and housing, and lack of other human consideration, it may be many years before the black ghettos are dissolved or integrated. In the meantime, school integration must be pursued as vigorously as possible. When black and white children are bussed into mixed classes of high quality, both groups gain from the experience. The moving of [black] children into schools that are predominantly white and a corresponding transporting of white pupils into schools that are predominantly black must be increased so that larger, meaningful numbers are involved. But two-way movement is in and of itself insufficient. It is a step toward integration, not integration in its social and psychological sense.

Teacher Preparation and School Integration

The problem of training teachers for schools in disadvantaged areas is not the same as the problem of preparing teachers to deal with racism in school and society. The teacher may be well prepared to work with children and parents who are victims of economic and social deprivation. He may know how to relate to them, to empathize with them, and he may understand quite fully the social and economic forces that cause their plight. He may correctly assess the experiential background of the children and tailor his instruction to their interests and needs. He may know what sort of content is most conducive to their development and he may know how to handle that content intellectually and with technological devices. He may know all these things and still be baffled by the problems in an integrated school which originate in racism.

He may not know how to handle discipline problems in a racially mixed group, especially if part of the group is from a culturally deprived area. If a [black] teacher is confronted by discipline problems with a white child in his classroom, the problem may be much more serious to him than the same conduct would be with a [black] child. He may be concerned with the reaction of the white parents, as well as the child, to the steps he takes. The same can be said of the white teacher who has an integrated class. In some integrated schools communication between the white and the black pupils is either nonexistent or has largely broken down. The problem of restoring communication in such a situation is one with which the whole school faculty must struggle.

The teacher must also face the question of racial prejudice in himself. The white teacher harbors many prejudices of which he is unaware. The [black] teacher may carry feelings of resentment and aggression that come with a feeling of imposed inferiority. It is necessary for the teacher to face his personal problems squarely and to include in his program of preparation experiences to shock him into realization of his prejudices and show him how to deal with them. Just as there are prejudices in the teacher's feelings and modes of thought, so too are these to be found in pupils and in the adults of the community.

Proper education of the teacher will lead him to examine his own human prejudices generally and, specifically, his racial prejudices and it will discipline him in the techniques of handling problems of interpersonal relations that arise from racial prejudices in his students and their parents.

SUMMARY

This chapter has been concerned with some of the current educational issues and problems that are related to the rapidly changing social environment in which the school now functions. Teachers face the challenge of understanding these problems and of aiding in their solutions as schools strive to fulfill their function in a democratic society.

Today's student desires less conformity and more participation in his development. He wants to be heard and to be treated as a human being. Failure to recognize these facts frequently has resulted in organized protests upon the part of students. One very positive response to students has been the attempts by school administrators and teachers to provide opportunities for students to participate increasingly and more meaningfully in school government. Such participation can help to make the schools more responsive to the needs of students and at the same time prepare them to become participating members of a democratic society.

The current public desire for accountability in education is, in part, a demand that teachers be able to determine exactly the degree to which instructional objectives are achieved. The demand for objective measurement has produced experimentation with performance contracting in which private firms have been delegated instructional responsibility with payment contingent on guaranteed pupil performance.

Great differences exist throughout the United States in the educational opportunities afforded students. Various attempts are being made to remedy these inequalities through federally supported programs. An increasing awareness of these inequalities has focused attention upon the need for a better method of financing public education as well as a program of national assessment.

Teachers are confronted with the task of working more effectively with disadvantaged students and with the problem of racism in schools and in society. Disadvantaged youth often are viewed as being emotionally and intellectually inferior, when in reality they basically are the same as all youth. The problem of educating disadvantaged students often becomes confused with problems related to racism. Hence, the teacher is faced with the responsibility of critically examining his feelings and modes of thought so that he may be able to eradicate any subtle aspects of racism in his interpersonal relationships.

QUESTIONS TO CONSIDER

1. What are some of the criticisms that elementary and secondary school students have of teachers and schools? How valid do these criticisms seem to be? What changes would you suggest?
2. To what extent are schools providing dehumanizing experiences for students? What are some examples of this dehumanization, and how would you correct each of them?
3. How do you propose to deal with some of the current educational problems such as student protests, relevance, student governance, drugs, and sex education?
4. In your opinion, what are the advantages and disadvantages of holding schools accountable for the achievement of pupils?
5. What are the arguments for and against performance contracting? What implications does it have for teachers and for the organization and administration of schools?
6. How will you attempt to foster a belief in the great American ideal of educational equality for all youth? Specifically, what changes in our educational system will you attempt to promote in order to make this ideal become more of a reality?
7. Upon what bases should public school authorities in large cities attempt to ensure that the public schools are racially balanced, even though this might result in students attending schools some distance from their homes?
8. What desirable and undesirable outcomes may result from the national assessment program? What possible effects may it have upon you as a teacher?
9. In addition to the many common characteristics to be found among children of minority groups, what differences may be found in the life-styles of Appalachian white, Mexican, blacks, and Indian children? How should the school attempt to respect these differences?
10. What are the arguments for and against bussing students to achieve racial balance in the schools? Which arguments do you think are sound? Unsound? Why?
11. Do you feel that teachers of culturally deprived children should be given some special type of training? Justify your position.
12. What are the most critical problems in the ghetto community? Which ones can the schools help solve? In what ways can the schools help solve them?
13. Define the term "racism." Have you seen racism in your high school? If yes, how did it manifest itself?
14. What competencies and qualities are needed by the white teacher to teach in a ghetto school? To which ones can teacher-education programs contribute most and how?
15. If you could do so today, what changes would you make in ghetto schools?

PROBLEM SITUATION FOR INQUIRY*

As Mrs. Jones goes into different rooms in her role as resource teacher in a predominantly black school, the children usually greet her with smiles and applause. She first encountered hostility when she met Nanette.

From their first encounter, Nanette was stonily, silently, aggressively uncooperative, like a demonstrator in a sit-in. Mrs. Jones used every technique she could think of for drawing her out, but Nanette refused to be moved.

One day Mrs. Jones was trying to tell the children an inspiring story about a great black American and his contributions to our country. Nanette slumped in her chair. Mrs. Jones looked at her and she thumbed her nose at Mrs. Jones. At this point, Mrs. Jones interrupted the story at its peak and gave Nanette a piece of her mind. "If you're not interested in what

*Adapted from "Classroom Incident," *Today's Education,* vol. 58, no. 7, National Education Association, Washington, October, 1969, p. 67.

your own people have done to help make our country great, you ought to be ashamed."

Mrs. Jones has been bothered ever since. Why couldn't she have treated Nanette the way she would have treated any other child who was misbehaving? Or had she done just that? Would she or wouldn't she have been just as angry if a white child had thumbed her nose at her?

Mrs. Jones worries about the fact that she is worried. Does the whole matter bother her because there is in her some latent, unrecognized racism? She rather doubts that. She feels comfortable with the rest of her pupils, and she loves them all. Can it be that she regards black students in the context of *they* and *theirs* rather than of *we* and *ours?* It seems to her that human beings are successful in bridging a gap only when they forget there is one. She wonders if anyone can tell her how to do that. Can you?

ACTIVITIES TO PURSUE

1. Interview some school dropouts, and attempt to determine the extent to which they feel that their school experiences were irrelevant.
2. Talk with school administrators and teachers regarding such problems as student protests, student governance, drugs, and sex education. Try to determine how they are attempting to deal with these problems.
3. If possible, visit a school that is using performance contracting. Talk with teachers, school administrators, pupils, and parents to determine how they feel about the use of performance contracting and its future role in education.
4. Organize a panel discussion on ways of equalizing educational opportunities throughout the United States.
5. Have a group of students collect data on the extent to which boys and girls in your state have equal educational opportunities. Discuss how any differences that exist may be corrected.
6. Make a careful study of the findings resulting from the national assessment program. What recommendations would you make to resolve some of the educational inequalities revealed in the data?
7. Visit some schools in which there are significant numbers of students from minority groups. In what ways are the teachers recognizing the needs of these students and providing appropriate educational experiences for them?
8. Visit in some ghetto schools and talk with students and teachers about evidences of racism. How will you attempt to avoid any racial tendencies in your interpersonal relationships when you become a teacher?
9. Select an American history, or English textbook, and study the table of contents, index, and pictures. What does the textbook contain on racial and ethnic groups in America? What do you think they should contain about racial and ethnic groups? Why?
10. Interview a black, Chicano, Indian, or Puerto Rican community leader to discover what he thinks are the critical educational needs of students and how well teachers are prepared to meet them.
11. Secure a listing of courses from a black studies or ethnic studies program. What courses do you think you should take in order to prepare for teaching in a school for students of the culturally different group chosen?
12. Secure a copy of *La Raza, The Liberator,* or the *Journal of American Indian Education* and read an article about one of the culturally different groups discussed in this chapter. Write a brief review of the article telling what you agree or disagree with and why.
13. Organize a panel of your classmates to discuss and deal with such topics as: the importance of quality education for urban students, ethnic studies in teacher education, needed improvements in the education of teachers for ghetto schools, community control of schools, and new conceptions of teachers and teaching for ghetto schools.

FIGURE CREDIT

FIGURE 9–1. (*Source: Statistical Abstract of the United States*, U.S. Department of Commerce, Bureau of the Census, Washington, 1970, p. 308.)

REFERENCES

1. *Agreement between the Board of Education of the School District of the City of Detroit and the Detroit Federation of Teachers, Local 231, American Federation of Teachers, AFL-CIO, July 1, 1969-July 1, 1971,* Detroit Public School Center, 5057 Woodward Avenue, Detroit, Michigan, 1969.
2. Alexander, William M.: *Are You a Good Teacher?* Holt, Rinehart and Winston, Inc., New York, 1959.
3. Alexander, William M.: *The Emergent Middle School,* Holt, Rinehart and Winston, Inc., New York, 1968.
4. Bain, Helen: "Self-governance Must Come First, Then Accountability," *Phi Delta Kappan,* vol. 51, no. 8, p. 413, Phi Delta Kappa, Bloomington, Ind., April, 1970.
5. Beggs, David, III: *Team Teaching: Bold New Venture,* Indiana University Press, Bloomington, Ind., 1964.
6. Bloom, Benjamin Samuel: *Stability and Change in Human Characteristics,* John Wiley and Sons, Inc., New York, 1964.
7. "Boardmen Reason: Share the Power with Students," *American School Board Journal,* vol. 157, no. 11, pp. 27–28, 30–31, National School Boards Association, Evanston, Ill., May, 1970.
8. Bruner, Jerome S.: *The Process of Education,* Harvard University Press, Cambridge, Mass., 1965.
9. Bushnell, Don D.: "Computers in Education," in Ronald Gross and Judith Murphy (eds.), *The Revolution in the Schools,* pp. 56–72, Harcourt, Brace and World, Inc., New York, 1964.
10. Chambers, M. M.: "No Teacher Surplus," *Phi Delta Kappan,* vol. 52, no. 2, pp. 118–119, Phi Delta Kappa, Bloomington, Ind., October, 1970.
11. "Citizenship Weaknesses Spotted by Assessment," *Education U.S.A.,* National School Public Relations Association, Washington, November 20, 1970.
12. "Class Size," *NEA Research Bulletin,* vol. 46, no. 2, pp. 35–36, National Education Association, Research Division, Washington, May, 1968.
13. "Classroom Teachers Speak on Differentiated Teaching Assignments," *Report of the Classroom Teachers National Study Conference,* National Education Association, Association of Classroom Teachers, Washington, 1969.
14. Combs, A. W.: *The Professional Education of Teachers,* Allyn and Bacon, Inc., Boston, Mass., 1965.
15. *Computers: New Era for Education,* National School Public Relations Association, Washington, 1968.
16. *The Contemporary Challenge to American Education,* National Education Association, Educational Policies Commission, Washington, 1958.
17. Darling, Charles M.: *Perspectives for the 70's and 80's: Tomorrow's Problems Confronting Today's Management,* National Industrial Conference Board, Inc., New York, 1970.
18. "Differentiated Staffing in Schools," *Education U.S.A. Special Report,* National School Public Relations Association, Washington, 1970.
19. "Drug Crisis Challenges Schools," *The Shape of Education for 1970–71,* vol. 12, pp. 9–14, National School Public Relations Association, Washington, 1970.
20. *Education Is Good Business,* American Association of School Administrators, Washington, 1966.
21. "Educational Technology," *New Directions for School Administrators,* California Association of School Administrators, Burlingame, California, January, 1969, pp. 25–31.
22. "Elementary Principals Set Policy Goals," *Education U.S.A.,* National School Public Relations Association, Washington, May 4, 1970.

23. Emans, Robert: "Teacher Attitudes As a Function of Values," *The Journal of Educational Research,* vol. 62, no. 10, pp. 459–463, Dembar Educational Research Services, Inc., Madison, Wis., July–August, 1969.

24. *Enforcement of the Code of Ethics of the Education Profession,* National Education Association, Committee on Professional Ethics, Washington, 1969.

25. Epstein, Benjamin: *The Principal's Role in Collective Negotiations Between Teachers and School Boards,* National Education Association, National Association of Secondary School Principals, Washington, 1965.

26. Eurich, Alvin C.: *America Is Opportunity: Effective Education for the Sixties,* an address at the 49th Annual Meeting, Chamber of Commerce of the United States, Washington, May, 1961.

27. "Facts on American Education," *NEA Research Bulletin,* vol. 48, no. 2, pp. 35–41, National Education Association, Research Division, Washington, May, 1970.

28. *Fall 1968 Statistics of Public Elementary and Secondary Day Schools,* U.S. Office of Education, Washington, 1969.

29. Fantini, Mario D., and Gerald Weinstein: *The Disadvantaged: Challenge to Education,* Harper and Row, Publishers, Inc., New York, 1968.

30. Finn, James D.: "The Good Guys and the Bad Guys," *Phi Delta Kappan,* vol. 40, no. 1, pp. 2–5, Phi Delta Kappa, Bloomington, Ind., October, 1958.

31. "First Assessment Results Analyzed," *Education U.S.A.,* National School Public Relations Association, Washington, August 3, 1970.

32. Flanders, Ned A.: *Teacher Influence, Pupil Attitudes and Achievement: Studies in Interaction Analysis,* U.S. Office of Education, Cooperative Research Project, no. 397, Washington, 1960.

33. Frasier, James E.: *An Introduction to the Study of Education,* 3d ed., Harper and Row, Publishers, Inc., New York, 1965.

34. Gallup, George: *How the Nation Views the Public Schools,* A CFK Ltd. Report, Gallup, International, Princeton, N.J., 1969.

35. Gallup, George: "Second Annual Survey of the Public's Attitude Toward the Public Schools," *Phi Delta Kappan,* vol. 52, no. 2, pp. 99–112, Phi Delta Kappa, Bloomington, Ind., October, 1970.

36. Gallup, George: "The Third Annual Survey of the Public's Attitudes Toward the Public Schools, 1971," *Phi Delta Kappan,* vol. 53, no. 1, pp. 30–44, Phi Delta Kappa, Bloomington, Ind., September, 1971.

37. "The Gallup Poll," *Washington Post,* Nov. 20, 1968, p. B 18.

38. Gardner, John W.: *Excellence: Can We Be Equal and Excellent Too?* Harper and Row, Publishers, Inc., New York, 1961.

39. Glass, Bentley: *The Time and the Timeless,* Basic Books, New York, 1970.

40. *Goals of the American Federation of Teachers AFL-CIO,* American Federation of Teachers, AFL-CIO, Washington, n.d.

41. Good, Thomas L., and Jere E. Brophy: "The Self-Fulfilling Prophecy," *Today's Education,* vol. 60, no. 4, pp. 52–53, National Education Association, Washington, April, 1971.

42. Goodlad, John I.: "The Future of Learning: Into the 21st Century," *AACTE Bulletin,* vol. 24, no. 1, pp. 1, 4–5, American Association of Colleges for Teacher Education, Washington, March, 1971.

43. Goodlad, John I., and Robert H. Anderson: *The Nongraded School,* Harcourt, Brace and World, Inc., New York, 1963.

44. Goodlad, John I., and Frances M. Klein: *Behind the Classroom Door,* Charles A. Jones Publishing Company, Worthington, Ohio, 1970.

45. "Governance for the Teaching Profession," *NEA National Commission on Teacher Education and Professional Standards,* no. 1, A working paper, National Education Association, Washington, November, 1970.

46. Graybeal, William S.: "Teacher Surplus and Teacher Shortage," *Phi Delta Kappan,* vol. 53, no. 2, pp. 82–85, Phi Delta Kappa, Bloomington, Ind., October, 1971.

47. Hamachek, Don: "Characteristics of Good Teachers and Implications for Teacher

Education," *Phi Delta Kappan,* vol. 50, no. 6, pp. 341–345, Phi Delta Kappa, Bloomington, Ind., February, 1969.

48. Harris, Norman C.: "Redoubled Efforts and Dimly Seen Goals," *Phi Delta Kappan,* vol. 46, no. 8, pp. 360–365, Phi Delta Kappa, Bloomington, Ind., April, 1965.

49. Heil, Louis, Marion Powell, and Irwin Feifer: *Characteristics of Teacher Behavior Related to the Achievement of Children in Several Elementary Grades,* Brooklyn College, Brooklyn, New York, 1960.

50. Hodgson, J. D.: "Manpower Patterns of the 70's," *Manpower,* vol. 3, no. 2, pp. 3–6, Superintendent of Documents, U.S. Government Printing Office, Washington, February, 1971.

51. *Hogs, Ax Handles and Woodpeckers,* American Association of School Administrators, Washington, 1958.

52. *How Much Are Students Learning?* A Report from the Committee on Assessing the Progress of Education, University of Michigan, Ann Arbor, Michigan, November, 1968.

53. Hughes, James Monroe: *Education in America,* 2d ed., Harper and Row, Publishers, Inc., New York, 1965.

54. *Imperatives in Education,* American Association of School Administrators, Washington, 1966.

55. *In Search of Excellence,* American Federation of Teachers, AFL-CIO, Washington, n.d.

56. Incollingo, Larry: "Sexplosion Erupts in U.S. Secondary Education," *Daily-Herald Telephone,* Section 2, p. 2, Bloomington, Ind., June 16, 1969.

57. "Innovations Fail to Reach Classroom, Study Says," *Education U.S.A.,* National School Public Relations Association, Washington, February 8, 1971.

58. "Instructional Technology," *Today's Education,* vol. 59, no. 8, pp. 33–40, National Education Association, Washington, November, 1970.

59. *An Introduction to Phi Delta Kappa,* Phi Delta Kappa, Bloomington, Ind. (brochure).

60. Reprinted by permission of the publishers from Arthur T. Jersild and Associates: *Education for Self-understanding: The Role of Psychology in the High School Program,* (New York: Teachers College Press, copyright 1953 by Teachers College, Columbia University), pp. 6 & 9.

61. Kirp, David L.: "The Poor, the Schools and Equal Protection," *Harvard Educational Review,* vol. 38, no. 4, pp. 635–688, Graduate School of Education, Harvard University, Cambridge, Mass., Fall, 1968.

62. Krech, David: "The Chemistry of Learning," *Saturday Review,* Saturday Review, Inc., N.Y., January 20, 1968.

63. Lambert, Sam M.: *Inaugural Address,* Presidential Room, Statler-Hilton Hotel, Washington, Oct. 20, 1967.

64. Lieberman, Myron: "Implications of the Coming NEA-AFT Merger," *Phi Delta Kappan,* vol. 50, no. 3, pp. 139–144, Phi Delta Kappa, Bloomington, Ind., November, 1968.

65. Little, Malcolm: *Malcolm X Speaks: Selected Speeches and Statements,* Merit Publishers, New York, 1965.

66. Locke, Robert W.: "Has the Education Industry Lost Its Nerve?" *Saturday Review,* Saturday Review, Inc., N.Y., January 16, 1971, pp. 42–44, 57, Copyright 1971.

67. "The Magnitude of the American Educational Establishment 1960–1970," *Saturday Review,* Saturday Review, Inc., N.Y., September 19, 1970, p. 67.

68. Mee, John F.: "The New Knowledge Industry," *The Review,* vol. 10, no. 2, pp. 10–22, Alumni Association of the College of Arts and Sciences—Graduate School, Indiana University, Bloomington, Ind., Winter, 1968.

69. "Methods of Evaluating Teachers," *NEA Research Bulletin,* vol. 43, no. 1, pp. 12–18, National Education Association, Research Division, Washington, February, 1965.

70. Michael, Donald N.: *The Next Generation: The Prospects Ahead for the Youth of Today and Tomorrow,* Random House, Inc., New York, 1965.

71. Michael, Donald N.: "Your Child and the World of Tomorrow," *NEA Journal,* vol.

55, no. 1, National Education Association, Washington, January, 1966 (supplement).

72. Miller, Harriett: "Santa Barbara Has a Student School Board," *American School Board Journal,* vol. 157, no. 11, p. 29, National School Boards Association, Evanston, Ill., May, 1970.

73. "National Assessment Spreading to States," *Education U.S.A.,* National School Relations Association, Washington, August 3, 1970.

74. *NEA Handbook for Local, State and National Associations 1970–71,* National Education Association, Washington, September, 1970.

75. *NEA Handbook for Local, State, and National Associations 1971–72,* National Education Association, Washington, October, 1971.

76. "Negotiations Moving to State Level?" *Convention Reporter,* American Association of School Administrators, Washington, February, 19, 1970.

77. "New Legislation to Spur Drug Education," *Washington Monitor, Education U.S.A.,* National School Public Relations Association, Washington, November 30, 1970, p. 77.

78. "News and Trends," *NEA Journal,* vol. 56, no. 2, pp. 3–4, National Education Association, Washington, February, 1967.

79. "News and Trends," *Today's Education,* vol. 58, no. 1, pp. 3–4, National Education Association, Washington, January, 1969.

80. "News Front," *Education U.S.A.,* National School Public Relations Association, Washington, September 29, 1969, p. 26.

81. "News Front," *Education U.S.A.,* National School Public Relations Association, Washington, May 11, 1970, p. 206.

82. "News Front," *Education U.S.A.,* National School Public Relations Association, Washington, September 7, 1970.

83. "News Front," *Education U.S.A.,* National School Public Relations Association, Washington, December 14, 1970, p. 86.

84. "News Front," *Education U.S.A.,* National School Public Relations Association, Washington, February 22, 1971.

85. "News Front," *Education U.S.A.,* National School Public Relations Association, Washington, March 22, 1971.

86. "Objectives of the National Congress of Parents and Teachers," *PTA Manual,* National Congress of Parents and Teachers, Chicago, 1965–66.

87. Olivero, James L., and Edward G. Buffie (eds), *Educational Manpower: From Aides to Differentiated Staff Patterns,* Indiana University Press, Bloomington, Ind., 1970.

88. "Opinion Surveys Pinpoint Student Views," *Education U.S.A.,* National School Public Relations Association, December 14, 1970, p. 85.

89. "Our Schools Aren't Good Enough," *The News Letter,* vol. 20, Bureau of Educational Research, Ohio State University, Columbus, Ohio, November, 1954.

90. "Panel Blasts Vocational Education Effort," *Washington Monitor, Education U.S.A.,* National School Public Relations Association, Washington, September 8, 1969.

91. *Policies and Criteria for the Approval of Secondary Schools,* North Central Association of Colleges and Secondary Schools, Chicago, 1966.

92. Polley, Ira: "What's Right with American Education?" *Phi Delta Kappan,* vol. 51, no. 1, pp. 13–15, Phi Delta Kappa, Bloomington, Ind;, September, 1969.

93. "Population Trends and School Enrollments," *NEA Research Bulletin,* vol. 47, no. 1, pp. 25–28, National Education Association, Research Division, Washington, March, 1969.

94. "Population Trends Signal School Needs," *NEA Research Bulletin,* vol. 46, no. 1, pp. 24–28, National Education Association, Research Division, Washington, March, 1968.

95. *Professional Organizations in American Education,* National Education Association, Educational Policies Commission, Washington, 1957.

96. "Profit and Loss in Education," *Saturday Review,* Saturday Review, Inc., N.Y., Aug. 15, 1970, p. 39.

97. *Projections of Educational Attainment in the United States: 1965 to 1985,* Current Population Reports, ser. P–25, no. 305, U.S. Bureau of the Census, Washington, April 14, 1965, pp. 1–16.

98. "Promising Innovations Hit Snags," *Education U.S.A.,* National School Public Relations Association, Washington, September 23, 1968.

99. "Purposes," *Educational Horizons,* vol. 43, no. 4, p.i, Pi Lambda Theta, Washington, Summer, 1965.

100. *The Pursuit of Excellence: Education and the Future of America.* Copyright 1958 by Rockefeller Brothers Fund, Inc. Reprinted with permission of Doubleday and Company, Inc.

101. "Rankings of the States, 1969," *Research Report 1969–R1,* National Education Association, Research Division, Washington, 1969.

102. "Rankings of the States, 1971," *Research Report 1971–R1,* National Education Association, Research Division, Washington, 1971.

103. Rathbone, M . J.: *Human Talent: The Great Investment,* Standard Oil Company (New Jersey), New Jersey, February 25, 1964.

104. "Reporting Pupil Progress," *NEA Research Bulletin,* vol. 47, no. 3, pp. 75–76, National Education Association, Research Division, Washington, October, 1969.

105. "Reporting Pupil Progress to Parents," *NEA Research Bulletin,* vol. 49, no. 3, pp. 81–82, National Education Association, Research Division, Washington, October, 1971.

106. Rosenthal, Robert, and Lenore Jacobson: *Pygmalion in the Classroom: Teacher Expectation and Pupils Intellectual Development,* Holt, Rinehart and Winston, New York, 1968.

107. Ryans, David G.: *Characteristics of Teachers,* American Council on Education, Washington, 1960. Used by permission.

108. Ryans, David G.: "Prediction of Teacher Effectiveness," *Encyclopedia of Educational Research,* 3d ed., The Macmillan Company, Toronto, Ontario, 1960, pp. 1,486–1,490.

109. Salz, Arthur E.: "Local Control vs. Professionalism," *Phi Delta Kappan,* vol. 50, no. 6, pp. 332–334, Phi Delta Kappa, Bloomington, Ind., February, 1969.

110. "School Enrollment," *Financial Facts,* National Consumer Finance Association, Educational Services Division, Washington, April, 1971.

111. *Schools for the Sixties,* Project on Instruction of the National Education Association, McGraw-Hill Book Company, New York, 1963.

112. "Serious Protest Found in 18% of High Schools," *Education U.S.A.,* National School Public Relations Association, Washington, March 2, 1970, p. 145.

113. *Sesame Street Newsletter, No. 11,* 1865 Broadway, New York, November 8, 1970.

114. "Sex Education in the Schools," *Education U.S.A. Special Report,* National School Public Relations Association, Washington, 1969.

115. Shaffer, Helen B.: "Discipline in Public Schools," *Editorial Research Report 2,* pp. 635–652, ERIC Clearing House on Educational Management, University of Oregon, Eugene, Oregon, Aug. 27, 1969.

116. Shane, Harold G.: "Future-planning As a Means of Shaping Educational Change," in Robert M. McClure, and Herman Richey (eds.), *The Curriculum: Retrospect and Prospect,* The Seventieth Yearbook of the National Society for the Study of Education, Part I, The University of Chicago Press, Chicago, Ill., 1971, pp. 185–218.

117. Shane, Harold G.: "Future Shock and the Curriculum," *Phi Delta Kappan,* vol. 49, no. 2, pp. 67–70, Phi Delta Kappa, Bloomington, Ind., October, 1967.

118. Shane, Harold G., and E. T. McSwain: *Evaluation and the Elementary Curriculum,* Holt, Rinehart and Winston, Inc., New York, 1958.

119. Shane, Harold G., and June Grant Shane: "Forecast for the 70's," *Today's Education,* vol. 58, no. 1, pp. 29–32, National Education Association, Washington, January, 1969.

120. Sheviakov, George V., and Fritz Redl: *Discipline for Today's Children and*

Youth, National Education Association, Association for Supervision and Curriculum Development, Washington, 1956.

121. Simon, Kenneth A., and Marie G. Fullam: *Projections of Educational Statistics to 1979–80,* U.S. Office of Education, Washington, 1971.

122. Smith, Louis M.: "Group Processes in Elementary and Secondary Schools," *What Research Says to the Teacher,* no. 19, National Education Association, Department of Classroom Teachers, American Educational Research Association, Washington, 1959.

123. Stinnett, T. M.: *Professional Problems of Teachers,* 3d ed., The Macmillan Company, Toronto, Ontario, 1969.

124. Stinnett, T. M.: "Reordering Goals and Roles: An Introduction," in *Unfinished Business of the Teaching Profession in the 1970's,* pp. 1–7, Phi Delta Kappa, Bloomington, Ind., 1971.

125. Stinnett, T. M.: "Teaching Professionalization: Challenge and Promise, Power of Professionalism in Teaching," *Bulletin of the School of Education,* vol. 40, no. 5, pp. 9–20, Indiana University, Bloomington, Ind., September, 1964.

126. Stinnett, T. M.: "What Is Relevant?" *The Inauguration of Sam M. Lambert,* National Education Association, Washington, October 20, 1967.

127. Stoddard, George D.: *The Dual Progress Plan,* Harper and Row, Publishers, Inc., New York, 1961.

128. "Study Praises Differentiated Staffing," *Education U.S.A.,* National School Public Relations Association, Washington, March 15, 1971.

129. "Swings of the Educational Pendulum," *NASSP Convention Reporter, Education U.S.A.,* National School Public Relations Association, Washington, January 23–27, 1971.

130. "Teacher Aides in Public Schools," *NEA Research Bulletin,* vol. 45, no. 2, pp. 37–39, National Education Association, Research Division, Washington, May, 1970.

131. "Teacher Job Shortage Ahead," *NEA Research Bulletin,* vol. 49, no. 3, pp. 69–74, National Education Association, Research Division, Washington, October, 1971.

132. "Teacher Mobility and Loss," *NEA Research Bulletin,* vol. 46, no. 6, pp. 118–126, National Education Association, Research Division, Washington, December, 1968.

133. "Teacher Opinion," *NEA Research Bulletin,* vol. 47, no. 3, pp. 70–72, National Education Association, Research Bulletin, Washington, October, 1969.

134. "Teacher Opinion Poll," *Today's Education,* vol. 60, no. 2, p. 27, National Education Association, Washington, February, 1971.

135. "Teacher Strikes, 1960–61 to 1969–70," *NEA Research Bulletin,* vol. 48, no. 3, pp. 69–72, National Education Association, Research Division, Washington, October, 1970.

136. "Teacher Supply and Demand in Public Schools, 1972," *Research Report 1972–R8,* National Education Association, Research Division, Washington, 1972.

137. "Teacher Supply and Demand in Universities, Colleges, and Junior Colleges, 1963–64 and 1964–65," *Research Report 1965–R4,* National Education Association, Research Division, Washington, April, 1965.

138. "Technology in Education," *Education U.S.A. Special Report,* National School Public Relations Association, Washington, 1967.

139. "Technology in Education," *NEA Research Memo 1969–4,* National Education Association, Research Division, Washington, February, 1969.

140. Thayer, V. T.: *The Role of the School in American Society,* Dodd, Mead and Company, Inc., New York, 1960.

141. Thomas, Steven C.: "Valley View's 45–15 Year-round School," *Today's Education,* vol. 60, no. 8, pp. 42–43, National Education Association, Washington, November, 1971.

142. Thompson, Ronald B.: *Projections of Enrollments: Public and Private Colleges and Universities, 1970–1987,* American Association of Collegiate Registrars and Admissions Officers Office, One Dupont Circle, N.W., Washington, December, 1970.

143. Toffler, Alvin: *Future Shock,* Random House, New York, 1970.
144. Trump, J. Lloyd: *Guide to Better Schools: Focus on Change,* Rand McNally and Company, Chicago, 1961.
145. *200 Million Americans,* U.S. Department of Commerce, Superintendent of Documents, U.S. Government Printing Office, Washington, November, 1967.
146. "Use of Drugs in Schools Poses Dread U.S. Problem," *Los Angeles Times,* Part 2, Los Angeles, Calif., February 19, 1970, p. 7.
147. Van Til, William: "The Key Word Is Relevance," *Today's Education,* vol. 58, no. 1, pp. 14–17, National Education Association, Washington, January, 1969.
148. "What the Kids Want," *Phi Delta Kappan,* vol. 51, no. 7, p. 407, Phi Delta Kappa, Bloomington, Ind., March, 1970.
149. Whitehead, Donald R.: "This Is Your Earth," *Indiana Alumni Magazine,* vol. 33, no. 6, pp. 10–13, Indiana University, Bloomington, Ind., March, 1970.
150. Williamson, John A.: "Seniors Comment on Their Best and Poorest Teachers," *Colorado Journal of Educational Research,* vol. 7, no. 2, pp. 3–7, Bureau of Research, Colorado State College, Greeley, Colorado, Spring, 1968.
151. Witty, Paul A.: "Mental Hygiene in Modern Education," *Fifty-fourth Yearbook of the National Society for the Study of Education, Part II,* The University of Chicago Press, Chicago, 1955.
152. Witty, Paul A.: "The Teacher Who Has Helped Me Most," *NEA Journal,* vol. 36, no. 5, p. 386, National Education Association, Washington, May, 1947.

INDEX

Abilities:
  appraisal of, 41–42, 45–46, 129–130
  needed by teachers (*see* Teachers, abilities
    needed by)
Ability to support education, 245–247
Academic freedom, 226–227
Accountability, 144, 243–244
Achievement, appraisal of, 100
Activities of teachers:
  in classroom, 96–102, 142–148
  in community, 105–107
  extraclass, 102
  within school, 96–102
Administrators, number of, 156
Adult education, 75, 88
Agency for International Development, 91
Alcoholics, number of, 17
Alexander, William, 103
All-year schools, 125–126
Allport-Vernon Scale of Values, 44
American Association of School Administrators,
    168, 232
American Association of University Professors,
    168
American Bar Association, 160
American Council of Education, 49
American culture, characteristics of, 13–18
American Dependent Schools Overseas, 91
American Educational Research Association, 168
American Federation of Teachers, 160,
    165–167, 174–177
  future of, 174–177
  goals of, 165–167
  history of, 165
  membership of, 165
  objectives of, 165–167
  publications of, 165
American Medical Association, 160
American Teachers Association, 160
American way of living, 11–18, 99
Anderson, Robert, 109

Appellate court system, 182–183
Applying for position, 47
Association for Childhood Education Interna-
    tional, 168
Association of Supervision and Curriculum De-
    velopment, 168
Associations (*see* Professional organizations)
Assumption of risk, 195
Attacks on education, 1–3, 140–145, 215–218,
    237–243
Attainment, educational, 11, 27–28, 217
Audio-visual materials in classrooms, 137–139
Automation, 13, 29–31
Autonomy, professional, 153–154

Bible reading, 221–226
Biological engineering, 33
Births, number of, 73–74, 79
Blacks (*see* Minority groups)
British Infant Schools, 145
Bruner, Jerome S., 108
Buffie, Edward, 114
Buildings, school: changes in, 140, 146–148
  early types of, 140

Cable TV (CATV), 136–137
Career decision making, 38–43
Career planning:
  importance of self-appraisal, 41–42
  influence of goals on, 39–41
  nature of, 39
  related to life plans, 38–39
Career requirements, importance of, 42
Cassette tapes, 136–137, 139, 143
Challenge of teaching, 1–35
Changes:
  in American life, 13–18
  in organizational patterns, 107–126, 140
  in role of teacher, 96–126, 146, 241–243

Changes:
in technology, 132–149, 247
Characteristics of teachers, 49–56, 65–67, 129–130
Checklist:
personality, 52–56, 67–69
public relations, 130–131
for teaching, 55–56, 64–65, 129–130
use of, 45
voice and speech, 57–58, 69–70
Children, culturally deprived, 24, 140, 156, 245–247, 249–259
Church and state, separation of, 221–226
Civil Rights Act, 229
Classes:
number taught, 97
size of, 72–73, 80
Classrooms:
environment of, 146–147
legal liabilities, 185–187
overcrowded, 80
Closed-circuit television, 136–137
Cocurricular activities of teachers, 102
legal liabilities, 191–192
Code of ethics:
enforcement of, 173–174, 177
for teaching profession, 151, 161, 171–173, 177
Cognitive learning, 142
Collective bargaining, 166, 174–176
College and university teachers, opportunities for, 83–86
Combination of teaching fields, 83
Combs, Arthur, 54
Commissions of the National Education Association, 162–163
Communism:
fear of teaching about, 226–227
and loyalty of teachers, 226
Community:
changing nature of, 13–18
world, interdependence of, 16–17
Community activities of teachers, 105–107
Community attitudes toward teachers, 105–107
Community expectation of teachers:
participating in activities, 105–107
political activity, 106
providing exemplary behavior, 106–107
reporting to parents, 100–102
working in community agencies, 105–107
Community relationships with teachers, 105–107
Competence, social, 26–27
Competencies for teaching, 47–57, 64–67, 129–130
characteristics of competent teachers, 65–67, 129–130
critical behavior, 49–51
effective behavior, 50, 129–130
identification of, 49–56, 129–130
implications for planning, 56–57
ineffective behavior, 50
methods of analyzing, 49–56
self-rating forms, 55–56, 64–65, 129–130
voice and speech, 57–58

Computer-assisted instruction, 1, 75, 134–135, 143
Conference with parents, 101–102
Conformity, pressures toward, 15–16
Constitution of the United States:
Fifteenth Amendment, 229
First Amendment, 222, 223
Fourteenth Amendment, 222
Construction of schools, 146
Continuing education (see Adult education)
Contract performance, 1–2
Contributions of schools, 3–13
Controversial issues and problems, 215–234, 237–259
Corporal punishment of pupils, 208–211
Counseling students, 97–98
Court actions, types of, 182–183
Courts, types of, 182–183
Critical behavior of teachers, 49–51
Criticism of education (see Education, criticisms of)
Culturally deprived children (see Children, culturally deprived)
Curriculum:
adaptation to change, 241–243
relevance of, 238–240
Cybernation, 29–31

Data processing, 134–135
Decision making, 58–59
De facto segregation, 230
Defamation of character, legal aspects of, 196–198
De jure segregation, 230
Demand of teachers (see Supply and demand of teachers)
Democracy:
educational implications of, 11–13
meaning of, 11–13
in modern world, 13–18
quality of teachers in, 12
Democratic citizenship, meaning of, 11–13, 99–100
Democratic concepts of education, 11–13, 99
Democratic society, characteristics of, 11–13, 99–100
Dependent schools abroad, 89, 91
Deprived children, culturally (see Children, culturally deprived)
Dewey, John, 99
Dial-access system, 138–139, 143
Differentiated staffing, 75, 113–116, 140, 143
Dignity of man, 5–6, 22–23
Disadvantaged children, culturally (see Children, culturally deprived)
Discipline, 99–100, 205–211
Discrimination and segregation, 140, 215, 227–231
Dress of pupils, 200–201
Dropouts, 6–7, 74, 217–218
Drug education, 241–243
Due process, 207–208

Duties of teachers:
  counseling students, 97–98
  disciplining students, 99–100
  evaluating pupil progress, 100–101
  guiding students, 97–98
  instructing, 96–97
  meeting professional responsibilities, 103
  reporting to parents, 100–102
  sponsoring extraclass activities, 102
  teaching classes, 96–97
  working with other school personnel, 104–105
  (*See also* Community activities of teachers)

Early childhood, importance of, 24
Economic growth and welfare, 8–10
Economic Opportunity Act, 247
Economic status of countries, 8–10
Education:
  adult (*see* Adult education)
  attacks on quality of, 1–3, 140–145, 215–218, 237–243
  attainment of people, 11, 27–28, 217
  challenge of the future, 18–35
  change in, 140–148
  contribution of, 3–13
  criticisms of, 1–3, 140–145, 215–218, 237–243
  democratic responsibilities of, 11–13
  and the dignity of man, 5–6, 22–23
  economic growth related to, 8–10
  equality of opportunity, 5–7, 227–231, 245–247
  higher (*see* Higher education)
  importance of, 1–13, 215–216
  in-service, 147
  international, 16–17, 167–168
  issues in, 215–234, 237–259
  legal liabilities and responsibilities of teachers, 180–212
  of minority groups, 227–231, 249–259
  national assessment of, 144, 247–249
  opportunities for, 5–7, 15
  problems and issues, 215–234, 237–259
  purposes of, 99–100, 142
  religious influences on, 221–226
  teacher (*see* Teacher education)
  in transition, 13–18
  and the unification of our nation, 4
  vocational, 147, 231–233
Educational Policies Commission, 158, 163–164
Educational television, 135–137, 142
Educational vouchers, 144–145
Electronic laboratories, 137–138
Elementary and Secondary Education Act, 247
Elementary schools:
  enrollments in, 74–75, 79–82, 92–93
  opportunities in, 78–82
Emergency teachers, 80–81
Engineering:
  biological, 33
  social, 32
Enrollments:
  college, 74, 84–85
  nonpublic, 75

Enrollments:
  public school, 74–75, 79, 92–93
Environmental controls, 27–28
Equality of opportunity, 6, 227–231, 245–247
Equipment of schools, 140, 145–148
Ethics for teachers, 151, 161, 171–174, 177, 196–198
  enforcement of, 173–174
Eurich, Alvin C., 12
European schools, 10
Evaluation of pupil progress, 100–101, 144
Evaluation of teachers, 103–104, 144
Exchange teachers, 91
Expulsion of pupils, 206–207
Extraclass activities of teachers, 102
  legal liabilities, 191–192

Family, educative influence of, 17, 23–24
Farms, decline in, 14–15
Field trips, legal liabilities, 189–191
Financial support for schools, 75, 147, 219–220
  federal aid, 147
  inequalities in, 5–7, 227–231, 245–247
Fitness for teaching, self-rating scale, 64–65
Flanders, Ned A., 53
Flexible scheduling, 116–118, 143
Freedom to teach, 226–227
Furniture in classrooms, 145–148
Future challenges, 18–35
Future Teachers of America, 164

Gardner, John W., 12
Glass, Bentley, 28
Goals:
  influence of, on career planning, 39–41
  relationship of, to values, 38–41
Goodlad, John, 23, 140–143
Government:
  changes in, 32–33
  student, 240–241
Grades in evaluating pupil progress, 101
Gross national product, 10
Group leader, characteristics of, 59–60
Group participation, 59
Grouping of pupils, 119–120, 123, 146
Guidance of pupils, 97–98
  class groups, 96–97, 146–148
  learning experiences, 146–148

Half-day sessions, 80
Hamachek, Don, 52–55
Handicapped children, 81
Head Start, Project, 247
Heil, Louis, 55
High schools (*see* Secondary schools)
Higher education:
  increased enrollment in, 74
  opportunities in, 83–86
Holding power of schools, 6–7, 74, 79, 217
Honorary education associations, 169–170

Human relationships, 52–55, 59–60
Humanism, 142

Identity, self, 22, 41–42, 142–143
Income related to level of education, 8–10
Independent study, 120–123
Indians (see Minority groups)
Individualized instruction, 120–123
Individually Prescribed Instruction, 122–123
Inequalities between schools, 227–231, 245–247
Informing the public, 219–221
Innovations in instruction, 107–126
In-service education, 147
Instruction:
    changes in, 107–126, 141–148
    computer-assisted, 134–135
Intellectual freedom, 226–227
Interdependence of people, 16–17
International education, 16–17, 167–168
Issues in education:
    current, 237–259
    recurring, 215–234

Jefferson, Thomas, 11, 222
Jersild, Arthur T., 41
John Dewey Society, 168

Kappa Delta Pi, 169
Kilpatrick, William H., 99
Kindergartens, 79

Latin grammar school, 145
Laws, sources of, 181
Least effective teachers, 50, 54
Legal bases of pupil control:
    academic punishments, 205–206
    assault and battery, 209
    corporal punishment, 208–211
    destruction of school property, 201
    dress, 200
    driving cars, 202
    due process, 207
    expulsion, 206–207
    leaving school premises, 202
    in loco parentis, 204–205
    marriages, 202–203
    off school grounds, 202
    pregnancy, 203–204
    reasonableness of punishment, 245
    reasonableness of rules, 198–199
    secret societies, 204
    suspension, 206–207
Legal cases:
    Brown v. Board of Education, 181, 229, 230
    Engel v. Vitale, 181, 223
    McCollum v. Board of Education, 222
    Plessy v. Ferguson, 228
    Sweatt v. Painter, 229

Legal cases:
    Tinker v. Des Moines Independent Community
        School District, 180, 227
    Zorach v. Clauson, 223
Legal liabilities, 180–212
Leisure time, 17, 26–27
Liability:
    for assumption of risk, 195
    for contributory negligence, 193–194
    for defamation of character, 196–198
    for proximate cause, 194–195
    for pupil injury: involving classroom activities,
        185–187
        involving cocurricular activities, 191–192
        involving defective equipment, 187–189
        involving errands and field trips, 189–191
        involving school patrols, 189
Life styles, changes in, 24–25
Locke, Robert, 145
Loco parentis, in, 204–205

Machines, teaching, 133–134
Management technology, 31–32
Mann, Horace, 49, 216
Manpower, use of, 109–110
Materials:
    programmed, 133–134, 142, 143
    teaching, 146–148
    visual, 137–139
Megalopoli, 22
Melbourne High School, 123
Men teachers in elementary schools, 75, 156–158
Mexican Americans (see Minority groups)
Michael, Donald, 19–20
Middle schools, 123–124, 142
Minority groups, 227–231, 249–259
Mobility of population, 16
Modern living, characteristics of, 13–18
Modular scheduling, 116–118
Moral development, 223
Multiage grouping, 120
Multigrade grouping, 119–120

National assessment, 144, 247–249
National Association of Elementary School Prin-
    cipals, 168, 175
National Association of Secondary School Prin-
    cipals, 168–175
National Commission of Teacher Education and
    Professional Standards, 154, 162–163
National Congress of Parents and Teachers, 170
National Council for Accreditation of Teacher
    Education, 78
National Council of the Social Studies, 168
National Education Association (NEA), 76, 103,
    106, 108, 160–165, 171, 173–174
    code of ethics, 151, 161, 171–173, 177
    commissions of, 162–163
    committees of, 162–163
    departments of, 162–163

National Education Association (NEA):
 future of, 174–177
 history of, 160–161
 membership of, 160–161
 Project on Instructional Programs in the Public Schools, 108–109, 231
 publications of, 161–162
 purposes of, 161–162
 recommendations of: on academic freedom, 227
   on performance contracting, 245
 research function of, 162
 Today's Education, 162
National Industrial Conference Board, 13, 19, 25
National Society for the Study of Education, 167
NEA (*see* National Education Association)
Negligence:
 contributory, 193–194
 criteria for, 185
 defense against, 192–193
 defined, 184
 proximate cause, 194–195
 standard of, 184–185
Nongraded schools, 118–119, 140, 143
Nonschool personnel contacts with, 105–107
North Central Association of Colleges and Secondary Schools, 97

Obligations of teachers:
 to community, 105–107
 to fellow staff members, 104–105
Occupations, changes in, 29–31
Office of Education, 244
Olivero, James, 114
Opportunities for teachers, 70–93
 in the business world, 91–93
 in college, 83–86, 93
 compared for men and women, 75, 156–158
 in elementary schools, 78–82, 92–93
 factors affecting, 71–76, 92
 imbalance in demand for, 76–78
 in junior colleges, 84–86, 93
 in kindergartens, 79, 93
 list of, 87–90
 new types, 90–91
 nonteaching, 81, 91–92, 156
 range of, 70, 86–92
 in secondary schools, 78–82, 92–93
 in special areas, 81, 86
Organizations, professional (*see* Professional organizations)

Parent-Teacher Association, 170–171
Parents:
 expectations of teachers, 105–107
 reporting to, 100–102
 responsibilities to children, 17, 23–24
Peace Corps, opportunities in, 89, 91
Performance approach to teacher education, 147

Performance contract, 144, 176, 244–245
Personal growth, 57–60
 making decisions, 58
 in oral communication, 57–58
 serving as group leader, 59–60
 using time effectively, 60
 voice and speech, 57–58, 69–70
 working with people, 59, 105–107
Personal qualities of teachers, 49–55, 107
 checklist of, 67–69
Phi Delta Kappa, 169
Physical environment of classrooms, 140, 145–148
Pi Lambda Theta, 169
Piaget, Jean, 144
Planning:
 appraisal of abilities, 41–42, 45–46
 approaches to, 38–39
 attitudes toward, 38
 of career (*see* Career planning)
 concepts of, 38
 for continued teaching, 47
 importance of, 38–39
   obtaining objective data, 45–46
 influence on: of goals, 39–41
   of opportunities, 42–43
 for in-service growth, 47
 interpretation of, 38–39
 for major periods in life, 46–47
 meaning of, 38–39
 nature of, 39
 procedures for, 39–47
 self-appraisal in, 41–42
 steps in, 39–47
 tests in, 45–46
 values in, 38–41, 44–45
 weaknesses in, 38
Planning paper, nature of, 43–44
Playground, legal liability, 187–189
Political activity of teachers, 101
Polley, Ira, 7
Pollution, 27
Population increases:
 United States, 20–21, 71
 world, 20
Prayer in school, 223–225
Prekindergarten education, 124, 147
Prestige of teachers, 154–155
Primary schools (*see* Elementary schools)
Principals, 104–105, 156
Private schools, growth of, 145
Profession:
 characteristics of, 151–152
 status of, 152–153
Professional associations (*see* Professional organizations)
Professional ethics, 151, 161, 171–173, 177
Professional negotiations, 174–175
Professional obligations of teachers, 151–177
Professional organizations, 157–177
 aims of, 158

Professional organizations:
American Federation of Teachers, 160, 165–167, 174–177
future of, 174–177
Future Teachers of America, 164
honorary, 169–170
international, 167–168
Kappa Delta Pi, 169
local, 158–159
merger of, 176
national, 160–164
(*See also* National Education Association)
Phi Delta Kappa, 169
Pi Lambda Theta, 169
state, 159–160
student, 164–165
Student National Education Association, 164–165
UNESCO, 167–168
World Confederation of Organizations of the Teaching Profession, 167
Professional sanctions, 174–176
Professional status of teaching, 152–154
Programmed learning, 1, 75, 133–134, 142, 143
Project Head Start, 247
Project on Instructional Programs in the Public Schools, NEA, 108–109, 231
Proximate cause:
defined, 194
examples of, 194–195
Psychograph, use of, 46
Public relations, 107, 130, 219–221
Puerto Ricans (*see* Minority groups)
Punishments:
academic, 205–206
cases involving, 210–211
corporal, 208–211
reasonableness of, 209–211
Pupil control, legal bases, 198–211
Pupil grouping, 98
Pupil progress, evaluation of, 100–101, 144
Pupil-teacher ratio, 72–73, 80
Pupils:
attitude toward teachers, 51–52, 54–55
dress and appearance, 200–201
grouping, 98, 119–120, 123, 146
guidance of (*see* Guidance of pupils)
married, 202–203
number of, 74
pregnancy of, 203–204
punishment of, 205–211
secret societies, 204
spiritual growth of, 221–226
suspension of, 206–207
Purposes of education, 99–100, 142

Qualifications for teaching (*see* Competencies for teaching; Teachers, personal qualities of)

Racism, 255–256
Released time, 222–223
Relevance, demand for, 237–243

Religion:
and education, 221–226
influence of, on early schools, 221–222
Religious activities of teachers, 106
Reporting to parents, 100–102
Ryans, David G., 49, 51, 54

Sanctions, 174–175
Scheduling, flexible, 116–118, 143
School law, 180–212
School patrol, legal liabilities, 189
Schools:
contributions of, 3–13
criticisms of, 1–3, 140–145, 215–218, 237–243
elementary (*see* Elementary schools)
equipment of, 140, 145–148
European, 10
function of, 4–13
holding power of, 6–7, 74, 217–218
inequalities between, 227–231, 245–247
middle (*see* Middle schools)
national assessment of, 144, 247–249
nongraded, 118–119, 140, 143
population increases in, 74
private, 145
relevance of, 237–243
religious instruction, 221–226
secondary (*see* Secondary schools)
summer (*see* Summer school)
tomorrow's, 145–148
Seating arrangement in classrooms, 146–147
Secondary school teachers:
opportunities for, 76–82
subject-area combinations for, 83
Secondary schools:
dropouts, 6–7, 74, 217–218
increased enrollment in, 6–7, 74–75, 78–83, 92–93
opportunities in, 76–82
Secret societies, 204
Segregation, 227–231, 256–258
Self-appraisal:
importance of, 41–42, 44–46
techniques of, 43–46
(*See also* Checklist)
Self concepts, 41–42, 142–143
Sesame Street, 136
Sex education, 226, 241–243
Shane, Harold G., 90, 141
Sheviakov, George V., 99
Social competence, demand for, 25–26
Social engineering, 32
Sources of law, 181–182
Sources of teacher supply, 76
Specialization in subject areas, 83
Speech, importance of, 57–58, 69
Spiritual growth of pupils, 221–226
Standard of living in the United States, 8–10, 14–15, 17
Stinnett, T. M., 2, 153
Strikes, teacher, 174–176
Student government, 239–240

Student National Education Association, 45, 164–165
Student protests, 237–243
Student teaching, 144
Subject combinations for secondary school teachers, 83
Subject matter, specialization for teachers, 83
Suicides, number of, 17
Summer school, 125–126
Supply and demand of teachers, 70–93
   general factors affecting, 71–76
   imbalance of, 76–78
Suspension of pupils, 206–207

Teacher aids, 110–111
Teacher education:
   exchange teachers, 91
   in-service, 147
   subject-matter specialization, 83
Teacher evaluation, 103–104
Teacher Exchange, 91
Teachers:
   abilities needed by, 42, 47–57, 64–67, 96–107, 129–130
   activities of (*see* Activities of teachers)
   age of, 156–157
   attitudes, 54–55
   best, 50–52
   challenge to, 1–35
   changing role of, 96–126, 145–148
   characteristics of, 49–56, 65–67, 129–130
   as citizens, 105–107
   classes taught by, number of, 97
   code of ethics for, 151, 161, 171–173, 177
   collective bargaining, 2, 166, 174–176
   college (*see* College and university teachers)
   community relationships, 105–107
   conduct of, 107
   criticisms of, 1–3, 140–145, 215–218, 237–243
   demand for (*see* Supply and demand of teachers)
   desirable traits for, 47–57, 129–130
     (*See also* Competencies for teaching)
   due process rights of, 207–208
   duties of (*see* Duties of teachers)
   effective, 50
   emergency, 80–81
   ethics for (*see* Ethics for teachers)
   and the freedom to teach, 226–227
   least successful, 50–53
   legal liabilities, 180–212
   in loco parentis, 204–205, 210
   men, 75, 156–157
   mobility of, 71
   negotiations, 174–176
   noneffective, 50
   number of, 156
   opportunities for (*see* Opportunities for teachers)
   outside interests of, 105–107
   personal qualities of, 40–55, 107
     checklist of, 67–69

Teachers:
   personality of, 49–56
   political rights of, 106
   preparation and training (*see* Teacher education)
   prestige of, 154–155
   problems facing, 215–234, 237–259
   professional organizations for, 157–177
   professional status of, 152–154
   and public relations, 107, 130–131, 219–221
   ratio of elementary to secondary, 75, 156–157
   relations of: with nonschool personnel, 105–107
     with other school personnel, 104–105
     with parents, 100–102, 219–221
     with pupils (*see* Pupils)
   religious activities of, 106
   responsibilities of, 96–107, 146, 151–152
   role of, 96–107, 146
   sanctions, 174
   secondary school (*see* Secondary school teachers)
   self-appraisal, 41–42, 44–45
   strikes, 174–176
   supply of (*see* Supply and demand of teachers)
   turnover, 71–72, 78–82
   unions, 165–167, 174–177
   university (*see* College and university teachers)
   willingness to teach again, 155
   working with people, 59–60, 104–107
Teaching:
   appraising, 103–104, 144
   artistic nature, 49
   career requirements for, 49–56
     (*See also* Competencies for teaching)
   challenge of, 1–35
   ethics in, 151, 161, 171–173, 177, 196–198
   freedom in, 226–227
   new techniques, 107–126, 145–148
   opportunities (*see* Opportunities for teachers)
   prestige, 154–155
   problems and issues in, 215–234, 237–259
   as profession, size of, 1, 156
   status of, 152–154
   team, 75, 111–113
Teaching machines, 134
Teaching materials (*see* Materials)
Team teaching, 75, 111–113
Technological changes, 17, 29–31, 132–149, 247
Television, educational, 135–137, 142
Temple City Model, 113–116
Tests:
   for evaluating pupil progress, 100
   for use in planning, 45–46
Time, use of, 60
Toffler, Alvin, 18–19, 142
Tort liability:
   defined, 183
   of teachers, 183–198
Totalitarianism, 17–18
Trump, J. Lloyd, 109, 140
Turnover of teachers, 71–72, 78–82

UNESCO (United Nations Educational, Scientific, and Cultural Organization), 167–168
Ungraded schools, 118–119, 140, 143
Unification of the nation, 4
Unions, 165–167, 174–177
United States aid to other countries, 91
University teachers (*see* College and university teachers)
Urbanization, 15, 21–22, 140

Values:
    Allport-Vernon Scale of Values, 44
    appraisal of, 44–45
    career planning, 39–41
    changing, 25
    clarification of, 44–45
    definition of, 39–41
    democratic, 11–18, 99
    effects of: on human behavior, 39–41
        on planning, 39–41
    importance of, 39–41, 43–45
    nature of, 39

Values:
    and objectives, relationship of, 39–41
    sources of, 39
Video tape, use of, 136–137, 139, 143
Visual materials, use of, 137–139
Vocational education, 147, 231–233
Voice, importance of, 57–58, 69
Vouchering, 144

Wilhelms, Fred T., 140–141
Witty, Paul A., 51
Women in labor force, 24
Work, dignity of, 12
World community, interdependence of, 16–17
World Confederation of Organizations of the Teaching Profession, 167

Year-round school programs, 125–126

Zorach case, 223